SO-ARY-954

Dr. Rubin, Please Make Me Happy

THE COMMON-SENSE BOOK OF MENTAL HEALTH

ALSO BY THEODORE I. RUBIN, M.D.

Jordi

Lisa and David

In the Life

Sweet Daddy

Cat

Platzo and the Mexican Pony Rider

The 29th Summer

Coming Out

The Winner's Notebook

The Thin Book by a Formerly Fat Psychiatrist

The Angry Book

Forever Thin

Emergency Room Diary

Dr. Rubin, Please Make Me Happy

THE COMMON-SENSE BOOK OF MENTAL HEALTH

Dr. Theodore I. Rubin, M.D.

 **ARBOR HOUSE** *New York*

Copyright © 1974 by El-Ted Rubin, Inc.

All rights reserved, including the right of reproduction
in whole or in part in any form. Published in the United States
by Arbor House Publishing Co., Inc., New York, and
simultaneously in Canada through Musson Book Co.

Library of Congress Catalog Card Number: 73-90111

ISBN: 0-87795-076-8

Manufactured in the United States of America

To Mary Fiore of the *Ladies' Home Journal*
and Barbara Lawrence of *McCall's*

Contents

III   Dealing with Society

Foreword

"Make me happy" is more than a common request psychiatrists in practice hear. It is probably at the heart of all requests, because, for whatever ostensible reason a person seeks help, at bottom all human beings desire happiness. The words themselves often convey more than their literal meaning. For many people, the words are actually a cry for help to resolve painful emotional problems. I believe that all people have a great natural talent and tendency for happiness. But we are also highly susceptible to combinations of emotional problems, from which extrication sometimes seems impossible. I suppose this is largely due to the extraordinary flexibility and creative possibility of the human psychic structure. Complexity is inevitable to the human condition. It can't be otherwise in a species that is so highly developed and consequently is at the same time the most adaptable and the most emotionally vulnerable of any on earth. Yes, our capacity for constructive development and activity relating to ourselves and each other is matched only by our potential destructive counterparts.

In practice and in life generally I have come to realize that the variety of emotional problems we find ourselves in is truly limitless. All involve the relationships we have with our very own selves. Few of us are exempt from distortions in our self-concepts. We often unfairly—to ourselves—see ourselves in the worst light, negating obvious assets and abilities, or ascribe to ourselves assets and talents we don't have and impose for ourselves standards that are impossible to meet. Most often we unconsciously combine both processes, which usually produces a sense of futility, of hopelessness, and at worst a measure of desperation and misery.

Faulty relationships to ourselves also must have repercussions in the wider scope of human encounter. One emotional morass produces others and we are all victims of victims. Consequently we

9

affect others and others affect us, and both healthy and unhealthy reverberations are thereby felt in our relationships with children, parents, mates, friends, business associates, and professional colleagues, as well as the very culture we live in. We each of us do, after all, contribute to the language, symbols, meanings, and value system of our culture and are in turn reciprocally effected by the culture. While we usually do manage to meet the increasingly difficult challenge of living, we also are increasingly prone to both internal and external emotional harassment.

This book is not intended as a panacea or an attempt to resolve the human dilemma. It is not a "do-it-yourself psychoanalysis." But through my years of writing I have amassed a huge correspondence with people who have been enormously generous in sharing a multitude of their common human problems with me. While it is impossible to document all emotional problems, through the years I have attempted to deal with and to write about those problems that to me seem especially representative of the on-going life business of being a person.

In this book, I deal with a large number of issues in a combination of essay and question-and-answer form. I believe and hope I've covered a large enough segment of those subjects of emotional value —including self, marriage, family, and occupation—so that there may be some value for almost any reader.

This is not a theoretical book. It contains almost no technical language or psychological jargon. It is, I hope, a common-sense and practical approach to subjects and problems that at least in part are common to all of us. I hope that nearly anyone can easily understand the material and will find it possible to apply it directly to their particular area of concern, so as to make them and other people they know happier and more effective in their everyday lives.

—T.I.R
Weston, Connecticut

Part I
Dealing with the Self

CHAPTER 1

How Do You Feel About Yourself?
Mind Image and Body Image

MIND IMAGE

The way you feel about yourself governs the way you deal with your own problems and successes, the way you deal with others, the way you make career choices, the way you go on a diet or go off it, and the way you buy your clothes. Everything you do, in fact, can eventually be tied in with your feelings of worth or of insecurity. If you basically like yourself, and are only secondarily concerned with what others think about you, your self-esteem will be high enough to handle daily anxieties and pressures that beset all of us. People with poor self-esteem, on the other hand, may find themselves engaged in a great deal of self-destructive behavior and fantasizing to make up for a less-than-satisfactory reality. Their image of themselves is a shaky one; consequently, they may find that they "don't fit in anywhere," that they must be compulsively early to appointments, that their house is just never clean enough, or that members of the opposite sex always intimidate them. If we can try to see ourselves in clearer perspective, we will be better able to sort out our real problems from our fantasized ones.

Fantasies that Make You Unhappy

At various times in our lives, all of us have been or will be disillusioned. Moderate disillusionment puts us in a bad mood and leaves us with a general feeling of disappointment. Acute disillusionment generates more serious depression and self-hate, and can even lead to suicide.

While all men and women suffer from disillusionment, few know that their state of disappointment is the result of the breakdown of an illusion they themselves. have manufactured. Disillusionment is never possible without fantasy—and the destructive strength of the disillusionment can never exceed the strength and energy that was used to create fantasy in the first place.

Everyone lives in two worlds: the real world (reality) and the superimposed world of illusion (fantasy). From childhood on, both men and women develop ideas and beliefs that are totally imaginary. Fantasies become a way of coping with pain, solving problems, or overcoming the difficulties that the real world presents. These fantasies magically allow their maker to escape from anxiety as well as reality—and the greater the need to escape, the more we cling to fantasy.

At first, fantasies seem harmless enough, but living in a fantasy world keeps a man or a woman from tapping the riches that reality has to offer. Dreaming of nonexistent cake does not fill the stomach with real bread; the result is starvation.

No woman (or man) can go from a fantasy world into a real world without some disillusionment, but the resulting psychological harm can be greatly lessened if the individual will realize three things:

First, it is a tough struggle to separate fantasy from reality. But the struggle is totally worthwhile because it represents emotional growth and happiness.

Second, she must hold only herself responsible for her illusions —and, therefore, she alone can make the escape from the fantasy world in which she has put herself. Difficult as it may be, it is infinitely preferable for a person to remove herself from her fantasy world than to wait and have reality do it for her. Reality has a way of striking back when people are vulnerable—when they are ill-prepared for change.

Third, there are several illusions that are particularly common in our culture. These illusions have been passed on from parents, and through books, movies, TV, songs, etc. And each person who has learned them sustains them and passes them on to others. Familiarity with these principal illusions will enable you to help rid yourself of them before reality does it for you.

I will list and briefly describe some of the most common and most destructive illusions. There are illusions that are particularly prevalent to men, but I will not go into those. The fantasies I have named below, though common to both sexes, tend to be more harmful to women:

1. *The Shangri-la Illusion.* This is the fantasy that somewhere there is a paradise on earth, a problem-free, carefree, ever-joyous place in which one may live forever—if one can only find the key to the door. Victims of this illusion (and we *all* are, to some degree) believe that there is a society of beautiful people who live somewhere in constant excitement and joy, free from ordinary burdens that lesser people must endure. The key to such a "heaven on earth" is often thought to come with money, fame, power, or beauty.

In reality, no such place exists. Psychoanalysts know only too well the severity of problems that affect people from all walks of life, including people who—by American standards—have "made it." Indeed, "making it" often brings reality and vast disillusionment to people when they realize that, after all, fame and fortune do not produce happiness, do not prevent aging or death. The simple fact is that life is tough for everyone.

2. *The Money Illusion.* I include here all the fantasies stemming from the belief that prestige, money, power, beauty, fame, etc., make for continued happiness and radically alter personal experiences. I do not underestimate the pleasures money can buy, but I also know that there is a point beyond which money has little effect. Inner peace, self-acceptance, self-esteem and respect, resolution of inner conflicts, the happiness that comes from real involvement in one's areas of interests, the ability to relate fruitfully and constructively to others—all these important-for-living things—are simply not markedly advanced by money.

3. *The Love Illusion.* Love is wonderful, but it is *not* the key or solution to the human difficulties that everyone must face. Our culture constantly promotes the love myth with songs, poems, and stories, but it remains just that—a myth. No matter how much in love you are, you will continue to have problems with yourself and your lover, with others, and with the world in general. Love makes it easier to face problems, but life remains difficult.

4. *The Marriage Illusion.* This illusion is particularly prevalent among very dependent women—women who lack a sense of identity, real self, and confidence. The fantasy here is that marriage will provide a woman with those qualities she lacks. In many cases, these women see marriage as the solution to all their problems—and as a means of attaining total security and safety in an otherwise dangerous world. To many women, marriage is further seen as the fulfillment of every childhood wish and fantasy: a substitute

for imperfect parents; a life of endless peace, fascination, and pleasure; an end to frustration and feelings of emptiness and loneliness.

The degree to which a bride believes the marriage fantasy will determine the degree of her ensuing disillusionment—and rage—when she discovers that her beliefs were just illusions. Marriage can and does provide many satisfactions, but it is never a solution to personal problems—nor is it a substitute for needed personal growth, development, and self-fulfillment.

Nor is marriage an antidote for loneliness. Having a husband and children may lessen feelings of loneliness, but self-development and learning to like oneself enough to feel in good company when alone are much more constructive ways of overcoming loneliness. Too many women have the illusion that marriage, with love, ought to be instantly successful and complete. Such an expectation can lead to enormous disappointment and disaster.

5. *The Children Illusion.* Fantasies about children run rampant. They include claims that children—especially one's own—are brilliant, misunderstood, talented, beautiful, good natured, and devoted, as well as selfish, inconsiderate, insensitive, uncaring, etc. Children are some of these, all of these, and more. The point is that they are human and, like the adults they will someday be, they are full of human inconsistencies and confusions.

One prevalent, usually unconscious, illusion is that children will never grow up and leave home—and that the family status quo will never change. There is another popular illusion that even though the children grow up and leave home, they will still maintain a childlike attachment and devotion to their parents. But children *do* grow up, leave home, and have families of their own—which then become their most immediate concern. Parents who are prepared for this evolutionary development and change are much better able to face the changes that come with middle age than those parents who harbor illusions. Parents who have no interests and involvement other than their children seem to age overnight when children grow up, leave home, and marry. With the shattering of their "children illusions," these parents feel that all worthwhile things have suddenly been taken from them.

6. *The Youth Fantasy.* Intellectually, we know that we are going to grow older—and that beauty will fade and health problems

develop. Yet, despite this, some women unconsciously harbor the illusion of everlasting youth. These women are prey to all kinds of charlatans who promise all kinds of youth treatments. Some desperate women will even engage in activities inappropriate to their health and age, activities that may result in sickness or death. Some women try to deny age by dressing and acting like teen-agers. Women who cling to the youth illusion hate themselves as they grow older and often become disturbed and depressed. In their continual quest for something that is no longer possible, these women cheat themselves of realistic, pleasurable activities that are more appropriate to their particular age and state of health.

7. *The Dependency Illusion.* Women are not naturally dependent and helpless. They are not incapable, illogical, highly emotional, or unbusinesslike. These are false, prejudicial characteristics that have been attributed to women for so long that many women believe them. However, I've seen highly competent, intelligent, and potentially independent women who, believing the "dependency illusion," spend their entire lives being dependent and unfulfilled.

All illusions—and there are many more—are the stuff that misery is made of. "Busting illusions" isn't easy, because it involves motivation, recognition, and struggle. Growing up isn't easy either, but it can result in greater happiness and can prevent emotional difficulties —even disaster. Therefore, let me close by inviting you to become an "illusion buster." I consider it one of the prime keys to mental health.

Q: *I spend a lot of time second-guessing or chastising myself. What can I do about it?*

A: Self-hate, whatever forms it takes, is much more than a waste of time; it lowers morale, depletes energy, clouds issues and prevents us from taking constructive steps in our lives. Unfortunately, we can't always recognize when we are being cruel to ourselves. Even when we can, we are sometimes helpless to stop it. Any step toward recognizing self-torture—and taking a stand against it—represents real progress.

Being kind to ourselves—regardless of failures, unattained goals or mistakes—is worthwhile. Such compassion leads to emotional growth, enhances the constructive forces inside us all and increases our emotional strength—all of which means a greater potential for happiness.

Q: *I am a thirty-four-year-old women with a rather odd complaint. I feel I don't fit in anywhere. When I look back, I realize that I felt this way at school, I felt this way when I worked in an office, and now I feel the same way at home. Someday I'd like to find my niche, but I'm beginning to wonder if I ever will.*

A: Your complaint is rather common and not at all "odd." The majority of people with your complaint do not have a problem "fitting in" as much as a problem of "getting involved." These people refuse to give up an aloof, superior attitude that prevents involvement and fitting in. They secretly enjoy the feeling of not fitting in, and unconsciously harbor an infantile yearning for a utopian condition in which they will fit. Since the human condition precludes utopia, many of these people will go through life never "fitting in." An effort at total involvement with a person, people, a position, or an activity may result in "fitting in" and much fun.

Some people, however, are so threatened by possible involvement and have been "detached" so long they cannot change without psychoanalytic help.

Q: *I have a strange problem. I don't know what to do with my time. Oh, I have plenty of work to do and plenty of personal interests; it's just that I do not know what to do when. I know this sounds crazy, but I wake up in the morning depressed and frustrated as I face each day, because no matter which job I decide to do, I always feel as if I should be doing something else.*

I serve as a professional assistant to my husband here at home; we are both in the same profession (except that he has a Ph.D. and I have only a B.S.) and I help him in his research here at home while he is at work. So I have plenty of work to do (besides my housework), especially now since we are involved in a big project. I do want time to develop my own interests, namely painting. But every time I steal a little time for myself during the day for such activities as painting or embroidery, I feel very guilty, as though I

were wasting time. And by evening I feel too tired to do any of
these things. I feel as though my life does not belong to me. What is
wrong with me and what can I do?

A: You sound as though you know very well what you would
like to do with your time and life. You mention painting and embroidery, and it wouldn't surprise me at all if you want to go on
and get your very own Ph.D., too. Doing it, however, requires taking yourself and your desires seriously. This means you are entitled
and healthfully ought to regard yourself (including your needs and
aspirations) as the most important person in your life. However much
a person is in love, sacrificing oneself to prove it inevitably produces
frustration, considerable self-hate and resentment. This in turn makes
for chronic fatigue as well as confusion concerning one's feelings and
desires.

Of course it is impossible to participate in every conceivable
activity all at the same time. Some priority is necessary and this
entails giving up one or more activities in favor of others. But this
is particularly difficult for people who feel deprived and who therefore feel that they must have it all immediately or nothing at all.
This is most likely to occur in people who are not loyal to themselves, who refuse to assert themselves in their own behalf. People
who feel that they "steal time for themselves" and who feel guilty
for participating in their own individual and personal enrichment
always find it difficult to make decisions regarding the use of their
time. Having lost the feeling of being the center of their own lives,
decisions regarding what to do with their lives, time, and energy
are blocked by confusions and guilt. Psychoanalytic therapy is often
necessary to restore the feeling of owning one's life so that personal
ambitions, satisfactions, and pleasures can be realized without feeling self-hating, guilty, and threatened by potential loss of love from
others.

Q: *At one time I was a celebrity. People everywhere knew my*
name. Today I am a "has-been." I have tried to face up to my pres-
ent situation, but I still think of how it used to be and I get terribly
upset. I know this is not a common problem, but I wish that you
could comment and perhaps make me feel better.

A: You are right, your problem is not a common one, because most of us never achieve fame. However, we all dwell on the past. In looking back everyone comes off badly: we all used to be younger, better looking, healthier—you name it. But this does not make us "has-beens." No one can be considered a "has-been." Life does not stand still—living is a continuing process. Being part of the life process makes us what we are here and now, and it is the here and now that is important.

Anyone can be knocked off a pedestal that rests on unrealistic, superficial foundations. But real human substance cannot be blown away by bad luck or an uncaring public. Compassion and appreciation for human struggle—and being alive in a tough world—connect us to the real substance of life. True growth and development result in true living experiences. These experiences make for a solid life foundation and not the flimsy life-basis that can disappear and make us feel like "has-beens."

My answer to the "has-been" feeling is: "Be here now!" *Be* means being, living. *Here* means wherever you actually are, not some fantasy place or situation. *Now* refers to the present, which is the only time that exists, the only time in which living takes place. The past is gone and the future is not yet here, so—Be Here Now! Goals achieved are not nearly as important as life itself. Nothing can measure up to the fact that you are living here and now. If your present life doesn't measure up to fantasies of the past or future, it indicates to me that you must involve yourself more in today's relationships and activities. Appreciate your past, anticipate your future —but *live* your life in the present.

Q: *My wife is driving me and our teen-age son and daughter crazy with her need for cleanliness. She never stops cleaning and she insists that we don't, either. Our house looks like a sterilized museum. I'm sure that some of our friends hate to visit us, because they feel they're imposing on my wife just by walking on the floor. She was always this way, but now it's getting worse. I can't reason with her about it, but I think (hope) she'll pay attention to what you say.*

A: Compulsive cleaners are invariably suffering from anxiety and self-hatred. Even the symptom is a kind of self-torture. These people cannot help themselves, because they usually have no idea what motivates them. Some, apparently, are trying to wash away unconscious childhood guilt; others, to be good and acceptable to parents long since gone; still others, to clean away "dirty" sexual feelings or repress hostile impulses, including the urge to let go, to let all the dirt come out. Some have an unconscious childish desire to wallow in filth and fling it all over the place. Understandably, they are frightened of what they feel and impose all kinds of restraint on themselves and others to avoid exposing these feelings.

As with other serious neurotic manifestations, age often brings increased anxiety and greater severity of symptoms. Psychoanalytic psychiatric treatment is what I would suggest for the relief of all concerned.

Q: *Would you mind saying something about the symptom, compulsive earliness? I get so anxious unless I leave early that I invariably arrive at all appointments much, much too soon and then have to wait around for ages.*

A: I'm glad you realize that there is a difference between arriving on time and compulsive early arrival at all appointments. One is motivated by normal courtesy, while the other is a function of neurotic anxiety. Compulsive early arrivals *must* go early; otherwise they have a feeling that their safety and security are being jeopardized. Here are a few of the problems that may be involved in compulsive early arriving at appointments:

1. The need to be liked and the fear of rejection and retribution.
2. Fears of authority that have not been resolved.
3. The need for perfection.
4. An inflexible and punitive attitude toward other people's limitations, shortcomings, and what is felt as slights directed at oneself.
5. The unconscious demand that others reward them for being such a "good" and "responsible" person.

Q: *I am twenty years old. I'm a junior in college and my grades are fairly good. But I have a terrible time writing papers. Once I get started, I'm all right. But I can sit like a dunce trying to organize my thoughts, and hours (literally) go by, with nothing happening.*

Since I'm hoping to go to graduate school, I am terribly concerned. Have you any practical suggestions?

A: Try *not* to organize your thoughts into logical, complete patterns. If you wait until it is all in mind perfectly, you may wait a long time!

Remember that one thought brings on another, associations bring on more associations. Our goal here is to start the associative machinery working.

How? The trick is to start. The solution lies in the *starting*.

How? Write whatever comes to mind pertaining to the subject, and utterly disregard logic, organization, grades, and teacher response. After, only after, there is considerable material—words on paper—take a look. Observe what you have. Do these thoughts lead to more thoughts? Are there any points of particular interest? Anything present deserving of more research? *After* this *start* has taken place, you may well find that a central theme presents itself, so that a logical assembly can now take place with relative ease.

Q: *My husband needs constant excitement—people, nightclubs, parties, movies—go, go, go. He is just never satisfied to sit at home occasionally and relax, and frankly, I don't think I can stand it much longer. Is there any explanation for this kind of person or any way to change him?*

A: Many people need this kind of constant stimulation to feel safely alive. Without excitement and anticipation of excitement, they feel cut off, depressed, and anxious. Being on the go is for them a major defense against feelings of inner deadness and emptiness. To be left alone, without people and stimulation, often feels like impending doom and can produce anxiety to the point of panic. The principal antidote for a feeling of inner deadness is, of course, confidence in oneself and one's values.

For these inner-dead, supercharged excitement seekers, psychoanalytic treatment is often necessary in order to achieve a real feeling for self and for others. Successful treatment can produce feelings of real aliveness. This will reduce the need for constant and increasing amounts of stimulation and thus be lifesaving.

Q: *As a director of high school plays, I have found that young people have difficulty with space relations. To put it simply, they are always bumping into each other or things. Is this due to lack of a fully mature neurological development or are there emotional reasons for such behavior?*

A: The behavior you describe is directly related to a person's concept of himself. This includes his feelings about who he is in relation to other people as well as his physical image of himself. These "self" concepts start developing in very early childhood and continue to evolve and change as the individual grows and gathers experiences of all kinds. The experiences that are particularly important are those that involve him with other people. Through his reactions to others and their reactions to him, the young person forms a concept of himself.

The relationships of early childhood are very important in the development of this feeling for "self." Most psychiatrists believe that the infant does not know where he ends and the rest of the world begins. He feels that he is the world and the world is him. Through experiences and frustrations, he learns that his skin separates him from the rest of the world and that he is, in fact, a whole, integral, separate human unit. But his emotional self—his combined feelings about himself as well as his self-esteem—continues to be related primarily to his emotional involvement with people; thus it is in a state of flux. This state of flux is at its greatest during adolescence, when all kinds of important physical changes are taking place. These changes have repercussions on the adolescent's bodily image or concept of his physical being. Thus the budding adult does not have a clear-cut concept of his body or its outer limits. He may feel large or small, just as his self-esteem may vary from day to day. He may "bump" into things physically just as he "bumps" into people emotionally. This is, after all, a period of emotional and physical reality testing. As time goes on, his concept of himself becomes more solidified and his physical movements—relative to the world around him—will reflect a new maturity.

Q: *I have a friend who owns about ten pets. Is it true that people who like animals usually find it difficult to relate to other people because of a lack of maturity?*

A: No! There are all kinds of people, mature and otherwise, who like animals, and there are all kinds who like people, and even some who like both and some who like neither.

Q: *I find that I can't buy anything for myself without feeling guilty or without asking myself first whether everyone else in the family has the same thing or the equivalent. Have you ever heard of this kind of disease?*

A: It is extremely common and is not a disease at all. It is a symptom—the symbol of a combination of difficulties in relating to oneself and to others. Again—as with all human behavior—the pattern of problems causing this symptom may vary from individual to individual. With this kind of symptom, we very often find poor self-esteem, a compulsive need to be liked and great difficulty in self-assertion. However, the pattern of the problems producing these difficulties is extremely intricate. The symptom usually will not disappear until these problems have been resolved, and this almost always entails either psychoanalysis or psychotherapy based on psychoanalytic theory.

Q: *I have a friend who is always giving gifts. She needs no pretense at all to buy people all kinds of things. She is famous among our crowd for her indiscriminant gift-giving. I wonder if there is any special reason for this that is not obvious?*

A: People give gifts for many reasons. Gift-giving can be symbolic of love, gratitude, warmth, a real desire to give and to share pleasure and good fortune. Compulsive gift-giving is not an uncommon phenomenon and may be based on a combination of healthy and neurotic factors. The compulsive gift-giver often remains unaware of her motivations in giving. Some of the common explanations (they are usually found in combination) are:

1. Attempting to buy love, friendship, and security.
2. Attempting to impress people with one's generosity in order to bolster one's ego. This, too, is really an attempt to allay subconscious feelings of insecurity.
3. Attempting to make people feel indebted so that they will

grant future favors requested. Giving is a way of asking for gifts in return.

4. There are people who do not feel entitled to anything unless close relatives or friends are provided for first. Giving gifts is a ritual necessary so that they can feel free to buy things for themselves.

5. Many people give gifts as payment for favors received—real or imagined. These people use gifts to make certain that they are in no way beholden to anyone. These are usually people who have a need for freedom from involvement with others. They really fear sustained emotional closeness.

6. Some people give gifts to friends and to charity as a form of penance to atone for and allay feelings of guilt.

7. There are people who give gifts as a magic ritual to ward off evil and to pay off the gods.

Q: *What do I do about a friend who bluntly asks me where I buy my clothes and how much I pay for them? Most of the time I'm so shocked, I just blurt out the answers, although I don't want to. Now she's begun asking about the furnishings in my house. My friend is an intelligent, stunning, well-dressed, well-off wife and mother.*

A: Chances are your friend secretly admires you a great deal. Actually, she probably idolizes you. Having unconsciously invested you with all kinds of ideal characteristics (she is not fully aware of her hero-worship, nor of the reasons that make her so curious about your personal business), she naturally is curious about everything you do, including your personal money matters. The more she knows about you, the greater her illusion of closeness. This makes it easier for her to identify with you. Identification with you (her ideal) gives her a greater feeling of adequacy and self-esteem. Though you describe your friend as an intelligent wife and mother, she herself probably feels quite inadequate. She has selected you as her standard of achievement in various areas and is attempting to emulate you and reach that ideal. Eventually, she will attempt to surpass her ideal (you). This makes for competition. So the more she knows about you, the easier it is for her to compete. This is another of her ways of trying to feel more adequate.

Someday she will undoubtedly find out that you have limitations, too. When she discovers that even gods have clay feet, chances are she will be grossly disappointed and will suddenly lose her obsessive interest in you and your private matters. She will then seek other heroines—unless, of course, she resolves those problems that are related to her lack of self-acceptance and strengthens her own feelings of personal taste, value and individuality.

Q: *I have a girl friend who is a wonderful person, but we always get into silly arguments about the same issue. She is a super patriot and hero-worshiper and for her, the USA, the President, and other famous people are always right no matter what. I, too, love my country but have not abandoned my critical sense nor my feeling that there is an obvious need for improvement in certain areas. Why are some people like my friend?*

A: A few factors may pertain. Some people, as they become adults, transfer their idealizations from parents to institutions, causes, religion, God, country, and people too remote from them to be examined closely. Of necessity they avoid hero-worshiping people they actually know because obvious human fallibility will destroy the idealizing process before it even gets started. This idealizing processing often begins as children disappointedly discover that their parents are human after all and do in fact have human limitations and fallibilities. Many people attempt to compensate for inner feelings of fragility by identifying with others outside themselves whom they imbue with unshakable beauty, truth, wisdom, purity, and righteousness. Criticism of any image to which they have given God-like proportions is seen as an attack on their shrine and strength and as a threat of possible exposure of feelings of weakness, uncertainty and fragility.

Q: *My brother is obviously interested in a friend of mine, but he simply can't bring himself to call her for a date. Why do some men have no trouble asking a woman out, while others go through torture before they muster the courage?*

A: Many sensitive, interesting, eligible men are extremely fearful of rejection; they cannot bear the blow to their pride. If they could be certain the woman would say "yes" to their invitation, many men would not hesitate to call for a date. Women who know this will very subtly let a man know that a call would be appreciated and a date accepted. An occasional woman, unfettered by convention and less fearful of rejection, will sometimes call an interesting man to reassure him of her interest—and/or to initiate a relationship. If your friend is one of these women, why not suggest that she make the call . . . or at least indicate to your brother that she will say "yes" if he phones.

Q: *My girl friend's twenty-year-old brother is intelligent, good-looking, and has a great personality. Yet in all the years I have known him, I've never seen him with a girl who is his equal physically or mentally. He always dates dull, plain girls. Why?*

A: Your evaluation of this man may be affected by your own feelings about him. Perhaps you have praised him too much and his girl friends too little. Are you projecting your own desires to date him?

If, however, you are being totally objective in the matter, there are some possible explanations for his actions. Some men (and women) choose to date people with whom they have little in common—to avoid forming a permanent relationship, which they view as a trap. Others shun and fear people whom they admire because they feel inferior to them ("So and so is much too marvelous to date me"). It would be impossible for me to tell you exactly why your friend acts as he does. The chemistry that draws people to one another is usually very complex and has deep roots in each individual's life history and development.

Q: *Why are some women so attracted to mean, almost sadistic men? I'm sure this is not universally true, but it is certainly so for me and several of my friends. I'm talking about men who are hard to get along with, who generally give a girl a hard time. One man I'm thinking of is always very critical and never fails to show how superior he feels to me. I would like to be attracted to a nice, considerate man, but as much as I try, I never succeed.*

A: This is an all-too-common problem, and of course there are various reasons and combinations of reasons behind it. Here are some that I've encountered:

1. People with this kind of problem often confuse contempt, arrogance, and cruelty with strength and dependability. Unfortunately, sadistic people usually are undependable and actually quite fragile.

2. Cruelty is also confused with masculinity and virility, whereas sadistic people usually have serious sexual problems, including fear of being sexually inadequate.

3. People with poor self-esteem see people who treat them contemptuously as "really knowing" them and thus as being wise indeed. They see people who treat them with respect as having been fooled and therefore as stupid. In light of this self-contempt, they further see decent treatment as inappropriate, dull, and a sign of "weakness."

4. People who feel "dead and empty" look for cruel treatment as a form of stimulation. They are often desperate to feel anything at all and seek pain as particularly stimulating and as evidence of much-needed attention.

Q: *Arrogant, mean, untrusting, and ruthless men always appeal to me. If a man is nice, I feel no physical attraction to him. What's my problem?*

A: Your opinion of yourself, and your idea of what constitutes masculinity, may need investigation and overhauling. Chances are that you are confusing meanness, arrogance, etc., with masculinity and strength. These characteristics do not denote masculinity. If anything, they are evidence of serious emotional impoverishment—and as you probably already know, they are also characteristics that can lead to disastrously painful man-woman relationships.

BODY IMAGE

Obesity is one of the most common manifestations of self-hate. People who simply cannot stop themselves from eating compulsively may say that they do not care about their appearance; actually they care deeply but dislike themselves too much to do something constructive about it. Women who dress like young girls, use too much perfume, wear sexually suggestive clothing, or spend fortunes on cosmetic surgery all have problems with their body image. Our mirrors tell us the truth about our bodies, but only we can change our appearance for better or worse and, more important, decide *why* we feel the particular change is necessary.

Q: *Exactly what is a compulsive eater?*

A: In simplest terms, a compulsive eater is a person who eats whether or not he (or she) is suffering from real hunger. Real hunger is when a person has a physiological *need* to eat. A compulsive eater suffers from what I call "mouth hunger." Mouth hunger has no connection with real hunger or the body's physiological need for food. Mouth hunger is invariably caused by the eater's emotional needs—a need that he or she displaces from its hidden or unconscious source to the mouth. This need can be satisfied momentarily by the tasting, chewing, swallowing, and ingesting of food. When the emotional need reappears, so does mouth hunger. Compulsive eaters are usually overweight, and it is almost impossible for them to diet successfully until they solve their emotional problems.

Q: *I am chronically overweight but I always manage to tell myself that obesity is a matter of body type, glands, heredity, and luck. What can I do about it?*

A: Stop fooling yourself! You are a food addict! Ninety-nine percent of the cases of chronic overweight are caused by chronic overeating. People eat compulsively because they feel nervous and anxious. In short, emotional problems cause the overeating that leads to overweight. Men and women who have been extremely obese most of their lives need help—psychoanalytic help. Pills, gimmick diets, and exercise will not help in the long run. Insight into one's emotional problems is necessary if sustained weight control is to take place. To get to the root of the problem, psychoanalytic psychotherapy is usually indicated.

Q: *I wake up almost every night at about 3 A.M., and I just can't stop eating whatever I find in the house. (I overeat during the day, too. I am very overweight.) Why do I eat at night?*

A: Most people who overeat so that they become chronically overweight do so because of anxiety. These people use food as a kind of tranquilizer; it makes them feel temporarily fuller, stronger, safer, and generally more adequate. As a result, they avoid the deeper problems that make them anxious in the first place. Some very anxious people have trouble sleeping because they often have revealing and frightening dreams. To avoid these painful dreams, which they cannot face, they wake up. When they wake up, they often turn to the only security blanket they know—food. In general, night eating is an indication of a deeper-than-normal emotionally caused obesity problem. I nearly always advise compulsive night-eaters to consult a properly trained psychoanalyst.

Q: *My husband is terribly overweight and is also a heavy smoker. Our doctor warned him that he may have a stroke or a heart attack if he doesn't diet immediately. My doctor does not believe in diet pills. My husband says he will go on a diet, but I just can't take him seriously because he has gone on and off diets a hundred times in the past with no success. I know you feel that obesity is an emotional illness—and I agree. But what can I do to help my husband?*

A: I agree with your doctor who is against pills and knows that dieting is the only answer to sustained weight loss. I feel that chronic obesity is a psychosomatic illness, and I am happy that you, too, realize that obesity is an emotional problem. Many sufferers require psychiatric help, but few, unfortunately, will respond to urging or nagging. Few obese people are motivated to get thin by health needs or threats of dire illness and impending doom—however realistic these may be. Obese people—including men—are more likely to respond to appeals to vanity. Showing your husband pictures of himself at a thinner, younger age may have some effect.

Here is a list of what I consider practical ways a wife can help her husband diet:

1. Take him seriously each time he talks about a diet. This is

not the time to talk of old failures—besides, this time it may work.

2. Be helpful and supportive. Never nag. If he breaks the diet, treat it as a momentary break, and remind him of his successes up to that point and encourage him to continue.

3. Clear the house of all foods that he must not eat. You cannot expect a "food addict" not to eat food that's around the house. The eating habits of the whole family must change to thinning ways if you want to save the breadwinner's life. Do not bring up family deprivation and sacrifice on this score. Chances are the whole family will be healthier for having removed fattening foods from their diet. Young children should be taught to eat minimally and healthfully. This will serve them well in later life.

4. Try to prepare the foods your husband can eat interestingly and in a variety of ways. There are several fine low-calorie cookbooks around. Keep a plentiful supply of food that he (and you, too) can eat in any quantity; these include celery, carrots, string beans, and mushrooms (but not sautéed).

5. Don't eat out or go to restaurants until your husband has lost at least seventy-five percent of his desired goal. Then go to restaurants infrequently and learn how to order proper food: fish, lean meat, salads, fresh fruit, and only low-calorie desserts.

6. Never, absolutely *never,* encourage your husband to break his diet. If you feel sorry for him and want to give him a little tidbit, don't do it. Be especially careful about this after he has lost large amounts of weight, and you think he looks pinched, pale, pained, etc. This may be just your unfamiliar view of him. We all feel more comfortable with the status quo, but a fat man's status quo will kill him. Never succumb to a desire to break his diet as an unconscious wish to keep him a fat but familiar-looking husband.

7. Be prepared to accept his irritation and anger. It will come, but it will pass.

8. Be particularly supporting and loving during any period of stress that may come at a time of business difficulty, family sickness, etc. Your husband will be especially vulnerable at these times. Affection and entertainment may mitigate a desire for food.

9. Don't expect him to give up smoking or any other habit while he's dieting. Breaking that habit will be much easier after he has gained considerable self-esteem from having won the battle to lose weight—the most important battle of his life.

Q: *I have been fighting a severe weight problem for most of my twenty-one years. I plan to marry a man who is also overweight. What are the chances that our children will be born with this same condition? I would rather adopt than put a child through the weight misery I've had.*

A: Basal metabolism, the rate at which we burn up food and accumulate weight, is largely controlled by our glandular systems, and our glandular systems are inherited. But very few fat people are fat because of inherited glandular problems. Therefore, it is extremely rare for children to inherit any kind of condition leading to obesity.

Overweight is almost always due to overeating, which in turn is almost always due to emotional difficulties and faulty upbringing with respect to eating habits.

There is a great risk that fat parents will provide the emotional environment and eating habits that make for obesity. That is why it is important that before you become parents, you and your husband resolve your eating problems—not only for your own sake, but for your future children's sake.

One of the greatest crimes parents commit is stuffing children with food. This is especially true of parents who have lost touch with what constitutes healthy eating habits and "normal" portions. Establishing good eating habits is vital to a family's well-being.

Keep in mind that it is almost impossible for children to acquire different eating habits from their parents', because they learn through identification and imitation.

Q: *I've been flitting from one diet to another with little success. Is there one diet that really works? Which one do you prefer?*

A: I favor a well-balanced, low-calorie, relatively high-protein, low-carbohydrate diet. I would also favor your facing the fact that "flitting from one diet to another" simply means breaking one diet after another. Under those conditions, no diet will work. The bitter truth is that most diets work, but not without the secret key: sticking to it.

Q: *I am an obese thin, largely due to your writings, especially the book,* Forever Thin, *which I regard as my bible. The insights and direction I have found are measureless. At thirty-seven I feel twenty-seven, look younger by many years than at my top weight of two-hundred-eighty-pounds. Thanks to you and Weight Watchers and a nonflakey psychiatrist, I now weigh one-hundred-forty-two and am aiming for one-hundred-thirty-four. I lecture to four classes weekly for Weight Watchers and feel born again.*

I would like to hear your comments on your appearance in the photo in the January, 1973, issue of the Ladies' Home Journal. *You have obviously taken a vacation from being forever thin—why?*

A: Congratulations on your dieting success and the happiness it has brought you. It is a good idea to maintain vigilance because weight does have a way of creeping back. But being *too* zealous can be destructive, too. Excessive demands for thinness sometimes lead to undermining one's physical and emotional health as well as to disappointment and renewed eating binges.

With due respect to my picture in the *Journal*, here are my "weight facts":

I am six feet, three inches tall. I weighed a maximum of two hundred sixty pounds over twenty years ago. I now weigh two hundred pounds. I would like to weigh between one hundred eighty-five and one hundred ninety-five but am wary of becoming discouraged because of not being able to reach or sustain an "ideal" weight. Two hundred and ten pounds is my danger point. Anytime I've reached it over the last twenty years I have immediately and successfully dieted down to two hundred or below. Having no illusion as regards my ability to overeat and overgain, I am always careful and therefore hope to continue to sustain my initial loss, which now is more than twenty years old.

Q: *My husband is both a compulsive eater and smoker. When he diets, he goes from two packs to three packs of cigarettes a day. And when he tries to stop smoking, he eats twice as much as usual. Do oversmoking and overeating stem from similar emotional problems?*

A: Both habits have much in common, including much underlying anxiety, considerable ruthlessness toward oneself, a tendency to oversimplify the problem, so as to avoid much-needed professional help, and increased oral or mouth activity as a way of relieving tension. Smoking involves the added complication of the habitual use and effect of a powerful drug—nicotine.

Q: *My brother is eighty-four pounds overweight, and we know he is lonely and unhappy. The truth is that a girl would be out of her mind to look at him. My mother, my husband, and I have tried to talk him into seeing a psychiatrist, since everything else has failed. He says he is not crazy and won't go. What can we do?*

A: Don't nag him! Point out (once only) that people who see psychiatrists have problems. Tell him that seeing a psychiatrist shows that they know they have problems and desire to do something about them. This is in itself evidence of not being crazy. Quite often, the healthiest people in a family are seeing a psychiatrist, while people with less health are not. If this doesn't work, an approach by a person for whom he has great respect may be helpful. Again, this must be done tactfully and without nagging.

And if this doesn't work, you may just have to wait until your brother musters up sufficient motivation to see a doctor. The area of motivation still remains one in which we psychiatrists are most helpless. The truism that half the battle is won when the patient steps into the office remains true. Unfortunately, the patient is the only one who can effectively bring himself into treatment, since his cooperation is absolutely necessary. Until such time as your brother becomes sufficiently motivated, may I suggest that the people around him indicate by example and cooperation that they will help him in better eating habits (dieting) in every possible way.

Q: *I'm terribly overweight, but I just can't stop eating. It is really the bane of my existence. I'm thirty-two, and I look fifty. I try to stop; but it just doesn't work, because no matter how much I eat, I still feel hungry. What can I do? I'm a hundred pounds overweight.*

A: I consider a hundred pounds of overweight a very serious physical and emotional condition. Compulsive eaters can't just stop. They are suffering from serious emotional disturbances, which must be treated accordingly. Willpower is not nearly as important or effective as insight. This insight is best achieved through psychoanalytic therapy with a competent psychiatrist. It is also very important to have a complete physical evaluation with a qualified physician who practices internal medicine.

Initially, the compulsive eater will find it almost impossible to stop eating, for this is his way of handling deep anxiety. Until the source of that anxiety is properly explored and one's tolerance to anxiety is increased, it is too much to expect him to stop overeating. Expect to go on overeating for a while, and prepare accordingly. Proper preparation means having on hand plenty of no- or low-calorie food that is commensurate with the diet prescribed by your internist. I call these foods "ammunition foods." It will also be of value to remove what I call "poison foods" from the house. These are foods that will result in certain weight gain. So—remember, fat people are anxious people who need to eat to cope with their anxiety. Eat ammunition foods, remove poison foods, and have proper consultations with an internist and a psychoanalytically trained psychiatrist.

Q: *I have a friend who is a health-food addict. She claims that one is what one eats and that certain foods affect people's emotions. She says that people would not be hostile if they stopped eating meat. Is there any evidence to support what she says?*

A: None that I am familiar with. But I do know of many cases of people who become hostile when they are hungry. I also know that many people hate themselves when they eat too much and get fat.

Q: *I used to be married to a man who bathed once a month. His excuse was that he caught colds easily. What was the real reason?*

A: There are several possibilities for your former husband's behavior. He himself may have no awareness of the connections between the reasons and his own phobia about bathing. Consciously, he may just be aware that he doesn't like to bathe, and rationalizes this by saying he catches colds easily. Others rationalize a phobia about bathing by saying they are clean, they do not do physical or "dirty" work, or they are saving money by not using soap and water. Subconsciously, the real reasons for the phobia may be:

1. The person may be so full of self-hate that he cannot tolerate the sight of his own body. Being naked in a bath puts one in theateningly close touch with physical and emotional being.

2. He may be terrified of being alone because it means being with nobody. There are people who do not consider themselves as "someone." In this case bathing is as terrifying as any other solitary activity.

3. Your former husband may find bathing too relaxing. This state of relaxation brings to his awareness thoughts he prefers to keep buried.

4. Bathing can feel sensuous, pleasurable, and sexually exciting. Some men find these feelings threatening to their confused notions of masculinity.

5. Your ex-husband may use body odor as an expression of hostility toward others. By bathing he would destroy what he considers distance-making, offensive weapons.

6. He may feel too self-hating to do anything that smacks of self-care and self-indulgence.

7. He may have been brought up in a cultural environment that ignores soap and water. It can be most difficult for such people to adopt new activities.

8. He may be afraid of feeling helpless. Nakedness in a bathtub makes some people feel stripped of all social accouterments, accomplishments, and standing. This makes them feel helpless and vulnerable.

9. Some people with a traumatic history of near-drowning feel threatened by any quantity of water larger than a glassful.

10. Some imaginative people who fear death equate a bathtub with a coffin. Others feel phobic about any tight space: elevators, small rooms, bathtubs, etc.

To find out which of these many factors apply to your ex-husband, it would be necessary to delve more deeply into his personal history.

Q: *I have a friend who is always looking at herself in a mirror. Even when we walk along the street, she is captivated by her reflection in store windows. What makes a woman so preoccupied with herself? Is she "in love with herself?"*

A: Obsessive preoccupation with one's own image is the opposite of self-love—it is more often related to self-hate. People who really like themselves have adequate self-esteem and confidence; they do not need mirrors to reassure them of their worth. Many chronic "reflection-seekers" are people who are most concerned about looks and the superficial impressions they convey because they have a deep sense of emptiness and worthlessness. Many of these people seek security and reassurance through being liked and admired by others. Unfortunately, however, real self-confidence is never dependent upon either self-admiration or the admiration of others, since admiration does not in any way alter one's basic insecurities, self-rejection or self-hate. Some particularly fragile people need to look at themselves as often as possible to reassure themselves that they actually do exist and that they are truly human, and to remind themselves who they are. This is a pathetic effort to establish a missing sense of self-identity. The degree to which a person is lacking an inner sense of substance and self is the degree to which that person is preoccupied with surface looks and impressions.

Q: *My friend is thirty-eight years old, bright, charming, and likable. However, she dresses like a little girl. Frankly, I'm fed up with the baby-doll look, especially when the teeny-bopper in boots, white stockings, pigtails and short skirts turns out to have a fifty-year-old face. My friend is not married, and I know she would like to be, but I don't think a mature man can look at the way she turns herself out and want to be seen with her. What makes seemingly bright women slaves to fashion even when it is totally inappropriate for them?*

A: There are several interrelated explanations for this.

1. Many of these women are repressed and not-so-repressed exhibitionists. They want to be seen and will dress or undress any way necessary in order to be seen. Much of their sexuality is dissipated in being seen rather than its being used in closer contact.

2. Many are extreme conformists. They don't think or feel for themselves but simply go along with a style, however inappropriate, in order to feel "safe" and "acceptable."

3. Many are more than ordinarily narcissistic, operating on an extremely superficial, materialistic basis with a minimum of real values or real involvement with people. Their lives and well-being are predicated on "looks," "things" and "making impressions" rather than on responsible emotional interchange with people.

4. Some are emotionally stunted and quite immature. They live in an unreal tinsel world of chronic teen-age fantasy. As they get older their infantile values and emotions become increasingly distant from their aging bodies. Many have not moved an emotional iota from the time of being "Daddy's little girl."

5. Sadly, some see themselves as dehumanized, pretty, decorated ornaments, whose sole value in life lies in the ability to stir admiration and sexual response.

6. They often make relationships with equally immature, superficial men. An initial sexual encounter with a man who is adult is almost never sustained, for he usually becomes bored with this kind of partner's immaturity, chronic need for admiration, and inner emptiness.

Q: *I see so many women on the street who dress in an openly seductive manner. My husband and I are curious to know if these women are really as sexy as they look. I mean, are they as interested in sex as their dress (and manner) would indicate?*

A: It has been said—and I agree—that you can't judge a book by its cover. Many women dress provocatively simply because it is "in fashion." And these days fashion is rather blatantly sexy with the no-bra look, etc. However, there are women who have such a low opinion of themselves that they must use openly sexual methods (including dress) to attract men—because they do not feel their other assets are adequate enough to do so. Many of these women completely dissipate their sexual feelings and responses by "showing off." Psychoanalytic investigation often reveals that, emotionally, these women have not progressed beyond a childish level of sexual development. Therefore, despite surface appearance, many highly exhibitionistic women have little interest in sex and find it difficult or even impossible to be responsive. However, here—as in all other areas of human behavior—exceptions do occur.

Let me point out that men, too, dissipate sexual feelings—or compensate for feelings of sexual inadequacy and demonstrate sexual infantilism—with exhibitionistic behavior. This usually takes the form of compulsive sex talk, joking, bragging, and revealing personal details of their sex lives.

Q: *My girlfriend will only wear far-out clothes, yet she is quite conventional in all other ways. She looks good—but kooky. Shopping with her is impossible, she is so intent on finding clothes that nobody else would wear. Why does she strive so hard to be "different"?*

A: Outlandish clothes may be the one area in which your friend dares to express her feelings of uniqueness and individuality. Her kooky clothes may be her attempt to be different outwardly because she feels an inner need to conform. I'm happy to hear that she looks good in her outfits. This would indicate that her drive for uniqueness takes a constructive rather than a destructive form.

Q: *Could you possibly tell me why my thirty-two-year-old daughter always buys clothes that are too small for her? She is not fat, but after two children, she doesn't have the figure she used to.*

A: There could be many reasons for her behavior. One or more of the following could apply:

1. Some women (and men) wear tight clothes because they think it makes them look sexier and more attractive.

2. Some women buy clothes in the size they used to wear in an attempt to deny the passing of time, the process of aging, or any weight increase.

3. We all have a conscious and unconscious physical image of ourselves. This image is formed very early in life, and sometimes it is impossible to modify it. Your daughter could be buying clothes that are too small for her because, without being aware of it, she is clothing her "physical image" rather than her real self.

4. Many women take pride in being able to wear a small size. They prefer to deny reality and wear a small size rather than suffer the hurt pride of having to ask for a larger one.

5. Your daughter may buy clothes that don't fit because she is highly suggestible and cannot say no to a salesperson—whether the clothes fit or not.

Q: *Why does a friend of mine absolutely douse herself with perfume? I've asked her about this and all she can say is that she likes it. The same woman is very attractive but also uses vast quantities of make-up.*

A: Some people do actually have a problem with how they smell. This is sometimes a response to anxiety which brings on excess sweating and an amonia-like odor. But many people with hidden but considerable self-contempt have the illusion that they emit distasteful odors and are frequently convinced that they also look repulsive. These people will do anything to hide and disguise themselves from what they are certain must be perceived as offensive by other people. Still other women in desperate need of reassurance concerning their sex appeal will exaggerate the use of perfumes, make-up, and bizarre clothes, in a compulsive attempt to be noticed. Of course there are cultures in which the use of huge amounts of perfumes is considered par for the course.

Q: *My mother-in-law has a very irritating habit. She buys me the exact same dresses and perfume she buys for herself. She has been doing this for eighteen years and I am at my wit's end. I have tried everything and cannot make her break this habit. I have even tried returning the dresses to the stores—but she begins all over again. Why does she do this and what can I do about it?*

A: It is impossible to have conclusive insight into this problem without knowing more about you and your mother-in-law. I do not, however, think that returning the dresses to the store is the solution. Obviously, your mother-in-law has some emotional reason for doing what she does. Perhaps she thinks of you more as a daughter than a daughter-in-law; perhaps she thinks of herself as her son's wife. I do not know. The best way to find a solution is to sit down and discuss the matter with your mother-in-law. A good heart-to-heart talk, during which you both let down your guard, would be helpful in clearing the air and bringing about a solution. If, however, it does not—and if you feel that you can no longer cope with the problem and that it interferes with your life to too great an extent—then I would suggest you have a consultation with a psychiatrist.

Q: *I have a friend who insists on getting her nose fixed. There is absolutely nothing wrong with her nose or, for that matter, with her looks. Why does she insist on this? I mean, why can't she see herself as she really is? And as we all see her?*

A: The image people have of themselves is no simple matter. It is comprised of everything they have felt about themselves since early childhood, plus all of the ways and things they feel they want to and ought to be. With people like your friend, no amount of reassurance, however objective, helps, because the way she sees herself is distorted by her general emotional feeling and evaluation of herself. She probably displaces much of her lack of self-acceptance and self-contempt to the area of her looks and thus sees herself as ugly. I have seen any number of people in consultations who have compulsively gone to a vast number of beauty experts, seeking "good looks," when what they in fact needed was improved self-esteem and self-acceptance. This included people in show business who made their living from obvious good looks and who had even won awards in beauty contests. Of course, the culture we live in does not help, inasmuch as it constantly stresses the value and importance of good looks, as well as other superficialities, as sure roads to happiness.

Some plastic surgeons know that a fair percentage of people seeking their help have serious emotional problems. A number of them even insist on a routine psychiatric consultation before any surgical decisions are made. I think this is an excellent precautionary measure, since it sometimes leads to the prevention of unnecessary surgery. It also can be helpful in preventing serious psychiatric manifestations, which sometimes follow such surgery in predisposed people who are already quite emotionally fragile. There are people whose emotional balance is very delicate and who must retain a status-quo situation to go on functioning. Some of these people need to complain and use their looks to complain about. This kind of sick complaining is a defense against anxiety; indiscriminately removing this defense can sometimes be the cause of dire repercussions.

Q: *Why are women such slaves to fashion?*

A: This compulsion is probably one of the most common known to man. It is born of a need to belong, to conform, and to take no chances whatsoever on the possibility of not being accepted. It also relieves one of the necessity of taking responsibility for individual feelings and taste for what is and isn't esthetic. Of course, there are many shades and degrees in compulsions, too. Women who absolutely must adopt the latest style immediately, without any individual preference and regardless of how it looks, are particularly insecure. They are people who have long forgotten about their inner resources and feelings and how to tap them. These women must don the uniform of the day to assure themselves that they are part of the in-style army and, therefore, safe. Please remember, however, that an over-reaction *against* style can be equally compulsive and will usually result in just another kind of uniform.

It is interesting to observe certain women in therapy and the changes in dress that occur as their feelings about themselves change. I have known women who, after several years of treatment, for the first time dared to be out of style. They no longer needed to conform or to rebel. This was usually accompanied by a heightened aware-ness of color and form and the particular style best suited for them.

Q: *A current beauty fad is the light eyebrow or no eyebrows at all, which means that some women will be shaving off their eyebrows in order to have the proper look. Isn't shaving eyebrows harmful? What makes women go that far for fashion?*

A: When I was an intern, I was told to avoid shaving eyebrows when suturing lacerations over the eye because, in some cases, shaved eyebrows don't grow back. If this still applies—and I can only assume it does—there will be panic when eyebrow styles change, as they surely will. Whatever the rationale, self-mutilation (like shaving eye-brows) indicates poor self-esteem, self-contempt, and self-rejection.

Such self-defacement is also characteristic of a decadent and regressive society. There's something sad when civilized people attempt to emulate primitive and barbaric people who have hardly left the Stone Age. I can only hope that the dictates of style do not one day include knocking out front teeth, stretching the lips to saucer size, putting plugs of wood through the nasal septum, or stretching earlobes to the chin.

Q: *Why do you think so many women today insist on wearing bikinis and even less at the beach, especially when a lot of them look just plain awful?*

A: Some look awful and some look awfully good. Much, of course, is directly related to the eye of the beholder. In any case, there are all kinds of swimsuits, all kinds of people and all kinds of motives in making a choice.

Some women like the freedom they feel in near nudity. Some need this freedom as a rebellion against strong feelings of constriction in other areas. Some women are avid sun-worshipers. Others feel they need near nudity to attract a man. Some women fear close emotional relationships and fully developed sexual encounters; they hide both and dissipate much sexual feeling with near-nude exhibitions—advertising sexual promises that will not be forthcoming. Interestingly, many well-covered-up ladies are more mature sexually (have greater potential for sexual responsiveness and a better integration of emotional relatedness and sexual feelings) than their near-nude sisters.

Q: *What do you believe motivates all those kids who go around in costume?—you know, the ones who wear Elizabethan outfits, Oriental dress, Nehru collars, and so on.*

A: A certain amount of exhibitionism, narcissism, compliance with current fads is evident. But the present costume fad, I think, has its special motivating force. Probably these people unconsciously find this time and place too hard to take. They would rather be part of another place and era. Perhaps they seek slower times and more exotic climes. Interestingly, they often choose costumes symbolic of impoverished or constricted eras. Elizabethan days were not famous for liberal attitudes. The Nehru collar is tight, and India is chronically besieged by famine. A sufficient distaste for present reality can lead to strange and paradoxical substitutes.

Q: *What is your opinion of these new see-through blouses and the women who wear them?*

A: Exhibitionistic cultures are not new; they are rather old. The Egyptians, the Romans, the ladies of Napoleon's era, all bared their breasts. The world spends years hiding parts of the body and years exposing parts of the body, all in a great effort to effect sexual stimulation. The present situation is at best fleeting and superficial. It is designed to arouse as many people as possible as quickly and as meaninglessly as possible. Its commercial counterpart is the striptease act. It has little connection with authentic sexual feeling and is usually the product of a culture that is becoming increasingly superficial, infantile, and lacking in adult human values. Most of the new (old) looks in fashion are, of course, a commercial device to make women dissatisfied enough constantly to "need" and buy new clothes. Women who slavishly comply with every fashion that comes along are frequently those who lack individual resources. If a woman is not self-accepting, she must constantly dress to be "in," since to be "out" means out with everyone, including herself, thus generating considerable anxiety and even depression. People who feel particularly "dead" often need the stimulation of exhibitionism, sometimes to the point of leaving nothing to the imagination. As deadness increases (dead feelings, a loss of feeling for self), stimuli go from the subtle to the blatant (hence breast cultures). This effort becomes increasingly compulsive and desperate as one attempts to excite others in order to feel less dead oneself.

CHAPTER 2
Love and Friendship

There is usually a very fine line separating feelings of friendship from those of love if the relationship is a good and solid one. Developing a close friendship involves accommodating oneself to another's wants and needs, without excessive neglect of self. Simply understanding that a petty disagreement is unimportant in the entire scope of the firm "partnership" of two people who care for one another can make life so much easier.

Simple consideration for others is the start of a friendship, as friendship can be the basis for a love relationship. Among members of a family, where love is too often taken for granted, consideration, trust, and affection must be carefully cultivated and acknowledged. Between man and woman, husband and wife, love and friendship often combine to make the best marriages, the best partnerships.

What Makes a Woman Lovable?

The woman who is lovable—the woman who has sex appeal—is the woman who "understands men." The ability to understand men is much more important than looks, talent or education in determining a woman's L.Q.—Lovability Quotient.

If you grew up with a brother, or if you like little boys, you are way ahead in the game of understanding men. This is especially true if you have observed a brother carefully and understand the various characteristics of his early years of development, because nearly all men retain some important aspects of childhood characteristics, problems, and needs throughout their lives.

The woman with a high, sustained L.Q. knows *men* and devotes much time and energy to understanding the individual characteristics of *her man*. While she may come by her knowledge through great sensitivity and great powers of observation (such as by not ignoring

45

her father and brothers when she was growing up), she will make it her business to learn still more.

At this point, let me make a list of some of the important things a woman with a high L.Q. knows. (She knows these things deep down where it counts, so that she reacts to this knowledge automatically without need for study or thought.)

1. Most men are in search of a "good mama." This means a woman will consider her man the most important person in her life. She will value him above all other people—including herself—and all things. While she appreciates and enjoys the things he brings home to her (just as a mother enjoys her son's good grades, school drawings, etc.), she will never place greater value on things (clothes, car, house, money—and all that money can buy) than on her man. She will never reject him in favor of her children, her mother, or anyone else. He loves the children and she loves them, but deep down he considers himself one of the children and will not see his wife as lovable if he is discriminated against in any way. Like all youngsters, he wants to know where mom is. He likes her to be there when he comes home and he likes her to give him all kinds of goodies in the form of tasty food. To him, these are all indications of caring. The feeling that she cares is extremely important to him since it gives him a sense of security and support. He is very dependent on his woman, and if she is dependable, this is most supportive to him and gives him a sense of security and reassurance. But he must never be reminded of this dependency; it must not be mentioned at all. He takes great pride in not being dependent, because he sees dependency as antimasculine—and a lovable wife knows this. She will gladly choose things like ties and color combinations for him, but she will never, never remind him of "all she is doing for him" or "his helplessness."

2. The lovable woman is not subtle about what is on her mind. When she is angry, she does not manipulate destructively, she does not subtly sabotage or sulk. She never uses sexual deprivation as punishment, nor does she use sexual availability as a reward. She does not nag. She says what she has to say, and forgives and forgets.

3. The lovable woman knows whether she is more assertive than her man, and who is the more aggressive. She knows that since the woman has the right to say "No," she must give her man cues that say "Yes." Otherwise, relationships will not even begin, let alone

develop. This means she must give some kind of subtle, almost un-detectable, sign that her man will pick up. This sign indicates clearly that he will not be rejected if he approaches her. She must make the first move even though she allows it to seem otherwise. The lovable woman doesn't wait for his approach; instead she initiates it by say-ing, in effect, "if you ask me, I'll say yes." She knows how sensitive a man is to even the most remote possibility of rejection and how great a role this assurance of acceptability plays in the all-important beginnings of man-woman relations.

4. The lovable woman knows that most men have an exceedingly poor tolerance for frustration. A man hates to wait, so she does not keep him waiting. He finds it particularly hard to wait for food when he is hungry. She knows that he will react very badly to sexual frustration. She never promises more than she will deliver.

5. The married lovable woman knows that sex plays an extremely important role in her husband's life. Therefore, she also knows the following:

a. Her husband has probably come to her with a poor sexual education. His ability as her lover will largely depend on what she teaches him, particularly what gratifies and pleases her. After she teaches him and only after she teaches him can he take over as a good lover. He will then be enormously pleased and grateful for the pleasure that he now has the power to give her.

b. The lovable wife knows that sexual refusal will be interpreted as complete rejection. She never refuses her husband. She knows that it is not necessary for husband and wife to always have equal and complete responses. If her desire sometimes does not coincide with his, this still does not prevent her from being a warm, loving participant on a more passive level than at other times.

c. The lovable wife knows that her husband will regard lack of feminine attention to herself as not caring about sex and, therefore, not caring about him. He much prefers that she spend more time on being sexually attractive than on keeping an attractive house. He takes pride in her sexuality, and will appreciate any attempt on her part to add to her allure. For example, any kind of attractive night-dress is especially appreciated when he does not have to ask her to make these efforts.

d. The lovable wife knows that her husband enjoys her attractive-ness and the attention it stirs among other people. But she also knows that he demands absolute sexual exclusivity, no matter how liberal he pretends to be in this area. He will keenly resent any flirtatiousness on her part. The lovable woman is interested in winning only his attention and not a popularity contest. She knows that he does not want to hear about old dates, or former sexual conquests.

e. The lovable wife knows that her husband responds to affection just as she does. He needs and enjoys hugs, kisses, presents, and the interest she shows in his life and work. She knows how much he appreciates her as an interested listener.

6. The lovable woman accepts without resentment the fact that men will be interested in sports and the company of other men. She does not see these interests as a detraction from herself. When men get together and talk about work or world affairs, they may seem to her like little boys talking about marbles—but she will be tolerant.

7. The lovable woman knows that men detest being manipulated through guilt and martyrdom. The unlovable woman does this by greeting her man at the door with a long list of problems she's confronted that day: the children, the shopkeepers, the plumbers, etc. Complaints of what she has "had to put up with" make her seem a martyr and her man seem guilty, so guilty that he can only make up for it by giving up something he wants to do—like watching a game on TV or spending the night out with the boys.

8. The lovable woman will never put her man in a double bind. She will not resent her husband working long hours while wanting her husband to give her the things working long hours can bring.

9. The lovable woman knows that few people can resist emotional involvement with someone who cares for them. The capacity to care about another human being and to have someone care in return is the very basis of human communication. When this exists, the lovable woman knows there is no greater reward in life.

10. The lovable woman loves herself. I don't mean in a vain, narcissistic, self-preoccupied way. I mean she has a good feel of who she is, what her values are and where she stands in this world. She has considerable self-esteem. This regard for herself is conveyed to people around her, and they respond to her the same way she does. In short, they find her lovable; she finds this natural and nice. While she keenly appreciates the words, "I love you," she does not need her man to tell her this a million times a day. Also, unlike people with a low Lovability Quotient, she does not constantly ask, "Am I beautiful? Am I attractive? Am I talented?" These questions are

really cries for reassurance that she can make it in this world. A lovable woman needs little such reassurance since she is blessed with a high degree of self-acceptance.

As a psychiatrist, I repeatedly hear unhappy women tell me, "I only married him because he said he loved me so." A lovable woman knows better. She knows a man's crush or fixation is not love. She knows that love is a give-and-take involvement between two mature people. There is much more to love than a fulfilled need for admiration or the immediate fulfillment of romantic fantasies. She knows that love can exist only when it can grow, and that it can only grow when there is much in common to share—especially a common caring about each other. This enables her to be close to a man and to be involved; thus she is able to get to know him better and make still further closeness possible. She does not have the impossible burden of requiring universal love. She knows nobody is universally loved. She wants only the love of one man.

As with all other aspects of human endeavor, the Lovability Quotient will vary from woman to woman. It is a quality that exists only on a relative basis. A woman's spontaneous, unassuming, natural lovability—uncluttered by overwhelming self-concern—develops along with her self-esteem and self-growth. To the extent that a woman finds herself lovable, so will others.

This is what makes for unconcerned lovability—and what makes a woman truly lovable.

What Makes a Man Lovable?

What makes a man lovable? First, it is necessary to distinguish between instant attraction (or quick sex appeal) and sustained attraction (or lovability). The chemistry that can instantly attract a woman to a man can be a hodgepodge of many things: his voice, a gesture, the way he holds a glass, a mood, or a mutual interest. Any attraction based only on these qualities will be short-lived unless the man has a high enough Lovability Quotient (L.Q.) to sustain a woman's interest.

Sustained attraction—the kind that makes for a long-term relationship between a man and a woman—can be based on several factors. Much depends on the character of the woman. A dependent woman may be attracted to a strong, independent man. A woman with a yearning to "mother" will often choose a boyish man. A shy woman will be drawn to a gregarious man.

In addition, there are other characteristics that most women feel are part and parcel of masculine appeal or lovability. Here are those most mentioned by women I have interviewed:

1. Looks certainly contribute to a man's instant appeal and, to a lesser extent, to sustained interest. A woman who places too high an emphasis on looks may be more interested in impressing people with her "catch" than in real love. The man who is movie-star handsome has appeal, but women are generally more attracted by "interesting" or "manly" looks. A man's face can have symbolic value to a woman. A rugged face may symbolize masculinity, might seem to say to a woman: "I can take care of myself—I can take care of *us*." Boyish looks can symbolize naïveté and the possibility of growing—together.

A woman may be particularly drawn to a man who looks like her father or the first man to whom she was attracted (and this includes gestures and mannerisms, as well as physical features). This is especially true if the woman idolized her father. While this feeling about her father may be unconscious on her part, it may exert a powerful influence. Women often marry men just like their fathers, despite their protests to the contrary.

2. The most important factor in a man's L.Q. is his ability to be genuinely interested in and involved with his wife and his children. A lovable man will never invest his total time, energy and emotional involvement in work alone. He will regard his wife and family as full partners, friends and allies. He will share his life's work, his happiness and his problems with them.

3. The lovable man is happy to be a student lover all of his life. He realizes that his wife is a complicated person whose sexual requirements, feelings and responses are part of her total being and are dependent on her general feelings, well-being, and moods. Unlike him, she sometimes cannot rise above other feelings and issues but must wait until they are resolved before she can participate in sex with full response. The lovable man is patient. He is happy to learn and to teach and to become more and more creative and inventive in bestowing affection and satisfaction. He is more interested in mutual closeness, pleasure, and happiness than in personal pride. He takes nothing for granted and knows that tender words and gestures are keenly appreciated. He is not afraid of words like "I love

you," nor is he afraid to show what he feels. He does not think feelings and tenderness are antimasculine. He knows the ability to express his strong feelings of love is evidence of masculinity, inner substance, and strength. He is not a flirt. He may appreciate other women but he saves his tenderest moments and words exclusively for his mate.

4. The lovable man is straightforward about what he thinks. He is able to cope with problems without sulking. He is capable and willing to make decisions, but includes his wife in on all decisions that affect family life. He also is willing to "talk things out," and honestly expresses anger when he feels it, so that the family lines of communication are continually open and clear. He is also willing to forgive and forget.

5. A lovable man considers his wife as a mature grown-up. He does not regard her as a financial idiot. He sees to it that she is free, capable, and well educated in family finances so she would be able to cope should anything happen to him.

6. The man with a high L.Q. has a keen appreciation of the enormity of his wife's job of running a house. He knows there is no responsibility more important or more taxing—and no job that requires more of one's full self than raising children. He knows this, and tells his wife so.

7. The lovable man does not view his wife as a symbol of bills, burdensome responsibility, or problems and pressures that occur in everyday living. He also knows that it is periodically necessary to leave the office, the children, and problems behind so that he and his wife can go off alone in order to indulge each other, exclusively.

8. A woman is especially sensitive and appreciative of a man who is tuned in to her moods, problems, whims, and needs. A lovable man has learned to operate on his mate's emotional wave length. He knows when something is not right and can get her to talk about it. Then he is willing to listen so he can share problems. If his wife is having a difficult time, if she is physically ill, he does not have a temper tantrum because he feels neglected or abandoned. On the contrary, he is mature enough "to be there in full" so as to be emotionally supportive.

9. The lovable man is not a mama's boy. However devoted he may be to mama, papa, sister, or brother, there is never any question or doubt that his first duty, loyalty and responsibility is toward his wife and family. And he keeps private that which is private between

him and his wife. He does not gripe to his mother or friends. If he and his wife are having personal difficulties, he will talk them out with his wife. If this doesn't work, he should be mature and open enough to get competent professional help.

10. A man with a high L.Q. likes women. He married his wife because he loves her, not because she seemed to be the least troublesome woman he knew. He did not marry for convenience sake, for appearances, for housekeeping services, for sexual services, or for the ego satisfaction of having children. He also respects women. He loves his wife enough so that he is willing to die for her—but, more important, he is willing to live for her. He takes care of himself (he does not work, smoke or drink himself to death), so that he'll be around to see the children grow up.

The truly lovable man—like the lovable woman—knows that a relationship isn't complete when boy meets girl and marries her. It is only a beginning. From that point on they must be open and willing to grow together and to emotionally contribute to each other so that their relationship also grows. It must grow or it dies. When it grows, its partners become more and more lovable to each other. It is this kind of relationship that lets children grow up in a healthy atmosphere, that will make them lovable, too.

Why Men Can't Say "I Love You"

Most women have a great need to hear the words "I love you." Men who know this (and many responsible men do) are still extremely hesitant about saying those words. In fact, many men love their wives but are inhibited to the point of paralysis when it comes to saying "I love you."

Why do women "need" to hear the words "I love you"? There are many reasons. Some women need constant reassurance of their lovability to mitigate feelings of inadequacy, self-doubt and self-contempt. These are women who are inordinately dependent, who believe their earthly salvation can only be found in an all-perfect love. The words "I love you" symbolize this all-perfect love—which, like all perfections, simply does not exist. Love neither resolves basic personality problems nor creates much-needed self-esteem.

But even relatively healthy women want to hear those magic words, because "I love you" has a special meaning. Let me list the most common meanings I have heard in my discussions with women. This is what a woman' *hears* when a man with whom she has a serious relationship says "I love you":

1. You exist as a person.

2. You are a woman. I accept and respect your femininity.

3. You are desirable. You are attractive sexually, intellectually, and in countless other ways.

4. I am interested in who you really are.

5. I accept your human liabilities as well as your human assets.

6. Ours is an exclusive relationship. There is no one else with whom we have the same quality or intensity of feelings. What we share is private and precious.

7. You are not alone. There is someone in this world—me—who cares about your well-being as much as he cares about his own.

8. Our relationship is one of mutual trust and interest.

9. I am interested, and I know that you are interested, in all creative aspects of our relationship. More than anything, our children represent our integrated creativity.

10. You are of primary importance to me. I do not take you for granted.

No one wants to be taken for granted, and to a woman, the words "I love you" are the antithesis of being taken for granted. Why, then, are men—even responsible men—reluctant to say them? Do they know the comfort and pleasure these words can bring to the woman they love?

Most women feel that if they have to ask their husbands to say "I love you," the whole thing is spoiled—the magic is destroyed because the situation becomes contrived and the words lose spontaneity and meaning. Other women feel so strongly about the words that any gesture, however romantic—even the most ardent love-making—still leaves a void if the words aren't said. So in desperation they will insist, even nag, their husbands to declare their love. Even then, getting the words out is like pulling teeth.

Why is it so difficult for a man to say "I love you"? There may be many reasons, and much, of course, depends on the man's personal history. For the most part, men are only aware of feeling stubborn, resistant, or silly when it comes to saying the words. They are totally unaware of the underlying forces that curtail the freedom to say them spontaneously. Here are the major factors I have found

most commonly involved even in relatively devoted lovers and husbands. Again, any combination of these factors may be present in
a particular man.

1. Some men have spoken the phrase so casually in the past,
sometimes as part of a seductive maneuver, that they feel that saying
it seriously has no meaning. Some of these men feel that it's just
too corny. Because of past experiences with the phrase, other men
may even feel that saying it will dilute and spoil the seriousness and
sincerity of a real relationship.

2. Some men are still unconsciously emotionally faithful to their
mothers. Not having resolved these infantile feelings, saying "I love
you" to any woman other than mama feels like a breach of fidelity
and threatens to produce guilt, anxiety and depression.

3. Some men suffering from much repressed, unconscious (they
are often totally unaware of their feelings) hostility toward women
will refrain from saying these words in order to "get even" with, or
frustrate, the woman they love. (On a conscious level, these man
may be somewhat aware of feeling a certain satisfaction in holding
back, but they don't know why.) These same men will be particularly reluctant to utter the phrase if their wives "insist" or "nag."
Some men in this group retain emotional residuals of the boy-hate-
girl stage of development.

4. To many men, saying "I love you" represents a final and
complete emotional letting go and coming out. To them this means
that they have now finally exposed their innermost emotional selves
to the person they love. This makes them feel exceedingly vulnerable
because it means that they are now in a position to be hurt. This
factor will be particularly prevalent in men who have been hurt and
disappointed by women in the past (particularly by their mothers)
and who feel fragile, untrusting and suspicious of other people's
motives—especially women's motives.

5. Some men feel that saying the words destroys the last vestige
of their independence and freedom. To them the words mean that
they are now *fully* committed to another person and have now fully
entered into a stamped and sealed emotional contract. They are
forever "trapped."

6. To some men, the admission—let alone the expression—of
strong, warm feelings is seen as a threat to their masculinity and
possible evidence of femininity and even homosexuality.

7. Some men feel that all "soft" feelings are so delicate and

fragile that utter privacy is indicated. They feel that these feelings should never be spoken but simply taken for granted. "Why spoil it with words?" is their motto.

8. To some men the words "I love you" represent a complete surrender of logic to emotion. This is viewed as loss of control and is considered a sign of weakness and potential danger.

Of course, many men are in touch with and accept all their feelings and can freely and openly express them. These men are very fortunate—and so are the women they love.

But what of the men who can't express their love in words, the ones who do not have sufficient trust and confidence to enter into a relatively complete state of emotional exchange? Obviously the dynamics involved can be quite complicated, and generally there is no simple solution. Some of these men and their wives would profit immeasurably from professional help. In some cases, the wife would help matters by realizing that her husband feels and means "I love you" and demonstrates it in many ways—even if he can't say it. Nagging and demanding doesn't help. It usually makes matters worse. *Explaining* and *discussing* sometimes helps, if it is done gently and supportively and *if the relationship is a well-developed and good one.*

Becoming coercive or vindictive will be ruinous; it will only "prove" that the husband's unconscious motives for inhibition were right in the first place. *Demonstrating* can be particularly helpful. If a woman says "I love you" freely, without shame—even if reciprocity is not immediately forthcoming—she can help her husband become a freer, more complete human being.

Do You Expect Too Much of Love?

No emotion is subjected to as much propaganda as the feeling, state or condition known as love. Even with all this preoccupation, love remains one of the most confusing of human feelings. This confusion has been passed down from generation to generation, so that by now society has been permeated by a "love mythology."

Women, especially, are victimized by this love myth, with extremely destructive consequences.

Feeling love, falling in love, being loved, and finding a loved one—all these "musts" are spoon-fed to girls from childhood on. They are told that these are the most important—in fact, the only really important—activities in their lives. This spoon-feeding amounts to brainwashing. Sometimes the brainwashing is blatant, sometimes subtle—but it is always present and chronic—and by chronic I mean it goes on and on.

Along with the love myth, girls are fed other nonsensical propaganda about the feminine role in life. As a result, feelings of femininity (which are confusing enough on their own) become less understandable.

Because femininity and love are so often considered one and the same, many women equate personal narcissism (the need to be attractive to men), self-effacement, compliancy, dependency, even helplessness, with femininity and/or love. Important feelings such as self-assertion, self-development, self-reliance and self-interest are seen as antifeminine and/or antilove, and are to be avoided by women at all costs.

Basically, what love boils down to in this scheme of things is passivity. It follows that it is much more important to be loved than to be in love.

In my psychiatric practice I have seen many women who have disastrous marriages to men with whom they have nothing in common. When I ask why one of these women ever married such a man in the first place, the answer almost always is: "He kept telling me that he loved me."

To the woman who has been raised in the "love myth" tradition, being loved is irresistible because she feels that it is the key to making her own personal love myth come true.

The love myth is also enforced outside the family. The media and some of the so-called arts contribute to the propaganda. Television, films, songs, and books give the impression that life is love, love is life, women and love are all one, and nothing else counts. One popular song tells us that what the world needs now is love, sweet love, and that there is enough of everything else. Small wonder that so many young women have been entranced by love and the "love child" movement. To these girls, lying around a park somewhere, being a love or flower child is actually mother's message—spoken or unspoken—carried to the ultimate: "Love alone is important, nothing else matters."

There are many families in which daughters are encouraged to go to college, to seek careers and "to make something of themselves." However, probing into these homes often reveals that here, too, the parents have an ulterior motive. They feel—and these feelings are often transmitted to the daughter—that if she betters herself with education, she will be able to find a "better" love partner and a "better" love. The message here is, "By all means go to school, develop yourself in all possible areas, but remember that doing all this has nothing to do with personal satisfaction, it has only to do with finding a loved one. . . . And if you should find this true love before your schooling is finished, then your academic career has been worthwhile and successful."

I do not mean to imply that the message is delivered in just these words, or in words at all. But make no mistake about it—the message is delivered and there is no escaping its effects.

Many young women who have not married, but who have been outstanding in their academic lives and subsequent careers, suffer from deep and painful depression. Their success means little or nothing because they have not achieved their "love myth." Not only have they remained unwed, but they have not found "true love." This feeling of failure engenders deep feelings of worthlessness, lack of self-esteem as a woman, and self-hate.

The situation is also frustrating to the mothers of unwed daughters; it makes their lives incomplete. Mothers honestly feel that only when their daughters are safely and securely married, only when their fantasy love myth is fulfilled, is a mother's work done.

A woman who has married, who has fulfilled her myth, can also have problems. Having been convinced of her unimportance (remember, love is *passivity*), she may try to counteract these feelings by wanting and expecting too much of love.

A woman's own feeling of unimportance makes it imperative that she be loved by all or at least *liked* by all and loved by one. This love becomes the mythical stepping stone to self-esteem, security, and happiness, as well as the magical solution to every problem. This love will connect this woman to a strong man who will give her a "self." His love will be the link through which strength will flow into her being to counteract the myth of feminine weakness in which she has been led to believe. This love will bind her and her man together into a pure and perfect oneness that can withstand whatever difficulties life has to offer. She expects a "perfect relationship" in which two people have instant and complete harmony.

These fantasies, unfortunately, are never fulfilled.

The late Dr. Karen Horney, the brilliant psychoanalyst, once detailed the claims people make on themselves and others on the basis of love. Dr. Horney included the following: "If you love me, you will be all powerful, all reliable, all forgiving, all understanding, and you will forgo all other activity or company to be with me."

When these impossible love myth demands are thwarted, as they always are, bitter disappointment, cynicism, hopelessness, and depression often result. Placing these demands on a man makes him feel possessed, drained and exploited. The result, of course, is that his love turns to bitterness or hate. A woman caught in this kind of confusion might well view it as evidence that she was indeed mistaken about the love she thought she found. She feels that the solution to her problem is very simple: find the "right" love.

Inevitably, any new relationship she enters into will lead to new frustrations (and possibly promiscuity) because the kind of love this woman seeks simply does not exist. What she needs to solve the problem is not a new and better love, but a reevaluation of herself and her concepts about love and love relationships.

Not every woman is a victim of love mythology. Much depends on her mother, her family, and her personal development.

A dependent, compliant woman should be especially careful that she does not exaggerate the importance of the power of love, and take care not to confuse sexual infatuation with love. She should also be wary of what I have come to call the "crush phenomenon." A crush is not love. A declaration of adoration by a man is not love. Love is an active, on-going process between two people. It involves emotional exchange—not image-worship from a distance. Realistic love involves two real people. Crushes involve people on whom nonexistent fantasy perfections have been projected.

Self-effacing women also tend to "fall in love" with their concept of "strong men." Often these men turn out to be rigid, stubborn, infantile, childish, cruel and, in fact, more emotionally fragile and weak than the dependent women who see them as strong in the first place.

Love is an extremely important emotion; it is a cornerstone of human relating. Being involved in a sustained, adult love relationship with a member of the opposite sex, which means caring about someone at least as much as about oneself, is one of the major highlights of human satisfaction and existence. In order to achieve this happiness, the love relationship must be viewed as a liaison between two separate people with individual needs and wants. It is also vital for them to have a minimum number of interests in common, plus a common frame of reference (backgrounds, culture, language, etc.) that makes human exchange possible. Both the man and the woman must be open to learn about themselves and each other and the world they live in. They should enjoy each other's company sexually, emotionally, and intellectually, and care about each other enough so as not to avoid common responsibilities—including the raising of children.

Most important, they must realize that while they love each other, they are still two separate human beings and that perfect communication and harmony is impossible whether or not two people love each other.

Love is necessary and it helps immeasurably, but it does not solve all problems within one's self, one's marriage, one's family or the world.

Q: *My boyfriend recently told me that he thought I "overrated" love. What did he mean by this?*

A: Being involved in a sustained love relationship with a member of the opposite sex—that is, being attracted to and caring about someone at least as much as you do about yourself—is one of the major elements of human existence. Love of people, causes, and work are important, too. Yet many of us overrate the importance and power of love. This invariably leads to disappointment. Two people may love each other as much as possible, but they are still two separate human beings, and perfect communication and harmony are not possible. Love is a basic human necessity, but it does not resolve all problems. Solving economic problems, medical problems, emotional problems, social problems, etc., takes more than love.

Q: *Six months ago, my eighteen-year-old daughter broke up with a boy she had been seeing for about four months. She has been quite depressed and seems to be getting over it only now. Why do young girls have such extreme reactions? Why should she be so* *upset about the breakup of a relationship that was, after all, only a short one? It's not as if she had lost a husband.*

A: 1. The intensity of a relationship is not always proportional to the length of time two people have been involved with each other. Some people develop very intense involvements in a relatively short period. Others hardly become involved at all, however long they are together. Much depends on the emotional investment people make in each other and the extent to which they exchange feelings.

2. The capacity and ability to exchange feelings and to care deeply about another human being are not predicated on age. Young people can love as intensely as adults. Likewise, mature and immature involvements can occur at all ages.

3. Young people often have very strong reactions, because they cast themselves totally into a relationship. The intensity of their feelings is not muted by years of various disillusionments and the subsequent development of cynicism. Unlike many adults, they have not learned to repress, dilute, and prevent strong feelings. They are vibrant, vital, alive, and intense, and they bring the considerable strength of their feelings to both their relationships and their disappointments.

4. Sometimes people react to the breakup of an affair severely because the failure of the relationship represents an enormous blow to pride and self-esteem. Since self-acceptance, in this case, is based on success—or at least maintenance—of the affair, its termination engenders self-rejection, self-hate, and depression.

5. Some people confuse love with dependency (indeed, both can exist at the same time). The breakup of a love affair is felt as a loss of the individual who provided sustenance, life, and a raison d'être. It is as if a treasured parent were lost precipitously when a child was ill-prepared to fend for herself. In effect, the person has transferred her unresolved infantile feelings and yearnings toward her parents to her loved one. His departure evokes the same (infantile) reaction as would the death of a father. This reaction can occur in either sex and at any age and particularly where there is much immaturity and dependency.

Q: *I am forty-two years old. My parents were the kind of people who never showed any feeling. I don't think I ever saw them kiss, and I can't remember their ever kissing me. I am married, and I must say that my husband has a hard time showing affection, too. I'm beginning to wonder if there is something wrong with me. I feel that I've never been loved. I suppose I'm silly to be concerned at my age.*

A: 1. You are not silly to want to love and be loved at any age. That you feel silly is an indication that some of your parents' "teachings" have rubbed off on you. This is further evidenced by your attraction to a man who has problems like your parents'.

2. Some people love strongly and deeply but have great difficulty expressing and demonstrating their feelings. Does your husband demonstrate his love in other ways—*e.g.,* by his concern and devotion?

3. Have you had an open discussion with your husband, indicating the importance to you of a show or expression of deeper feelings?

4. How much do you like yourself? Perhaps if you liked yourself more, you would be less dependent on other people's demonstrations.

5. Have you considered consultation with a psychiatrist specializing in marriage counseling?

Q: *Is there anything I can do to improve feelings among members of my family? I am seventeen years old and hardly ever look forward to being at home because everyone there is always so sullen and irritated with each other.*

A: It may be very valuable to talk things out with your entire family, telling them honestly how you feel about them in a clear, concise, and courteous fashion. By courteous, I mean everybody in the family should have his chance to be heard and everyone should be attentive when someone else is talking. Take nothing for granted in this discussion. Convey your own feelings so that you are understood, and, hopefully, others will follow your example by being equally honest and open when it is their turn to speak. Each family member should be nonjudging and nonvindictive. As you talk, you may find that some family members share your feelings; some will be surprised to find you feel as you do; still others may interpret family happenings in a totally different way. Their revelations should give you new insights. This "clearing the air" discussion may initiate new understanding, reparations, growth, and improved family atmosphere. There is no substitute for speech. People may be completely blind to your feelings unless you tell them.

Family problems and relationships, however, can sometimes be so complicated as to require the special help of professional family therapists, including psychiatrists who specialize in the field and social workers attached to agencies like Catholic Charities or the Jewish Family Service. You might try seeking such help if relations do not improve.   •

Q: *So many of my friends' children are on drugs or become "love" children or are school dropouts. I know that individual problems are involved and also that the world has become an increasingly complicated place to live in. But why do you think so many children from good families are so disturbed today?*

A: I'm not sure that emotional disturbances are more prevalent either in the young or among children from good families. I do agree with you that problems are highly individual and that the culture we live in plays a large role. Another key to the situation, in my opinion, is the confusion women feel about their role as mothers. Many women no longer take pride in motherhood. For these women, having and raising children is certainly not felt as a highly creative occupation. Mothers who feel unfulfilled in potential career expectations and conflicted as to identity and purpose must also have more than usually confused feelings toward their children. Their children are often unconsciously seen as obstacles to activities that would produce self-acceptance. These mothers, and there are many of them, are unable to give their children enough uncomplicated, fundamental love. Proper actions and proper words cannot compensate for feelings. And without a great deal of love and feeling, people grow up with extraordinary yearnings and problems—many of them infantile. I feel, for example, that many so-called love children are obsessed with love to compensate for a lack of love at home.

While momism may have been the curse of yesteryear, many current-day difficulties are due to the opposite extreme.

Q: *We are expecting our first child in six months. We have been very happily married for three years and we are very excited about my pregnancy. There is only one small problem. Both of us were raised as Roman Catholics but we have since quietly fallen away from the Catholic Church for personal reasons. However, my husband's parents are very strict Catholics and have already brought up the subject of a Catholic baptism for our baby. I feel that we should not baptize our child just to please his parents. He thinks we should. I love his parents and I can understand his reasons for not wanting to hurt them. But, I'm not sure that baptizing the baby is the right thing to do. What do you think?*

A: First, congratulations and much health and happiness to all of you!

Since you left the Church and they stayed I assume that at this point baptism symbolically means much more to them than it does to you. If you feel solid in your own beliefs, why invest the symbol with disproportionate importance now? Baptizing the baby but raising him as you desire are not mutually exclusive, regardless of what religious or irreligious beliefs and values we apply. This is compassionate action and not hypocrisy. Compassion invariably serves human purposes the best for all concerned wherever it is possible to apply it.

Q: *How important is it to have had a close, sustained relationship?*

A: If you can say you've had at least one, you are way ahead of the game. A close relationship, in which two people can share and exchange feelings and interests, is one of life's great satisfactions. The ability to be friends over long periods of time should not be taken for granted. Close relationships usually bring out one's neurotic characteristics and many people are too sick to relate on more than a fleeting basis. The ability to have friends is often related to liking people and liking one's self. Friendship and mutual caring is evidence of mental health.

Q: *How do you feel about the use of computers to match people up?*

A: I'm prejudiced by my dislike and distrust of mechanization when it is applied to human resources. I am not at all convinced that human emotions, feelings for each other, and potential relatedness can be computerized. We know a great deal about how *neurotic* components in people complement each other. (Neurotically compliant people somehow find neurotically dominant people, and vice versa.) But we still know very little about the chemistry—the spark of attraction and reaction—that goes on between healthy people. How useful can computers be if we can't feed them this indispensable information?

Q: *My friends put me down, treat me poorly and leave me feeling demoralized and depressed. What can I do about it?*

A: You'd better look to your self-esteem. Friends don't just happen—friends are chosen. Often this choice seems casual or accidental, but it is not. People who choose friends who are cruel to them invariably have little self-esteem, a lot of self-contempt, and an unconscious need to be punished. As an individual's self-esteem improves (as a result of psychotherapy, for example), he or she will refuse to tolerate poor treatment at anybody's hands. Feeling better about themselves, such people either alter old relationships or end them and seek more equitable, constructive friendships.

Q: *I'm an interior decorator. I get along well with people, but I find it almost impossible to please some of my clients. They are as demanding as infants, change their minds at the drop of a hat and expect me to be on call constantly. What makes grown people act this way?*

A: People whose work involves service and personal contact, such as doctors, dentists, hairdressers, lawyers, accountants—and especially interior decorators—all voice complaints similar to yours. Many people who think they want professional expertise are really seeking psychotherapy. Thus your clients will look upon you as 10 percent decorator and 90 percent psychotherapist. Many people are in deep conflict: they want to conform, but they want to be individuals; they are afraid of feeling empty and dead, but they are also afraid to show strong feelings, opinions, and tastes. For some, psychiatric treatment is abhorrent because it means admitting that they need help. So the needed therapy takes place between an untrained "therapist" (in this case, you) and an unwilling patient—neither of whom is aware that any treatment is occurring. They similarly do not know that furniture or teeth or whatever have now taken on deeper meanings and implications. Of course, this kind of relationship is bound to be stormy and frustrating; quite often it will seem irrational to the decorator, the dentist, or whomever the therapy-seeking client has inflicted herself upon.

Q: *Help! I tell people who are practically strangers details of my personal and private life. I've noticed that because I have made myself vulnerable, they later feel free to say things to me in a manner they would not ordinarily have used and start giving me their criticisms—which in turn make me angry. Why say anything to them, you may ask. Well, I don't know why—it's a habit. I've tried to stop, but inevitably my conversation winds up on myself—and only on the negative side. Why?*

A: Your problem is very common and usually involves one or more of the following interrelated factors.

1. Poor self-esteem, feelings of inadequacy, and self-contempt.
2. An attempt to entertain, to please, and to impress people in order to compensate for feeling anxious and inadequate.
3. An attempt to cover up feelings of being uncomfortable and threatened by people.
4. An attempt to cover up feelings of anger toward people.
5. An attempt to gain instant recognition and admiration.
6. An attempt to establish instant and complete relationships and friendships to lessen feelings of anxiety and loneliness.

Q: *I have a friend who is never serious. She is a reliable, responible person, and I like her very much—but no matter what we talk about, she always manages to convert it into a joke. Lately, I find this very annoying. I value her friendship, but what can I do?*

A: Compulsive joking is often used to keep distance between the joker and anyone else—especially someone the joker may find threatening in some way. This is particularly true of anyone of whom your friend may be secretly jealous or envious. Chronic joking is usually used to cover up one's real feelings, especially hostile feelings. If, as you say, you value this friendship, it might be important enough for you to clear the air. Tell your friend exactly how you feel. This means informing her gently but firmly that she is always joking, that you find this habit annoying and that you like her enough to want to know what she is really like underneath the jovial "cover-up" that she is always using.

Q: *I'm a rather reserved person. I am not withdrawn, but I must say that I am not exactly the life of the party. I guess I am just not a small-talker and do at times like to be by myself. My husband says that I ought to try to be more outgoing, that that's healthier than being the way I am. Do you agree?*

A: The ability to become involved in relationships, causes, and activities may be a sign of emotional health. But real involvement on an emotional level does not at all mean relating to great numbers of people. A single meaningful relationship is, unfortunately, more than many people experience in an entire lifetime. Superficial, gregarious, bubbling, compulsively outgoing behavior is often confused with healthy involvement and is, of course, no such thing. A compulsive need to be the life of the party often masks a feeling of great inner deadness and self-contempt. The ability and desire to sometimes be alone with oneself can be a great asset. It is often an indication of self-respect—that is, seeing oneself as company worth being with—undiluted. However, this, too, must not be confused with an obsessive fear of people and a compelling need to withdraw from them and from most social situations. Our culture overstresses the importance of small talk, gregarious behavior, and popularity. I do not believe that this kind of behavior makes for mature relationships or happiness. It generally represents superficial living—with much activity and little accomplishment in the area of real involvement.

Q: *What's the explanation for so-called nice people who come to your parties, slop their drinks all over the place, and grind cigarettes into tables, floors, and rugs?*

A: Poor upbringing, bad manners, hostility, selfishness, ruthlessness, jealousy, envy, and, like a dog, a desire to leave an identifying spoor. Also, alienation from their own feelings and those of others, sometimes to the point of severe emotional disturbance, so that they can't differentiate a rug from an ashtray.

Obviously, I have shared your experience.

Q: *Why are some people only foul-weather friends? I know several people who are around only when things are going badly. At those times, they are particularly helpful and couldn't be better friends. As soon as things go well, they disappear. Why?*

A: First of all, you must understand that many of these people are genuinely unaware that they react in this way. The motivation for their particular action remains on a completely unconscious level.

Many people are extremely competitive and at the same time very fragile and vulnerable. They experience anybody else's good fortune and success as a challenge and a threat to their own status. This is sometimes too painful to endure. Problems and suffering on the part of others remove the competitive factor. In other words, friends in trouble are out of the running and are, therefore, safe.

Q: *For twenty-five years, my friend and I have gotten along beautifully; we have always helped each other, and found much joy and comfort in our friendship. About three months ago, my friend did something that hurt me deeply and we stopped talking. She called a few weeks ago, apologized, and asked to resume our friendship. While I miss her very much, I am disappointed in her and wonder if I am better off without her friendship. What do you think?*

A: I think that a relationship that has been so full of mutual benefits for so long is indeed a rich and wonderful one. The problem here is that you had unrealistic expectations about your friend. You expected her to be perfect and she turned out to be human—with human faults. You are now suffering from hurt pride. The question is: do you want to cater to this pride and deprive yourself of further enriching experiences with a proven friend? Pride and welfare are not on the same wavelength. I suggest that you put down your pride and cater to yourself. Good friendships are not easily established. Perfect friendships do not exist at all. If your friend's apology does not suffice, this kind of friendship deserves an open confrontation and clearing of the air so that the friendship can be resumed and all that was good between you can take place once more.

Q: *My husband and I have friends who have a demoralizing, depressing effect on me. I'm referring to one particular couple who never fail to put me down. My husband agrees that these people are capable of being arrogant and sarcastic, but he feels that it is wrong to terminate a friendship that has been going on for as long as this one has. What do you think we should do?*

A: I think that our first duty must be to ourselves. Just as there is little in life that is as enriching as a good friendship (even though a good friendship is never perfect), there is little in life that is as self-destructive as a bad relationship. I believe that it is just as constructive to terminate destructive relationships as it is to begin new ones and sustain old ones. It is an excellent idea to take stock of friends periodically, reviewing how you relate to them and how they relate to you. Friendships with people who consistently fill you with self-hate, destroy your self-esteem, and make you feel unhappy should be terminated.

CHAPTER 3

Anger, Jealousy, and Fear

Within each of us lies the capacity and potential for the strong and sometimes hurtful and harmful emotions: anger, jealousy, and fear. It is dangerous to deny that these emotions exist within us—like love and joy and compassion, they must also be acknowledged and openly expressed. When rage or terror are bottled up inside, they do not lie dormant; instead, they fester and take on importance totally out of proportion to their cause. From the moment we are born and wrenched from our comfortable uterine home, we feel rage; as soon as we recognize our mother's affection for our father, we feel jealousy; when we sense that we are separate individuals from both of our parents and that they may abandon us, we feel fear. But none of these emotions need be too terrible to cope with. Through growth and maturity, we can gain a realistic perspective about each of them.

ANGER

It is difficult for many of us to express anger: to really let go and yell at a friend, husband, or wife. Many people feel that this kind of outburst may jeopardize the relationship, when, in fact, a healthy argument can often strengthen ties between people. When anger is not expressed, it emerges in many defensive, destructive actions: gossiping, for example, or continually being late to appointments. A wife who always burns her husband's dinner or a brother who constantly teases his sister may be trying to say something quite important in a very indirect and hostile manner.

What Gossiping Reveals About You

Women have no priority on gossip. Men gossip, too. In fact, nearly everyone gossips to some extent, but some people carry it too far. To them, gossip becomes a chronic way of life that cannot be altered without psychiatric help.

What really makes men and women gossip? What makes them want to disclose private information about people they sometimes don't even know? There are many reasons.

Some men and women are chronic "mouth movers." Much of their concentration and sensation centers about the mouth. These mouth movers either over-eat or over-talk and sometimes they do both. They tend to be particularly mouth-active when they are anxious. Their gossip has no special goal other than to keep their mouths moving.

Boredom and apathy also breed gossip. Idle talk becomes a filler to compensate for empty hours. Lonely people whose lives have become dull and devoid of interests use gossip as a form of reaching out or relating. Because they are not sufficiently involved with current events or issues they cannot talk about them, and they feel that talking about themselves is dull and useless—so they gossip about others. They read items about celebrities and relate these tidbits to friends, often adding their own exaggerations to those already described. It doesn't matter that the gossip doesn't know the people she is gossiping about; all that matters is that she can live vicariously through the gossip. Elderly parents will often gossip about their children in an effort to produce self-stimulation and vicarous experiences. All these lonely, bored people are so involved in gossip that they don't always realize they are telling tales or exaggerating. In short, they believe their own fabrications.

Repressed anger is perhaps the most common cause of malicious gossip. Many angry men or women cannot admit or accept their anger, nor can they express it directly. Instead, they let it out with gossip. These angry people want desperately to be universally liked, and they feel that any expression of anger would destroy their "angel" image. If openly confronted, they will deny feeling angry at the very same people they are verbally destroying. And if the anger is very pent up, the gossip will not only tattle about those with whom they are angry, but they will strike out against anyone to relieve their anger and self-hate. Unreleased, these emotions result in deep depression.

Jealousy and envy are intimately related to repressed anger and are common motives for gossip. Some unfortunate people go through life feeling deprived and think others unjustifiably possess more than they do. They crave what others have and live in terror that someone will take something away from them. The subject of the gossip here is usually the individual who seems threatening to the person gossiping, or a person who owns what the gossip craves. The object of the gossip is to put down the person so as to remove the craving for what that person owns. In knocking down the subject, the gossip feels she is raising up herself and compensating for her own poor self-esteem. Because of this knocking-down-building-up cycle, envy and jealousy produce the most vicious gossip.

Basically those are the emotional ingredients that make people gossip. Now let's categorize the various kinds of gossips:

The "insecure gossip" is similar to a small child who wants to play with only one playmate at a time. The single playmate becomes the friend who is *there*, and all other playmates become potential enemies who are to be gossiped about in an attempt to destroy them. This need for exclusive friendship stems from the feeling that if any other playmates were present, they most certainly would prove more interesting than the gossip herself. In adults, this exclusive friendship is largely due to profound feelings of inadequacy coupled with the feeling that one has only a limited amount of loyalty and interest that must not be dissipated by speaking to more than one person at one time.

The "lovable gossip" has an inordinate need to be liked. This is her only way of feeling safe. She brings gifts in the form of disclosures about other people's affairs in order to be liked. In effect she says: "I give you all this confidential information that I'm sure you want to hear so that you'll like me." Of course, the lovable gossip tries her very best to tell people anything she thinks they want to hear.

The "entertaining gossip" gives information in order to be admired. Admiration is more important to her than likability or love. Admiration is her principal compensation for low self-esteem. This gossip will try to provide entertainment with smart, shocking, exotic, private, or funny information—anything to convey the impression that she has access and proximity to important people: anything for a laugh or applause or any other reaction that can be interpreted as admiration.

A "trader gossip" has an insatiable curiosity to know other people's business. She lives vicariously through other people's affairs, and the more she knows about them the greater her fund for synthetic living. In effect she says: "I'll tell you and you are going to feel obligated to tell me. We will trade, and the juicier you make your tidbits, the juicier I'll make mine."

The "temptress gossip" uses gossip to tease and flirt in a sad effort to be a coquette. She often gossips to men as an aberrant form of sexual play. In effect she says: "Be nice to me and I'll tell you lots more."

The "holier-than-thou gossip" sometimes honestly believes she has a saintly mission to purify the world. Her gossip is an act of condemnation and is punishment against those people she feels are less virtuous than herself. Secretly, however, she envies their freedom and wants to do the same things they have the freedom to do. Gossip and condemnation are her principal means of repressing her powerful temptations, unrequited yearnings, and unresolved conflicts.

The "honest gossip" will gossip for any and all of the above reasons, but she almost never exaggerates or lies. She is perfectly capable of devastating her victim with honesty. She must utter only the truth because this is her way of rationalizing away both her reasons for gossiping and the fact that she gossips at all. She is saying: "Gossip? I never gossip. I only tell the truth." She does not allow herself to become aware that she uses truth to verbally assault and destroy.

As you can see, the subject and material a gossip uses gives ample insight into the gossip's motives and personality. If you listen closely to others (as well as to your own gossip), you will see a pattern emerge that will give you sufficient information to make a gossip-type diagnosis.

It must be pointed out that gossip is always more damaging to the one who spreads it than to the person being gossiped about. Gossips are usually "found out" and suffer the kind of ostracism common to bores and other offensive people. Chronic gossips are unhappy people, and gossip only serves to increase their feelings of self-hate. Gossip involves a vicious cycle that can only leave one feeling more emotionally depleted, emptier and deader than before.

Q: *Do you have any suggestions for a "big mouth"? I keep promising myself that I'm not going to tell people about my troubles and things, but the next thing I know, I've told everything. I don't gossip, I just blab things about myself that I really don't want to reveal. I've gotten myself in trouble this way, and I've even lost friends because of it. Help!*

A: Many people cope with nervousness and anxiety with a good deal of mouth movement. They eat a lot, smoke a lot, talk a lot, but unfortunately still can't control their anxiety.

A talkative person is usually a person who suffers from low self-esteem. To compensate for not liking one's self, the person attempts to make other people like her by being entertaining. She entertains by giving information about herself (or about others) that she feels is interesting. (This can be likened to giving gifts in exchange for love.) The "talker" also hopes to manufacture intimacy and friendship (the rationale being, "I'm telling you what I would only tell a friend, so you are my friend").

Self-acceptance is the key to resolving this kind of problem. The best way to achieve self-acceptance is through self-exploration. Constructive self-exploration is seldom possible without professional help, since people with low self-esteem tend to berate themselves when attempting self-help.

Take yourself as a case in point. You have a problem that is painful, disturbing, and destructive to your relationships with other people. You know this, and you want to do something about it. These facts put you ahead of the game. But then you call yourself a "big mouth"—an expression of self-contempt. Resolution of emotional problems cannot take place when we are at war with ourselves. To resolve any problem we need to be as gentle and kind to ourselves as we would be to others. Every person needs her own love and friendship. If she doesn't have this, then she needs outside help to achieve it.

Q: *I always find myself giving out unasked-for information. It doesn't seem to matter whether I'm with a close friend or somebody I hardly know. In no time at all, I tell about private things I ought to keep quiet about. Afterward I feel awful and worry about it for days. But then I go and open my big mouth all over again. Why do I do this?*

A: Yours is a very common symptom, but, like some other emotional problems, can stem from one or a number of roots. Let me list just a few.

1. A repressed (hidden) need to express hostility and to hurt others through malicious gossip.

2. A repressed need to hurt oneself, due to unconscious self-hatred.

3. A need to be entertaining and to be admired.

4. A need to be liked: "Look, I'm giving you something—secret information—so please like me." I believe this is the most common one.

5. Curiosity about other people's private affairs. "I'm giving you secret information, so please give me some, too, even though I won't ask you in so many words."

6. A repressed desire to exhibit oneself. This one is often linked to sexual stimulation, and the talk here is often about sexual matters.

Q: *My husband and I have a friend who is thirty-seven, single and good-looking, but I hesitate to introduce him to my single girl friends because of a disconcerting habit: He constantly brags about his "conquests." What would make him "kiss and tell"? Do you think I should introduce him as a possible marriage partner?*

A: When this kind of habit extends far into adult life, it is no longer a habit but a compulsive need. Your friend's compulsion is rather common, and the motives are often complicated and unconscious. Though your friend is unaware of the forces that move him, moved he is, and he has no choice but to seek out people and reveal his conquests to them.

Despite an outward veneer of liking, even loving women, some men are unconsciously extremely hostile to them. Though they are unaware of this distrust and hatred of the opposite sex, they have a powerful need repeatedly to downgrade women. This need often takes the form of "kissing and telling." In this way, they are revealing to themselves and others that women are untrustworthy and bad.

This lets them rationalize sexual exploitation without long-standing relationships.

Many of these men had difficult childhoods and were mistreated by castigating, exploitative mothers. They need repeated conquests —and advertisement of these conquests—to counteract fears of inadequacy, lack of desirability, lack of masculinity, loss of potency and/or the hidden fear of homosexuality. These men feel that friends might see the "truth."

In order to avoid that, they try to delude friends with stories of exploits, many of which are as false as their professed "love of women." As with many neurotic symptoms, the attempt at camouflage is, in itself, most revealing. No, your bachelor friend is not husband material. He is not ready for marriage—nor will he be until he receives psychiatric treatment to resolve his underlying problems.

Q: *I have a girlfriend who always seemed to be a relatively serious and deep-feeling person. But she can't seem to keep from giggling and laughing, especially at inappropriate times or even in the middle of tragic and sad events. Why?*

A: This is the way some people react to embarrassment, tension, anxiety, and fear, and sometimes to repressed anger. The display of inappropriate emotion is often used as a cover-up for fear of displaying how they actually feel. At the same time, however inappropriate it may seem in a given situation, giggling is an active expression of feeling and as such relieves tension.

Q: *I've just about had it with a woman to whom I have been introduced at least six separate times at a mutual friend's home. About one hour after each introduction, this woman invariably stops the conversation to ask me, "What is your name again? I just can't remember it." I might add that, as far as I can tell, she has no trouble remembering other names. Why have I been singled out for such rude treatment?*

A: There are several possible reasons for this woman's irritating habit:

1. She may be too preoccupied with herself to be interested enough to remember the name of anyone who can't be of benefit to her in some way.

2. She may have some hostile feelings toward you because of what she may feel you represent or what she may have heard about you.

3. She may feel threatened by you because of your position in the community or your profession or just because you are you.

4. She may be chronically anxious or depressed and thus unable to concentrate on the names of people she sees intermittently.

5. You may remind her of someone she long ago decided to forget.

6. You may in some way bring to mind an event, time or place that is too painful for her to remember.

Q: *My husband and I have been married less than a year. Whenever we fight, which is no more often than most couples, my husband insists that we kiss and make up before we go to sleep that night. However, I do not always feel like kissing and making up. It isn't that I want to hold a grudge, but sometimes my anger simply does not disappear as quickly as his—and, since my own anger hasn't really gone, I feel that kissing and making up is phony. My husband says that it is much better for our mental health—and our marriage—if we do not go to sleep angry. We have both agreed to abide by your advice. What do you think?*

A: I'm strictly with you. I see nothing wrong with going to sleep "still mad." I'm all for people expressing their anger verbally —because this is infinitely healthier than a cold, silent war which can be destructive to communication and warmth. Making a pact never to go to bed angry quite often just manages to produce more anger. A contrived act of pretending not to be angry merely pushes angry feelings down to the point where they may become hidden, exaggerated, and destructive. It is best to get gripes and disagreements over with, but this sometimes takes days. Dissipating anger on a natural basis—without rules, contrivances, or phony rituals— ultimately prevents chronic simmering hate and coldness.

Q: *Can you tell me why my wife always burns my food? She's been doing it for twenty years. We've had all kinds of arguments about this and she invariably promises to change—but doesn't. When we have guests, my wife prepares a perfect meal—nothing gets burned at all. It really gets to me!*

A: Your wife burns your food because she is "burned up." People who are very angry sometimes resort to secret or not-so-secret sabotage. Your wife is sending you a message, and she's been successful in transmitting it. Your statement, "it really gets to me," proves that. What you are getting is more than burned food. Your wife is also serving you her anger, her vindictiveness and her unhappiness. Cooking lessons won't help, but efforts at better husband-wife communication will. Marriage counseling may also be helpful.

Q: *My wife's snoring drives me crazy. Is it possible that she snores because, unconsciously, she is angry at me? We discussed this and she denies any such feeling. She also turns down my suggestion that she see a hypnotist or a psychoanalyst to find out if I am right. What do you think would be the best thing for us to do about it?*

A: I think your money would be better spent on a consultation with an ear, nose, and throat specialist for your wife—and a pair of ear stoppers for you.

Q: *My eighteen-year-old son is always picking on and teasing his thirteen-year-old sister. It doesn't bother her a bit, but it does bother me. What makes a brother act that way toward a sister who simply adores him?*

A: This is very common behavior among siblings, and there may be many reasons for your son's actions.

It is not uncommon for an older child to feel angry at a younger sibling whom he feels is attempting to usurp his favored and exclusive position with his parents. He simply does not want to share his parents' affection with a latecomer. While such anger is often quite overt in young children, it can persist on a relatively unconscious level in older children, and it has been known to continue into adulthood.

Young boys are often embarrassed by the affection they may feel toward their sisters, and this embarrassment may coexist with jealous feelings. The boy may use teasing both to express and to cover up these feelings.

Your son's teasing may not bother your daughter because she views his barbs as attention and is flattered and grateful to be noticed by her older brother. It is important to keep in mind that the family provides the earliest possible opportunity for boys and girls to relate to each other. While the participants may not consciously know it, teasing between brothers and sisters is often practice for approaching and relating to the opposite sex outside the family.

Some boys who are unable to express anger or affection, or both, toward their mothers will feel safer in unconsciously displacing these feelings onto a sister. You say that in teasing his sister your son makes you angry. This could be precisely what he wants. Thus by teasing his sister he unconsciously accomplishes several things: he expresses attention and affection toward his sister, who responds accordingly, and he discharges hostility by irritating you—who respond accordingly.

Q: *I am thirty-five years old, have two sons and think of myself as happily married; but from time to time I have dreams in which my husband dies. Do you think this has any special meaning?*

A: All dreams have meaning. But their meaning is invariably linked to the individual doing the dreaming. One cannot interpret a dream validly without a good deal of knowledge about the dreamer's personality and history. The symbols in a dream become meaningful only when the dreamer associates to them and tells us, through his associations and feelings, what they represent in his life.

Your dream is one of the most common and is reported again and again. It can have a variety of interpretations—again dependent on the dreamer. Very frequently the dreamer has considerable repressed or unexpressed anger toward the person he dreams about.

Q: *My wife is late. She is always late, and she often manages to make me late, too. I honestly think that she goes out of her way to be late. Is there any rhyme or reason to this kind of irritating behavior?*

A: I agree with you that your wife goes out of her way to be late. *But* please keep in mind that chances are excellent that she is unaware of her compulsion to be late. This kind of unconscious need or compulsion always has rhyme and reason. But the reasons for it are varied and complicated. Here are some that I have encountered.

1. A poorly developed sense of responsibility and regard for others.

2. Extreme sensitivity to coercion and the unconscious feeling that being on time or keeping an appointment is giving in to coercion.

3. A need to rebel against any symbol of authority and considering appointments as authority symbols.

4. Repressed anger and an unconscious need to retaliate, to be vindictive, to tease and to provoke. Breaking appointments serves these needs as a kind of displaced temper tantrum.

5. Hidden self-hatred and a need to hurt themselves as well as others. These people will often arrive late or break appointments in an unconscious determination to put their worst foot forward.

6. A need constantly to test other people—in effect saying, "If you love me, show me how much social delinquency you will take from me."

Q: *Why do I hate to write letters? I find it almost impossible to sit down to write or answer a letter. I've alienated friends, but even this doesn't make me change. Could there be a psychological reason for my action?*

A: There could well be a psychological reason for your not wanting to write letters, but I would have to know much more about you in order to understand your actions. However, aversion to letter-writing is quite common, and in most cases could be due to one or more of the following:

1. A need to be perfect. Perfectionists often can't write letters

because they feel they might produce a letter that lacks literary style. To avoid this possible imperfection, they simply do not write the letter.

2. A fear of their own feelings and/or commitment. People who are afraid to express feelings and commit them to paper—thereby putting them on record—seldom write letters. They fear that putting something down in writing makes it irrevocable.

3. A fear of hostility. Some people fear that a letter will reveal personal aspects that they much prefer to hide—particularly hostile feelings.

4. A need to rebel. People who have trouble with authority and who are secretly quite rebellious see letter-writing as a duty. Such people look upon letter-writing in much the same way that a rebellious child looks upon homework . . . and they respond accordingly.

Q: *Sometimes a friend does something that really infuriates me, and I don't realize it until much later. Is this common?*

A: I'm sure you are not always aware of your anger—nobody is. Most of us hide our feelings of anger from ourselves. We do this so quickly and automatically that we aren't aware we are doing it. But we pay a physical and emotional price for hidden anger. Often suppressed anger asserts itself in other ways: headaches, high blood pressure, ulcers, nervousness, depression, etc. Why are people afraid to express anger? Mostly they fear they will be disliked if they let their anger show. Yet the more we permit ourselves to feel angry, whether or not there is a rational reason for anger, and whether or not we express it, the healthier we are emotionally.

Q: *Do you agree with those who say that man is naturally aggressive and hostile and that all the violence in the world—wars, power struggles, etc.—are only an excuse to let out this natural rage?*

A: There are schools of psychoanalytic thought in which the belief is held that aggression is instinctive and basic to the human condition. I and my colleagues at the American Institute for Psychoanalysis feel otherwise. We believe, as Dr. Karen Horney did, that man is not basically hostile, aggressive or self-destructive. We believe that these characteristics are the result of emotional disturbance,

Anger, Jealousy and Fear   81

poor communication, and "sick" cultures. We feel that man has the potential for better communication—that is, for greater maturity and for better and peaceful emotional exchange.

This does not mean that health negates anger. Anger, like love, is a warm and human emotion, and there are times when anger is a completely appropriate response. But I speak here of a short-lived, nondestructive anger rather than a murderous, cold, vindictive rage.

Please do not confuse aggression with self-assertion. Aggression is compulsively motivated by neurotic needs and is designed to put the next person down—to master and to achieve a vindictive triumph. Self-assertion springs from a healthy need to do things for oneself in the service of self-realization, with no satisfaction derived from hurting or manipulating anyone else.

Q: *It seems to me that I'm a pretty good-natured guy. I always give the edge to a friend, or let others get ahead of me in line. Somehow, I always finish last, though, and no one ever appreciates what I've done for them. What's the matter with me, anyway?*

A: It is time you climbed down from your saintly pedestal and joined the rest of the world. You are probably no better natured than anyone else; more likely, you have been repressing all kinds of resentments, hurts, and angers, and suffer, as a result, from all kinds of headaches—literally and figuratively.

You should give up your fictitious saintly image, which probably makes you more of a nuisance to your friends than you realize. They would much prefer to relate to a *real* person. So join us plain folks who become irritated once in a while, even lash out at people occasionally. Be a person who sometimes acts considerately and sometimes selfishly. In short, be a human—and be happy.

Q: *Sometimes I have utterly crazy, destructive thoughts. Is something the matter with me?*

A: You're not losing your mind. We all have peculiar thoughts and fantasies of extreme violence that involve strangers as well as loved ones. These thoughts are almost always caused by repressed feelings of hostility. For example: feeling guilty, you may try to repress feelings of momentary hate for a loved one. The more you try to repress these feelings, the more exaggerated they become. When they finally emerge (as they always do), they will often appear in highly exaggerated and distorted words or fantasies. They must be exaggerated in order to break through your censoring efforts and to make you aware of them. Since 99 percent of our thoughts do not become actions, chances are you have nothing to fear. The more we can accept and admit our feelings, the less we will have "crazy" thoughts.

JEALOUSY

Jealousy, we have been told, is the "green-eyed monster." If we fear that something of our own may be taken from us by another, we become jealous. We feel envious if we covet something that we want desperately but that belongs to another. When we can successfully separate those needs that are attainable in reality from those that are totally inaccessible to us, we are better able to handle feelings of jealousy and envy.

How Do You Handle a Jealous Husband?

Jealousy and envy are very common, complex emotions, but because most people consider them unpleasant, even "sinful" feelings, few take the time and trouble to understand them.

Attaching moral judgment to these feelings—or to any other human emotions—usually hinders the possibility of understanding them and often destroys any chance of obtaining the very changes desired.

It is also destructive to tell a jealous or envious person that he or she can avoid these "sinful" feelings by a simple act of willpower. How many times has a well-meaning friend said, "All you have to do is make up your mind that you won't feel such and such an emotion, and you won't. You can just will these feelings away if you want to."

People who suffer intense feelings of jealousy or envy are very unhappy individuals who need understanding and insight into their problems. They do not need friends who make moral judgments or give them unworkable pep talks about willpower.

Emotions are human, and thus there are bound to be times for each of us when we feel jealous or envious.

It is easy to confuse these two feelings because they usually go hand in hand, and their root causes are often identical. I explain the difference this way:

Jealousy is the threat or fear that something or someone will (totally or in some measure) be taken away from the jealous person.

Envy? The envious individual feels that he would like to have something or someone or some situation or status that he thinks is possessed by the person he envies.

Jealousy and envy are neither male nor female characteristics: women can be as jealous or envious as men—and vice versa. But in this article I will talk only about the male—specifically the jealous husband.

Jealousy is *not* a function of love. A jealous husband does not necessarily love his wife more than a nonjealous husband. Jealousy and envy are more often functions of possessiveness, and they result from feelings of insecurity and inadequacy. The possessive husband may love or may even be in love, but feeling possessive enough to suffer jealousy usually stems from feeling dependent and threatened.

When does a husband feel dependent or threatened? Perhaps his business has been bad. Perhaps his children are doing poorly in school. A parent may die or require surgery. Perhaps the husband suddenly realizes that he has reached the age that he has always considered "middle age." Children may marry or move out on their own, etc. These are also times in a husband's life when he may feel particularly jealous or envious.

Feelings of jealousy and envy may or may not have some basis in reality. Men can be jealous when there is no actual or real threat. They can also be envious of others who do not, in truth, have the things or the position the envious man thinks they have. The envious husband may well realize that his thinking is distorted, but he may still feel jealous or envious. This makes sense if you realize that these feelings are born in us and are projections of something that goes on inside us rather than objective responses to things that occur outside ourselves.

Let me give you some examples of jealous or envious husbands and what happened in each case:

Peter started to become very jealous whenever his wife Mary spoke to other men. Even though Peter knew that Mary loved him and that her conversations with other men represented no threat to his marriage, he felt vaguely uneasy and slightly threatened whenever he saw his wife chatting with another man. Then, without realizing why, Peter began questioning his wife's fidelity. He didn't even understand his own doubts, questions and self-torture. He began to wonder, "Did Mary ever love me? How could she love me? Did she know other men before me? Did she really want to marry me or did she just want to get married?"

At the same time he began questioning her fidelity, Peter became more dependent on Mary. He recognized this increased dependency and considered it "unmasculine," torturing himself even more. He also felt possessive of his children and his home.

Then, just as suddenly as these jealous, possessive feelings had begun, they disappeared. Peter became his old self again.

What had happened was this: During the period of his jealous attack, Peter had failed in several important business deals. As a result, he felt wounded and inadequate. For this period he did not like himself and projected his feelings onto his wife. Subconsciously, he felt that if he did not like himself, how could Mary like him?

Whenever a man feels inner emptiness and weakness, he tends to want to "own" people or to exert exclusive and complete ownership of things outside himself. This is how he compensates for his feelings of inner weakness.

So Peter knew outwardly that Mary was faithful, but inwardly, because of his own feelings of weakness and self-douts, he thought that perhaps she was not.

Envy works in much the same way. If a man feels inadequate, he may desire another man's lot, even though the other man's position is, in reality, inferior to his own. A man in an envious state will imagine that anybody else's grass is greener. This unrealistic attitude is usually accompanied by the feeling that the other person does not deserve his imaginary good fortune. Again, such thoughts are possible because they are based on inner feelings of inadequacy rather than on actual truths.

Such was the case of the husband I'll call Fred. Fred became very envious when he overheard his wife congratulating a neighbor on his promotion. Fred's job was far better than his neighbor's, yet Fred's inner feelings of inadequacy caused him to suffer an attack of envy.

Through discussion, it was learned that Fred's feelings of inadequacy had been brought on by his recent loss of an election at his golf club.

Yet another husband, Alex, stood by stony-faced while his wife Ellie told a neighbor how handsome he looked since he had dieted off twenty-five pounds. Alex was exceedingly envious because he had failed in his own secret attempt to lose weight. Truthfully, he was not overweight, and his wife had never berated him for being heavy; it was an unrealistic goal that he had set for himself, made worse by his unrealistic attack of envy.

All attacks of jealousy and envy are painful for the sufferer and create difficulty for a spouse. The wife who does not understand the attack can feel terribly hurt and may interpret her partner's jealousy or envy as a sign that he does not love her. Overpossessiveness on the husband's part may, of course, make the wife feel constricted. The pair will then become quite irritated with each other; hostility can develop and can have a destructive effect on the marriage. In this way, a relatively simple problem can mushroom into a gigantic one. Worry, depression, anxiety, fatigue—all corrosive emotions—begin to pop up. After that, the attack can get out of hand. The victim continues to torture himself and his sometimes imagined adversary, and the attack becomes a never-ending cycle.

Usually a wife's reassurance that her husband's fears are unreal will not be enough to stop an attack. At best, reassurance brings only a brief respite that is usually followed by a new siege of envy.

Understanding the nature of the jealousy-envy process can be very valuable because it might cut short an attack. Whenever a person —man or woman—feels a jealousy-envy attack coming on, the best treatment is to look inward for the cause. Has anything happened recently that might have jolted your feeling of security? Why has there been a sudden ebb of self-esteem? Is your current position —economically, socially, emotionally, etc.—really so poor that a trade with someone else seems desirable?

If the sufferer could be helped to go directly to the source of the threat (business failure for Peter; loss of an election for Fred; failure to reach an unrealistic goal for Alex), then the attack of jealousy or envy would be short-lived. Valuable time and energy wasted on these emotions would be used to bring the victim closer to the solution instead of further away from it.

Jealousy and envy create self-contempt, which destroys morale, because secretly we know that the difficulty lies within ourselves rather than with the people we choose to see as threatening. This kind of morale-breaking effect makes us feel more jealous and envious, thus creating that never-ending cycle.

The key to defeating jealousy and envy is to look within ourselves and to find the real solution at the very beginning before things get out of hand.

If things do get out of hand, if the attacks are constant and painful, then psychoanalytic psychiatric treatment is advisable. However, one should not wait until it is impossible to tell the real from the imagined before seeking professional help.

Q: *Sometimes I feel terribly jealous or envious of a friend and I hate myself for it. What can I do?*

A: We are all susceptible to attacks of jealousy and envy when we feel particularly weak, vulnerable or fragile because of a business setback, a rejection, hurt pride, etc. However, some people always feel fragile, vulnerable and self-hating—and, therefore, suffer from chronic jealousy and envy. This has a corrosive effect on their potential for happiness and is most destructive to their relationships. Such people can gain much from professional psychiatric help; it will make life more bearable for themselves as well as for their friends and relatives.

FEAR

Fear can be a crippling emotion, totally paralyzing a logical mind and a functioning body. It can cause an individual to retreat into himself and away from society, to resort to compulsive and ritualistic behavior in order to ward off potential danger, or to panic and lose all control. Often, of course, we are confronted by real, frightening situations. A person about to undergo a serious operation or someone confronted with an armed criminal in a dark alley will experience real terror. But very often, anxiety attacks may occur when the cause is consciously unknown. A remembrance of a bad automobile accident may frighten a driver so badly he cannot get behind the wheel again, the mere thought of a dinner party may give the hostess a headache. Other fears are deeper in the psyche, of course. Why should a pregnant woman be fearful of bearing a son, or a reasonable man have a terrible phobia about tunnels, trains, and elevators? Only by dealing with our fears on all levels will we be able to recognize the real dangers from the imaginary ones.

Q: *I'm afraid of being frightened. Is this an unusual fear?*

A: Too many of us are embarrassed to admit that we're scared. Too many men and women equate fear with being immature, weak, and cowardly. As a result, we teach our children that to be scared is not grown up. This is poor advice. Being frightened is a human condition, and to deny that it exists is inhuman and leads to self-hate whenever fear arises—as it must.

Being scared in certain situations is entirely appropriate and healthy. This reaction is all-important and at times can be life-saving. While constant, inappropriate fear is evidence of an emotional problem, the ability to become afraid at times is one of our most constructive facilities and must not be destroyed.

Q: *Can you tell me why my thirty-six-year-old daughter is afraid to drive over bridges? She gets so nervous that her hands shake.*

A: As with most phobias, the object or activity feared has little or no conscious rationale. Logic can only be found on an unconscious level. In other words, your daughter's real, subconscious fear has been transferred to a conscious surface object—a bridge.

Fear of bridges is rather common. Sometimes the real fear is of height, of inner feelings of insecurity, of crossing from one phase of life to another. In any case, each individual's fear can only be understood and worked out in terms of that person's life, values and emotional situation. For such an undertaking, psychoanalytic investigation is almost always necessary.

Q: *I'm a good driver but I have a continual fear of skidding, even though it has never happened. I even dream about it. In these dreams the car goes out of control and I spin around and around all over the road. Can you make any sense out of my fear?*

A: "Irrational fears" such as yours seldom have anything to do with the situation that is feared. "Car dreams" are very common and are usually symbols of deeper meaning than what appears on the surface. To understand a fear, fantasy or dream it is necessary to have considerable detailed information about the individual involved. However, your kind of fear (skidding) often is found in people who are afraid to fully experience their feelings. They are afraid of losing control (as when a car skids out of control) and letting go with whatever it is they really feel. A fear of losing control over feelings is especially applicable to anger and rage. The solution to the problem means resolution of the underlying cause or causes. Resolution involves full awareness and acceptance of all feelings, especially feelings of anger or rage. Being able to express one's feelings to others, and to express anger, may bring considerable relief from symptoms. This kind of resolution may require psychoanalytic psychotherapy. The goal of such treatment would be more than getting rid of the troublesome symptoms; it would include freedom from the underlying problem—in this case, freedom to accept and tap all feelings, including anger. Such therapy would also contribute to feeling more comfortable with one's self and would increase the potential for feeling alive and happy.

Q: *My husband would like to take trips to distant places, and frankly, so would I. But I cannot bring myself to go on airplanes. This limits us greatly, because we don't have enough time to travel by train or boat. Looking back, I know I have always felt queasy in high places. I suspect that this is a common fear; but is there a common basis and solution for it?*

A: You are right. Extreme fear of high places, particularly airplanes, is very common. As with nearly all psychological problems, the basis and solution are highly individual. There are, however, certain facts that come up again and again and that many people have in common. Let me describe just a few of the types of people I've known who have this fear of high places and airplanes.

1. Those who are afraid of falling from their own idealized or glorious concept of themselves.

2. Those to whom control and mastery are a way of life. They are threatened by any potential loss of control and helplessness. Some of these people can fly if they are at the controls, but cannot sit as "helpless" passengers while another person flies the plane.

3. People who are afraid of hidden self-contempt and self-destruction and hostile impulses and the urge to jump.

4. People who feel particularly fragile when confronted with the unfamiliar and who require the familiar feel of earth under their feet for a sense of solidity, identification, and self-confidence.

5. People who need confining landmarks around them for a sense of security and who get the feeling that they are "coming apart" when they are in wide-open spaces.

6. People for whom the confinement of a plane cabin represents their own inner tyrannies, coercion, pressures, and lack of freedom. These people have an inordinate need for freedom of movement and direction.

Q: *My husband has a terrible fear of tunnels, bridges, elevators and trains. Because of this, we cannot go very far from home and our social life amounts to almost nothing. Also, he cannot earn nearly as much as he could if he could travel. Our family doctor tells us that symptoms of this kind are due to some kind of nervous-system upset. He says that talk treatments don't help, because my husband didn't get sick through talk and won't get well through talk. He wants us to go to a man who specializes in drugs and electric-shock treatments. Could you please give me your opinion?*

A: People in fairly large numbers suffer from illogical fears, known as phobias. There is a great variety of phobias, and your husband's fear of closed and confining places (claustrophobia) is one of the commonest. I have yet to see a phobic patient with any kind of demonstrable (adequate evidence) nervous-system-disease symptom or dysfunction. People suffering from phobias are invariably suffering from a complex emotional disturbance. This evolves from a disturbed way of relating to themselves and to other people. It is true that they did not get sick through talk and will not get well through talk—but they did not get sick through drugs or electricity and will not get well through drugs or electricity. They get sick through difficulty in their early emotional development, resulting from problems in early family relationships.

They can best be helped by psychoanalytic treatment. In this treatment, talk takes place. For human beings, talk is very important. We use talk to communicate ideas, needs, information and, most important, *emotions*. The talking that takes place in psychoanalysis is special and particularly important. This is so because it affords the possibility of insight. It enables the patient to see where, what, and how he operates in relation to himself and others. It pinpoints his pitfalls and his assets and enables him to reduce the former and develop the latter in a constructive move toward self-realization, health, and, in the case of phobias, freedom!

Q: *I had a car accident several months ago, and since it happened, I just can't bring myself to drive. I've been driving for ten years. I've always considered myself a very reasonable person, but I just can't get behind the wheel. I sit down in the driver's seat and actually get the shakes. What can I do?*

A: An anxiety reaction following an accident is sometimes called a traumatic neurosis. Quite often, the anxiety symptoms clear up of themselves several months after the trauma or accident. But sometimes the symptoms linger on. This is largely due to the fact that the trauma attacks self-confidence and in a complicated way stimulates old problems as well as hidden reservoirs of self-doubt. Thus the trauma is the straw, but old (unconscious) neurotic attitudes and problems comprise the load that breaks the proverbial camel's back. Therefore, my suggestion is that you stop trying to be so "reasonable" and get some psychiatric help.

Q: *I am about to have an eye operation, after which I must keep my eyes closed for several weeks. I am terrified. Is this a common fear?*

A: Indeed it is. It is particularly frightening for people whose sense of security and well-being depends a great deal on mastery and control of their immediate environment. Please consult a competent psychoananyst and have your ophthalmologist contact him, too. A combination of psychotherapy and tranquilizers may be helpful in mitigating emotional pain and trauma before and after this kind of surgery.

Q: *I'm considered normal and healthy, but I always get a bad headache the night before I give a dinner party. I've asked myself every conceivable question about why this happens, but it doesn't help. I'd be grateful for a little light on the subject, since I give quite a number of parties each year.*

A: Have you asked yourself any of the following questions?

1. Do you, in fact, *want* to give the number of parties you do, or somewhere do you feel that they are an imposition and that you are coerced?

2. Do you like the people you invite, or do you invite them as a kind of repayment or out of a sense of obligation or duty?

3. How perfectionistic are you? Are you trying to be a combination of best American cook, entertainer, raconteur of the year, or are you content to provide a pleasant evening for friends whose company you enjoy?

4. Are you in competition with your guests for praise, admiration, etc.?

5. Are you in any way embarrassed by your home—the circumstances in which you live?

6. Do you feel responsible for complete peace and compatibility among your guests? Are you afraid of strong discussions or strong expressions of feeling?

Q: *I am thirty-four years old, relatively sophisticated (I think), have given birth to two children, have had abdominal surgery (gall bladder) without any hysteria. But I'm absolutely terrified of going to the dentist. I just found out, for example, that I must lose two teeth. I know it's stupid and childish to react this way, but the whole thing is giving me the horrors.*

A: Fears of this kind are neither stupid nor childish. Inordinate fears are very common and have individual, complicated, and sometimes very obscure roots. Fear of going to the dentist—in all degrees—is a particularly prevalent one. Let me list a few of the possible dynamics, which may exist singly or in combination.

1. Most people are frightened of unfamiliar situations, and a dental office to many people is the quintessence of unfamiliarity.

2. Some people are particularly afraid of being in any kind of "helpless" situation. Allowing anyone other than themselves to be in charge or in control is particularly threatening.

3. The sight of any kind of instrument can be very disturbing to many people, often reminiscent of early hospital experiences (visiting sick or dying relatives as a child, having had a fractured limb or a tonsillectomy). People sometimes see the instruments as potential vehicles of torture—and as almost having a life of their own.

4. The loss of a tooth often represents the loss of a part of oneself. This kind of fear is particularly prevalent in people who have a shaky concept of themselves to begin with and who feel that they can afford no loss whatsoever. This, in turn, is often linked to the feeling that a loss of teeth represents loss of youth, loss of health, loss of beauty, etc. In extreme cases, the individual may inappropriately see the loss of a tooth as the beginning of a general decline or collapse.

5. The mouth connects us to the outside world. With the mouth, we eat the food—of the world—and with the mouth we talk to people outside ourselves. To many people dental work represents an assault on the mouth and, as such, an attack on our principal instrument of communication. This is unconsciously seen as an act that will isolate us from our fellows and, as such, can produce considerable anxiety.

In most cases of "dental fear," a mild tranquilizer or sedative (prescribed by your doctor only!) taken before a dental visit can be very helpful. Some people, however, require psychotherapy, which concomitantly helps them with other problems, too.

Q: *During my first pregnancy I subconsciously longed for a daughter, but I made myself believe that I would be delighted with a healthy child of either sex. When my daughter was born, I was flooded with relief. She is now three years old and in the next few years my husband and I would like to have a second daughter. Al-*

though my husband would prefer another girl, I know a boy would be equally acceptable to him. But I have no brothers and no knowledge of little-boy activities. The sons of my friends and neighbors do not appeal to me at all. I am actually afraid to become pregnant again for fear of having a son. Feeling the way I do, how could I be a good mother to a son? I don't want our daughter to be an only child, but the possibility of having a son just repels me. I feel like a terrible person. How do I cope with these feelings?

A: You have a serious problem. But having a serious problem does not make you a terrible person, and you should not feel that it does. Berating yourself only generates self-hate at a time when you need your own humanity and compassion. The fact that you recognize, and openly admit to yourself, that you have a problem is very constructive. Your problem is complicated because it involves more than just not wanting a son. Your problem is serious because it springs from deep roots and indicates disturbed feelings toward yourself and toward males and maleness in general. Such feelings often stem from difficulties with one's parents and from a disturbed relationship between parents. These feelings may also indicate latent jealousy, envy, and hostility toward men and what you think constitutes the male role. For obvious reasons, therefore, I would strongly suggest you see a psychiatrist before becoming pregnant a second time. Therapy would probably help you to resolve these problems on all levels (with your husband and daughter, too) and will be fruitful and enlightening.

Q: *I am twenty, and my fiancé is twenty-four. We are getting married next spring. Every time we talk about the actual wedding plans, he gets jittery. He tells me that he is frightened of all the pomp and ceremony and reassures me that his fear has nothing to do with our marriage. I believe him, because we have known each other for three years and we love each other. But I can't help wondering why the wedding itself makes him nervous.*

A: Wedding-ceremony and party jitters in young prospective grooms are extremely common. Many men would rather go into battle than be the center of attention of a large group of friends, relatives and strangers. However, the reasons vary with individuals, so that generalizations do not apply. I'll list just a few possibilities.

1. In our culture, men—unlike women—are not brought up to relish and take pride in the wedding ceremony or the attainment of the marital state. For women, there is psychologically much more prestige in getting a man than vice versa.

2. Women are both subtly and blatantly trained to be home- and family-oriented, and much of their life energy goes into getting a husband. Since the wedding ceremony represents this attainment, it is utterly desirable. Women want to show everybody. Men are trained not to hurry into family involvement, responsibility, and loss of freedom. To many, the wedding ceremony is an outward manifestation (to the world) that they have been "caught"—of which the less evidence the better.

3. Women in our culture generally enjoy pomp and ceremony more than men do. Particularly shy men find being the center of attention very difficult—especially when there is even the slightest reference to anticipated sexual things.

4. There are men (and women, too) who are very detached and who are terribly afraid of sustained contractual involvement. For them, a loss of freedom is greatly magnified, and anticipation of the marriage ceremony and its symbolic representation can cause severe enough panic to require psychiatric treatment.

Q: *I have been told that I have a talent for painting, but when I'm doing a picture I can't sleep or I have bad dreams. Why do I get so anxious?*

A: Many creative people have anxiety-producing manifestations because creative work often stirs up unconscious memories and feelings that have been locked away. Some memories may be happy, but some are laden with pain. Creative work such as painting and writing is similar to the process of pregnancy and birth, because it involves the maximum use of one's self and a struggle to tap one's innermost feelings and resources. While the finished product may be beautiful and fulfilling, the struggle to produce it has not been without pain—however constructive that pain may be.

Q: *Sometimes I experience anxiety attacks for no reason at all. Is this normal?*

A: I've never met anybody who doesn't have them. Many people—including many physicians—don't recognize an anxiety attack for what it is. Anxiety attacks occur when we try to repress anger, when we suffer hurt pride, and when we try to escape facing conflicts about important emotional issues in our lives. Sometimes anxiety feels like nervousness, increased tension, a feeling of apprehension or of potential danger and disaster—all without apparent cause. Very often anxiety attacks take various forms that are not immediately recognizable as anxiety. For example: panic ("I'm driving along and suddenly I feel that I'm losing myself"), severe chest pain, very rapid heartbeat, headache, stomach upset, peculiar and seemingly unrelated thoughts, frightening dreams and fantasies, etc. If these attacks are prolonged it is important to seek proper treatment.

CHAPTER 4

Loneliness and Depression

People have always traveled in groups. The family is the nuclear unit, of course, and the society in which men and women work together has formed itself around that unit. But everyone must at some point have a place and time to himself or herself. To be alone, however, is not the same as being lonely, and the healthy individual will welcome whatever periods of time he spends with himself. Many people find being alone very difficult, though, and experience loneliness and often depression whether they are by themselves or in a group. A large cocktail party, for example, can be the loneliest of places. And, on the other hand, being alone can be a rewarding, enriching experience.

LONELINESS

We all feel lonely at one time or other. When we are nostalgic for a city we once lived in or a group of friends now distant, and when we have no immediate replacement for the enjoyment we felt in those past situations, we may often feel isolated, split off from the rest of humanity. This is a time to remember not to abandon ourselves. This is a good time to be good to ourselves in whatever ways we have learned through the years. It can be helpful to seek out a sympathetic friend or relative or, better still, to comfort someone worse off than ourselves.

Everyone Feels Lonely Sometimes

The first step in resolving a problem is to understand the nature of that problem. Loneliness is a very common human condition. Every man and woman feels lonely at one time or another.

There are varying degrees of loneliness. While some women (or men) may seldom feel lonely, for other unfortunate people loneliness has become so malignant and chronic that life is miserable.

All human beings must experience human emotions such as loneliness, anger, love, etc. Neither age, personal history, wealth nor marital status precludes loneliness—any more than these factors do away with anger or love. Even those women (and men, too) who have wonderful relationships, devoted families, excellent and involved social lives and careers still, at times, experience loneliness. No matter how involved or interested a person may be in another person, no matter how much a human being loves or is loved, there are times when he feels lonely—just as that person feels anger, contentment, exhilaration or any other emotion.

Loneliness, I think, is closely related to nostalgia and a sense of longing. Nobody can go through life without occasionally yearning for a time gone by, for people long since gone, for a place that no longer exists, for appetites, desires, feelings, tastes and goals that vanished with the end of childhood. All of these past experiences have been stored up in a memory bank and they can crop up in our conscious mind at any time, quite unexpectedly, no matter how full or busy or happy life may be today. These memories create a sense of longing and often a feeling of distance from things desired and things unreachable. The gap between desire and ability to satisfy that desire makes a person feel somewhat distant, isolated, alone; it makes for a feeling of loneliness.

These lonely feelings will be strongest during times of stress or change in the family status. People tend to feel intensely lonely immediately after a son or daughter marries. Sometimes we feel lonely in anticipation of our children's growing up and going off on their own.

When you feel lonely there is nothing wrong with seeking warmth from loved ones. It is nice to have someone's hand to hold or someone's arms around you when lonely feelings arise. But it is more important to understand that these feelings are proof positive that you are indeed a warm, sensitive, feeling human being. It is also important not to become frantic or self-hating because of lonely feelings. Again, remember, these feelings are in fact perfectly human.

Once you accept loneliness as a perfectly human feeling, the lonely feelings will almost certainly pass. They will be replaced by another kind of mood or feeling. It is a fact of life that these feelings will come and go. Not accepting this fact, expecting to live in a constant state of euphoria will only result in disappointment or bitterness.

Loneliness and being alone are not always related. Many people live alone and spend a good deal of time alone but are seldom lonely. These people usually have a strong sense of self-esteem; they consider themselves as persons—and, therefore, as company. (They are not alone, they are with someone—they are with *themselves*.) Men and women who feel this way are usually people who live full, useful lives, people who can make a worthwhile emotional investment in other people and activities. While they spend much time alone, they nevertheless have rich, meaningful, and caring relationships with other people.

On the other hand, some men and women are seldom alone but still suffer from intense and desperate feelings of loneliness. Many people who are severely lonely—who have almost totally unrequited desires to relate to another human being—do not know they are lonely. They are so fearful of their lonely feelings that they camouflage them in many destructive ways. Here are some of the most common and neurotic (that is, distorted) ways in which people try to cope with loneliness. (These symptoms can also exist in other conditions, where loneliness may not be the prime problems.):

1. Depression and anxiety.

2. Severe and compulsive overeating, leading to gross and dangerous overweight.

3. Oversleeping and/or insomnia. (There may be intermittent periods of each.)

4. The use of drugs, including barbiturates, amphetamines, or alcohol, as well as any combination of destructive possibilities.

5. Serious tendency to be a hypochondriac, with enormous concentration on self and fear of any number of illnesses.

6. Forming all kinds of superficial, inappropriate, and often destructive relationships. Some of the most popular people you know can be the loneliest. Often they "know" many people but don't really know anyone.

7. Chronic infantilism and dependency on parents or other relatives, and fear of the responsibility of having one's own home.

8. Chronic, compulsive promiscuity, in which sex is used as payment for fleeting contacts and in frustrated attempts to feel liked.

9. Psychosomatic illnesses: gastric disturbances, asthmatic attacks, skin eruptions, etc.

10. Hyperactivity, in which the person embarks on a constant merry-go-round of energy-wasting, superficial action without sustained emotional investment or involvement.

Many people who suffer from loneliness are frightened of the closeness that would permit them to develop meaningful relationships. Some of these frightened people feel they have too little to give and that closeness would deplete them and engulf them. They fear the loss of individuality and identity. Others value an imaginary freedom too highly to become involved with another person or persons, but they nevertheless crave such involvement to soften their intense feelings of loneliness. This conflict—needing people and at the same time being afraid of people—is quite common. Most people who feel this way truthfully cry out for a relationship to ease their loneliness—but, at the same time, they unwittingly put every conceivable block in the way of realizing such a possibility. These men and women, including those who suffer from the ten symptoms I've listed, often require psychoanalytic treatment in order to resolve long-standing personality and related problems.

Many of the loneliest women in the world are women who are married—women who, on the surface, seem to enjoy full lives. Even though they have husbands, these women still lack a meaningful one-to-one relationship, one in which an emotional investment (caring for each other) and an emotional exchanging (listening to each other) takes place. Unrealized potential makes these married women's loneliness sadder and more frustrating. These wives and husbands have gradually slipped into separate, encapsulated lives in which they live together and talk together, but fail to share what they actually *feel*. In short, they are not operating on the same emotional wavelength; they are not communicating emotionally.

In some cases these husbands and wives can rebuild their emotional bridges by actively joining in all kinds of mutually interesting activities and social endeavors. Going on vacations together, without the children, or taking the time to try to get to know each other again (or for the first time) may be helpful if the couple honestly wants to get back on the same emotional level. To effect such an emotional reconciliation, it is vital for the couple to be open and honest with one another. Some people, unfortunately, can't cope with their neurotic pride and, therefore, can't be open enough to tell each other of their loneliness, unhappiness, and need for closer relating. If this neurotic pride has existed for too long, it is often necessary to seek marriage or family therapy with a psychoanalytically trained psychiatrist who specializes in treating couples or working with an entire family unit.

For the recently widowed or divorced person, loneliness can be quite frequent. In such cases, it can be useful to let friends know that you are lonely and that you want to meet new people. It may be difficult to admit this to yourself, let alone to a friend, but it is important to do so. Friends do not want to embarrass or push, so they will often do nothing about introducing a widow or a recently divorced woman to other men—or men to women—unless the person asks them to do so.

It may be difficult at first to "get back into the swing of things," to engage in social situations or go on vacations alone. But it gets easier with practice. Remember, the sight of a man or a woman alone is getting more and more common in our society. Political clubs, museums, concerts, causes, etc., are all indirect but effective ways of meeting people with similar interests.

Lastly, there are those people—the sick, the handicapped, the aged, the hospitalized—who suffer from chronic situational loneliness. They need help wherever and whenever the not-so-unfortunate can provide it. Reaching out to other people in need will almost always work wonders toward conquering your own loneliness. Try it and see.

Q: *I am twenty-four, happily married and generally outgoing. In fact, my big problem is that I can't stand being alone even for a few hours. I so envy people who enjoy going to a movie or even to lunch alone. Is this a common problem? I'd like to get over it if I could.*

A: People who hate to be alone, even for a little while, don't regard *themselves* as company. When they are with themselves, they feel that they are with nobody at all. They therefore need other people for friction and reflections to feel a sense of self. This overdependence on other people for a sense of well-being is often related to poor self-esteem, lack of solid interests and involvements, and generally feeling "empty."

Q: *I am thirty-three and single. What can I do to meet a man?*

A: Some women secretly do everything to negate meeting men. Some seek martyrdom through loneliness. Others are really fearful of involved and sustained relationships. Others have too much pride to ask for help. Help means telling friends that you want to meet someone. Married friends are the best source of introductions. Most husbands have bachelor friends, but they have to get the go-ahead sign from you before any introduction can take place.

Q: *I have a friend who starts conversations with anybody at the drop of a hat. She does this on trains, standing in line to buy a movie ticket, in the store. She never sees these people again, but she simply can't resist getting into conversation with whomever she happens to be near. Why does she do this?*

A: Your friendly friend—like so many other people who do this—may be very lonely and may get very anxious when she has to be alone with herself. Many people unfortunately do not consider themselves as company at all and find it very frightening and a great burden to be alone. This may be particularly true of your friend when she is away from her home, especially if she finds herself in unfamiliar surroundings. Being in the presence of people may not be meaningful to her unless a conversational bridge is formed to another person. Conversation means momentary contact with another human being—anyone at all—and however superficial or fleeting this may be, it serves its purpose in that it relieves her anxiety and loneliness.

DEPRESSION

Depression can range from a state of vague anxiety—what we call "the blues"—to a serious lack of interest in life itself. Certain situations can trigger depression: for example, holidays upset many people. With all the commercial gaiety and forced holiday cheer, it can be hard to accept being alone or feeling anxious about oneself. Depression may begin for a mother after the birth of a new child, or for a soldier after his return to civilian life, or for any of us after the death of a close relative. Many people experience depression with menopause, the change of life occurring sometime around middle age—and this condition is equally as prevalent in men as it is in women, although the physiological changes are not as drastic. Whatever the cause or the symptoms, depression should be evaluated, and if necessary, treated by a competent psychiatrist.

Q: *What can one do when one feels somewhat depressed? I'm aware that constant depression can be complicated and may require psychiatric help. But if someone is just feeling low or has the "blues," what would help?*

A: Choose a friend who, at the moment, is in greater emotional need than you are. Dedicate yourself to her for the day, even though in your mood it may take considerable effort. Try to cheer her up, take her out on the town for the day, spend time with her and exclusively for her. Use your total energy, however depleted you may feel, for *her* welfare and for making *her* feel better. This bit of mental hygiene can be quite effective in treating a simple case of the "blues."

Q: *I have been feeling very anxious for several months, so that I've lost my appetite and can't sleep. My family doctor has been giving me tranquilizers, but they don't help. He is a very nice man and a good doctor, and I've known him since childhood. He says, "Just make up your mind to snap out of it, and you will be all right." I try, but I just can't convince him that I don't have enough willpower to get better. What can I do?*

A: Stop trying to convince him. Get an expert psychiatric consultation at once!

Q: *I am a fifteen-year-old girl, and it seems to me I'm always blue and depressed. I know that girls my age have moods. But mine are really bad. Not so long ago, I started to cut my wrists. Why I stopped, I don't know. I guess I was afraid. I just can't talk to my folks. They wouldn't understand. What can I do?*

A: Try, try to talk to your parents. They may be more understanding than you think. If you can't do that, how about your minister or your family doctor? Is there a psychologist or a guidance counselor in your school to whom you can talk? Do you have a teacher whom you feel is understanding? How about an older brother, sister, aunt, or uncle? If you can talk to one of them, perhaps then you and your doctor, minister, or teacher can have a talk with your parents. It is most important that you have a talk with your folks, so that they can get you help through a competent psychiatrist. It is important to get help, so that some of your problems can be resolved. They may not be nearly as insoluble as you think, and it would be a shame for you to go on suffering when relief is available.

Q: *I'm so tired all the time; I have no vitality at all. I'm thirty-five and I know that I'm in excellent health—my doctor gave me a thorough examination and found no physical reasons for my continual fatigue. He suggested that my tiredness may be emotional in origin. Could this be possible?*

A: Yes. Chronic fatigue is often the result of repressed anger, tension, emotional conflict, anxiety, depression, and just plain boredom. Increased tension and anxiety often cause muscles to contract. This means that people who are tense or nervous hold their bodies stiff, and in doing so, unconsciously expend muscular energy, which produces fatigue. Relaxation usually permits the body to resume its normal pace of muscular expenditure, reduces energy output, and increases one's feeling of vitality.

Q: *I have a friend who wakes up feeling out of sorts and has a very difficult time getting started for the day. She spends her mornings feeling weighed down and rather blue. As the day wears on she feels much better and is just fine by the time evening arrives. Is this a common malady? Is it a sign of anything in particular?*

A: This "malady" you describe is exceedingly common. The symptom is characteristic of underlying depression. People who are depressed often find mornings much more difficult than evenings—largely because facing an entire day and its multiple duties seems impossibly burdensome and difficult when one is depressed. Evening and the promise of relief that comes with sleep is most welcome and uplifting. If this "malady" continues, consultation with a psychiatrist is indicated. Depression (and resolution of its underlying causes) is easier to treat before it becomes severe and chronic.

Q: *My daughter is being graduated from high school in June. I know I should be delighted, but I am nervous about it. I felt the same way when my son was graduated—and everything turned out fine. Is there some hidden meaning to graduation?*

A: June is a joyous month of weddings, graduations, flowers, etc. But June can also be a month filled with anxiety for many mothers. Graduation is the start of something new, which means the old way of life is being upset. The status quo, which you have come to know and work within, is changing. The change will undoubtedly be a happy one, but it signals that you are not the same, that time is passing, your children are growing up, and you are growing older. Graduation and weddings are full of sentiment, and sentiment makes for anxiety by recalling times past and by reaffirming your present status. It is only human to be anxious. Accept it and it will pass.

Q: *Why does a happily married woman like me always feel depressed on Valentine's Day?*

A: Many people are depressed on holidays because they have vast expectations that cannot possibly be fulfilled. These unrealistic expectations often exist on an unconscious level and have their origins in early childhood fantasies. Valentine's Day is a highly symbolic time that for many people brings out unrealistic, unrequited yearnings. As trite as it may sound, I suggest that you use Valentine's Day to count your blessings.

Q: *Is it common for people to get depressed during holidays? I am thirty-three years old, married, have two wonderful children, and I'm reasonably healthy and happy; but at the beginning of the Christmas season each year, I find myself getting despondent. Actually, I enjoy Christmas itself, so I really can't understand my depressed feelings.*

A: There's nothing odd about your reaction. You see it as odd only because you don't understand it. It is a completely human reaction and one that is shared by thousands of people. Unfortunately, no general explanation clarifies everybody's problem in this area. While the symptom is common and shared by many, the reasons for it are highly varied and sometimes very complicated. Some people become very depressed during certain holidays, others during any holiday, others whenever they have vacations and leisure time. Let me list just a few of the dynamics of this kind of depression that I have come across in my own practice.

1. There are people who find it particularly difficult to adjust to any new situation or unfamiliar set of things and people. During a holiday, things change around the house. The whole feel of the place is different. Your children are home instead of in school. Your husband is home. Although there is a pleasant, festive atmosphere, this is a change, and for these people adaptation to change and new routine always brings temporary difficulty.

2. During a holiday, there also may be people present with whom you are not particularly comfortable. I remember a woman who felt that she should have her parents as house guests every Christmas. But she found their continued presence a great burden and an intrusion on her much needed privacy. This produced enormous conflict (of which she was unaware). If she did not invite her parents, she felt guilty and depressed. If she *did* invite them, she felt terribly coerced, full of self-hate and also depressed. When she became aware of her dilemma and realized that she couldn't have it both ways, she resolved her conflict (she chose to have her parents for briefer periods).

3. There are people who feel they should be working all the time. Leisure makes them feel guilty as well as bored, a combination that is soon converted into self-hate and depression.

4. There are people who have forgotten some terrible event in

their lives that occurred at a particular season; the pain is revitalized each time this season of the year arrives.

5. And there are those who feel they should have such enormous enjoyment during a holiday that they become depressed anticipating their inevitable disappointment. Yes, having to enjoy themselves can be burden enough to kill the enjoyment!

Q: *I have a sister who became depressed and quite disturbed after the birth of her second child. Why does this happen so frequently?*

A: I don't know. Some doctors think that emotional disturbances following childbirth (postpartum reactions) are physiological in origin and are due to hormonal changes associated with pregnancy and birth. Some psychiatrists trace these reactions to longstanding personality difficulties that are rooted in the individual's early family relationships. And some doctors think that women who are frightened of adult responsibility are prone to react this way. The problem is so serious and common that there have been much research and many theories about it. I do not believe there is enough evidence to warrant any one conclusion. The women I've seen in consultation suffering from postpartum reactions had diverse personalities and diverse problems. I, for one, do not think this kind of reaction is inherited.

Q: *My mother went through a very difficult menopausal period, even requiring psychiatric hospitalization. I am thirty-nine years old, and frankly I am frightened. Does every woman have to endure some kind of psychiatric symptoms at menopause? Are severe symptoms during this period hereditary?*

A: Absolutely not.
Women who have not had severe emotional problems during their lives are not predisposed to menopausal psychiatric reactions. It is not the straw that breaks the camel's back but the load under the straw. So it is with menopause, which in an already problem-ridden woman can trigger a severe disturbance. In some cases, even the fear of menopause can cause difficulty. It is therefore a good

idea to discuss the subject freely and thoroughly with one's gynecologist, to learn what and what not to expect. Many women, incidentally, make more than an adequate adjustment and even prefer the postmenopausal condition to the premenopausal one. If a woman has a history of emotional disturbance, with frequent depressions and anxiety attacks or seemingly uncontrollable emotional outbursts or phobias or compulsions, it is a good idea for her to have a psychiatric consultation (for the purpose of possible treatment) long before menopause begins.

I do not believe that heredity plays a role in menopausal symptoms. If menopausal problems are common in a family, this is probably a "learned" reaction. I mean that it is due to particular neurotic problems members of that family have in common and is not connected to inherited structure.

Q: *Do men go through a period equivalent to female menopause?*

A: I certainly believe they do. While a physiological similarity may be lacking, men invariably feel all kinds of emotional repercussions at an equivalent age.

The Male Menopause

I receive many letters asking: (a) How can men go through menopause when they don't have a menstrual cycle? and (b) Since there is no physical signal to guide her, how can a wife tell when her husband is going through male menopause?

Physiologically, menopause *is* strictly a female phenomenon. Only the female has a menstrual cycle that begins and ends at specific points in her life. Yet, even without a comparable physiological syndrome, men between the ages of thirty-five and fifty-five do go through an emotional menopause.

As with women and female menopause, the reactions to male menopause can vary from man to man. For some men, change of life can be a time of emotional storms that can affect their wives, their children and their marriages—as well as themselves. For others, the change will come, but will result in no more than a ripple on the so-called sea of life.

In my practice I have seen many middle-aged men who are frightened by symptoms they can't explain. One patient once told me he was "coming apart at the seams"; he couldn't make decisions as easily as he once had; he had great doubts about himself as a worker, a husband, and a man.

As we talked, it became obvious that he had some of the more common symptoms of male menopause. In subsequent consultations, the patient was relieved to learn the truth about his symptoms and to discover that they are quite common among middle-aged men.

The symptoms of male menopause include: fatigue, headaches, increased moodiness, impatience, worry, touchiness, and hypochondria. Psychosomatic problems include: indigestion, upset stomach, heartburn, rapid or irregular heartbeat, urinary problems, respiratory difficulties, and insomnia. Inability to make decisions and new or increased feelings of self-doubt (especially as to sexual ability) are also common complaints. Emotional depression causes guilt feelings, feelings of worthlessness, loss of appetite, preoccupation with thoughts of aging, thoughts of suicide, as well as actual suicide attempts.

These symptoms, which women may also suffer during menopause, are largely a response to the person's anxiety over the loss of youth.

The exact age at which these symptoms occur varies according to the man in question. When a man reaches the age that he alone considers the turning point in his life, he may suddenly feel "old." Actually, this change-of-life reaction may have been developing unnoticed for some time. The "trauma" that brings it out can be one or more of the following (coupled with reaching a specific age):

1. A serious physical illness, particularly a sudden heart attack. Illness makes a man feel that he is human after all, and that he is subject to human limitations, including the reality of eventual death.

2. A sudden business reversal that threatens to change a man's financial status. A man who has a great emotional investment in his business ability may suffer a considerable blow to his pride, especially if he is the type of man who unrealistically equates money with security, social acceptance, and health.

3. The death of a wife, parent, or child can set off a change-of-life reaction. Men are very dependent on their wives for a sense of

emotional well-being. When a wife dies (or becomes ill), the husband may feel weak and vulnerable and decide that he lacks a reason to go on. A similar reaction may occur when a child or a parent dies.

4. The marriage of a child can make a highly sensitive man feel that his family is breaking up. This change in the status quo can signal the beginning of old age. Becoming a grandparent, however happy it makes a man feel at the moment, can also cause old-age trauma.

5. Retirement can initiate a change-of-life reaction that has been delayed by a man's involvement in business affairs. Retirement can be a blow to a man's self-esteem and feelings of usefulness.

The preceding five points can bring on an anxiety reaction or depression in men of all ages—particularly, as I've pointed out, at that symbolic change-of-life age that everyone has in his own mind.

Men (and women) going through a change-of-life period share similar thoughts and feelings about themselves and their lives. Some of the most common of these thoughts are:

1. "What was my life all about, anyway? It went by like a shot and here I am—old."

2. "I know now that I won't make it after all. It just doesn't add up." When questioned about what "it" means, men are extremely vague. They feel a sense of loss and longing but don't really know what "it" was or is.

3. Many men feel that they've "missed the boat." They vaguely feel that what they wanted to be has somehow eluded them.

4. Many men complain about unfulfilled adolescent fantasies, fantasies that are related to self-glorification. Yet those men who have managed to achieve some self-glorification feel at this point in their lives that glory is disappointing after all.

5. Many men feel that life is not fair, that things should be different: people shouldn't grow old; loved ones shouldn't die; children should remain loyal; and happiness should prevail.

6. For the first time in their lives, some men are really aware of life as it exists—with pleasure and pain, ugliness and beauty, simplicity and complexity. These men realize that much of what they once thought important is not important and that it is the little things that count. For some, these realizations are painful, but for others, such thoughts can lead to an inner peace that they have never before experienced.

The ease or panic with which a man faces change of life depends on a number of factors. The more love he has had and the more love he has given, the easier he can face middle age. The degree to which the man has accepted himself is also important. By this I mean that the man who has accepted his faults as wisely as he has accepted his strengths will find the going simpler. How has he come through other storm periods in his life? Has he come to regard himself and others with compassion? Have his relationships with people been enriching? If the answers are yes, the going will be less painful.

Does he have a high tolerance level for frustration and anxiety? Men who cannot tolerate the anxiety generated at change of life will attempt to run away in some form; some will become dependent on alcohol; some will resort to drugs; others will become promiscuous in order to prove their potency.

In change-of-life trauma, a man may divorce his wife in order to disengage himself from all that is "old." He will marry a much younger woman and start a new family to prove his virility and to try to gain new youth. In another change-of-life action, some men will change their jobs; some show good judgment; others show no judgment at all.

Unlike a woman going through menopause, a man has no physical symptoms on which to concentrate; his symptoms are all psychological, and thus they are harder for him to pinpoint and face. In our culture, men are supposed to take pride in their strength, independence, perpetual sexual ability, and control of feelings. Modern man has been taught to avoid showing softness, fear, helplessness, and warmth. Men, therefore, view emotional upheaval as weak and feminine, so that it is hard for them to seek help when such upheaval occurs. Men also tend to repress much of their feelings all their lives, and when these repressed feelings surface during the change-of-life period, they are frightening. The man feels as if he doesn't know who he is. As painful and confusing as this can be, it may, for the first time, permit a man to confront his true self.

A husband and wife need each other very much during this change-of-life period. How they relate to each other can determine the outcome of their life together. Middle age is a time when they both need patience, compassion, humor, and a love for themselves and for each other. Love from another person can stir up much needed love for ourselves—and love for ourselves is desperately needed during emotional storms. If psychiatric help is needed, it ought to be encouraged and certainly should be sought should any rash move be contemplated.

Couples going through this period together may grow closer, wiser, and happier with themselves, with each other, with their children and with the small, everyday satisfactions the world offers. I agree with Dr. Karen Horney, who felt that self-growth can take place at *all* ages in our lives.

Q: *I think my husband (forty-eight years old) is going through "male menopause." He is quite depressed much of the time and for the first time since I've known him, he suddenly seems to have lost all interest in sex. Some friends of ours suggest that taking male hormones, testesterone, I believe, may be helpful. What is your opinion?*

A: Lack of sexual interest often accompanies emotional depression and often has no physiological basis at all. Hormone treatment must be handled with great care. This is especially true of testesterone treatment in middle-aged and older men. Malignancy of the prostate gland is fairly common in older men, and improper use of hormones can accelerate growth and spread. If sexual difficulty has its basis in emotional disturbance, then it is probably best to treat the underlying causes. Psychoanalytic psychotherapy is usually helpful and the treatment of choice in depression, and that includes depression found in either female menopause or its equivalent in men. Some doctors use antidepressant drugs along with psychotherapy, both of which are usually preferable to hormone treatment in terms of efficiency and fewer complications. In any case, I think it would be advisable for your husband to have a proper psychiatric consultation before any treatment at all is initiated.

Q: *I have heard that there are new drugs that can cure depression. Can these drugs help a middle-aged woman who has suffered spells of depression for twenty-five years?*

A: Drugs may be helpful in calming anxiety and relieving depression. However, chronic periodic depression such as you describe is usually the product of self-hate and self-rejection. It stems from a person's poor relationship with herself and sometimes with other people as well. Such complex emotional problems can't be resolved by drugs alone. Drugs can only relieve symptoms; they can never eradicate the causes of the problem. Only psychoanalytic psychotherapy can do that. Therapy can help the individual to get to know, and eventually value chronic depression, and such herself. Self-acceptance is the key to relieving, self-acceptance and emotional growth is best attained through psychotherapy. Let me point out that psychotherapy means hard work for both patient and psychiatrist. It is also important to know that such therapy is effective for people of all ages, provided they are strongly motivated to seek help and work hard to resolve their problems.

Q: *I have a friend who takes tranquilizers for her nervousness. Do these pills really calm her down, or is it the fact that she has taken the pill that calms her down? What I mean is: Are tranquilizers merely a psychological placebo—or do they medically work?*

A: Studies indicate that tranquilizers have both a placebo effect and a physiological (medical) one. In other words, one way or another, they do what they are supposed to do—calm the patient. However, tranquilizers cannot resolve the basic problems that cause your friend's anxiety or nervousness; only therapy can do that.

Q: *As happy as my husband and I were to have our twenty-year-old son safely home from Vietnam, he has since made us very sad. He just sits around the house all day, talking to nobody, drinking, and smoking pot. I don't know what scares me more—my son's behavior or my husband's threats to turn him over to the authorities for smoking pot. I cannot let him turn our son in. What can I do?*

A: War affects everyone. It is impossible for me to know how much Vietnam has affected your son since I have no way of knowing what he was like before he went to war. I have, however, always been against taking legal action in an attempt to solve emotional problems. It sounds to me as if your son would benefit from psychiatric counseling. I might add that threats and insinuations are useless in this case. Your son is a man home from war and must be treated as an adult with a problem, not a child to be threatened by the police or spanked by daddy. If you and your husband can't talk calmly with your son about straightening out his life (and he himself must make the decision to seek psychiatric help), then perhaps there is a doctor, priest, rabbi, or good friend who can help. This should be done as soon as possible—for your son's benefit and yours.

Q: *I have a friend who, at age forty-three, gave up a fantastic fashion career to marry. Her husband never asked her to give up her work, she just did. She became a demure, clinging wife who lived and breathed for her husband. Five years later he died, and she went into a "state" that has lasted now for four years. Friends have tried to help her, have tried to interest her in returning to work (she has had offers), but to no avail. She constantly asks me what she should do, and no matter what I say (and I have suggested psychiatric help), she says, "Yes, I'll do it tomorrow." Then she does nothing. My husband feels I should give her up as a lost cause. Is he right? Is there anything I can do to help her?*

A: Let me respond to your statements and questions in "steps":

1. Involvement with a friend makes it very difficult to evaluate objectively the friend's emotional condition. We are inadvertently prejudiced by our own needs and expectations, which we tend to project to our friends.

2. You imply that your friend made a sacrifice in giving up "a fantastic fashion career" in order to marry. I doubt there was any sacrifice here. People choose one road over another because of preference. This particular sacrifice of career for marriage comes up in women again and again. The fact is, most women still prefer marriage to any career, however "fantastic." Those who feel otherwise don't get married, or marry and continue with a career, too. Too many women use the "I gave up a career for you" as a guilt-producing weapon that is unrealistic but highly destructive to marriage.

You state, "Her husband never asked her to give up her work" —and I believe it. But to what extent do your feelings about "husband-exploited, self-sacrificing wives" cloud the picture?

3. You say "she became a demure, clinging, etc." I doubt that she became anything that she had not been before. The way an individual relates to herself and to other people is well established

long before marriage. Marriage may accentuate already existing patterns, but it does not create new ones, nor does it miraculously produce a metamorphosis or new individual—other than babies, of course.

4. People respond to the death of a loved one in highly individual ways. There is no "normal" or established way of mourning or any particular length of time that can be considered "normal."

5. People do not seek psychiatric help unless they are self-motivated. Sales talk, pushing, logic, etc., very often have a reverse effect.

6. Is your friend a lost cause or are the expectations, goals, and time schedules you have for her a lost cause? Sometimes people give up on a friend in need because they are disappointed with the results of their efforts. These expectations are often based on exorbitant goals. The helper often gets angry at the one to be helped because, by not responding, the helper's pride in being a helper is wounded. You must answer this question: Are you more interested in your self-glorification as a great helper, or in helping your friend, however limited the results?

7. To help: Don't push; don't pull; don't sell. Do be there, listen, engage her when you can in social activities that are not threatening —and try to be patient. The bells toll for us all, so don't give up on her lest you give up on part of yourself. Give up your goals for her. Let her seek her own comfortable level.

Q: *My mother passed away eleven years ago yet I still "tear up" whenever I speak about her. Why?*

A: Tears can indicate a range of emotion from gentle warmth to overly deep grief. Because I do not know you, I cannot say where, in this range, your emotions fall. However, the more mature a person, the more readily he or she accepts death as a fact of life. I have found that those who were most dependent on their parents are those who grieve the longest. If you are hindered or embarrassed by your tears, you might want to discuss the situation with a psychiatrist.

CHAPTER 5

Illness and Health:
Physical and Psychosomatic Ailments

A great many factors, emotional and physiological, are involved in an individual's capacity for health and resistance to illness. Age and changing body processes are, of course, extremely influential on the physical being, yet a person's feelings of self-worth can make a great difference in the balance between health and illness. How many people do you know who are constantly complaining about the way they feel? How much of it is real and how much is imagined? Actually, some of those you might classify as "hypochondriacs" are not just faking it. Their symptoms are real, all right, although the physical problem may derive from a far deeper psychological one. A person may experience severe headaches or heart palpitations with no somatic cause, or he may suffer from insomnia or be unable to stay "on the wagon." These and other questions of illness and health are nearly always important psychotherapeutic issues.

Q: *How important is one's physical health to one's mental health?*

A: Very important. It's all happening in one person. Physical health and well-being certainly contribute to a sense of emotional well-being and vice versa. Physical exercise (not in excess) can be emotionally therapeutic—relaxing. This is especially true for those of us who happen to be engaged in sedentary pursuits and much intellectual activity.

But it is also possible to be in fairly good physical health and mentally ill, and to be in fairly good mental health and physically ill. Please note my use of the word "fairly." This is because I feel that poor physical health *always* has emotional counterparts and repercussions and that emotional problems always affect us physically —however minimal these effects may be.

Also, please do not confuse good physical health with being a health faddist. Some physical-health faddists or fetishists suffer complete emotional collapse when any physical impairment at all takes place. They are often extremely narcissistic and find the physical limitations of old age particularly hard to take. This is easily understandable when we consider that most of their emotional involvement is with their own bodies rather than with other people.

Of course, no amount of exercise, however vigorously and religiously performed, and no amount of health food, however well chewed and digested, will resolve anybody's emotional problems.

Q: *I suffer from insomnia. Most nights, I hardly sleep at all. But this isn't my real complaint. Over the years, I've found out that I can get along on very little sleep, and I seem to be healthy. What bothers me are the awful thoughts and fantasies I have when I can't sleep. Many of them revolve around all kinds of terrible things happening to my husband and children, whom I love dearly. It has reached a point where I dread going to bed at night. Do you think a psychiatrist could help me?*

A: You say that if you could sleep, you wouldn't have the thoughts. While this may be true, the other aspect of this vicious cycle is much more important. *If you didn't have the thoughts, you could sleep.* Thoughts, especially the kinds of thoughts you describe, come from *feelings*—feelings that we would frequently rather not have. These very often involve anger at people we love. Please remember that love does not preclude anger. We can love somebody deeply and still get very angry at him or her. In any case, very strong feelings that have been repressed for a long time often tend to emerge as thoughts, especially when we are alone, with no distractions and with our guards down. These conditions prevail almost ideally just before we go to sleep.

Of course, acceptance of ourselves as less than angelic and ideal is the desired goal here, as elsewhere. This means accepting all our feelings—including angry ones. However, this often involves some complicated insights and changes, best arrived at through psychotherapy. Thus, I must say an *emphatic* yes, a psychoanalytically trained psychiatrist may indeed be helpful to you.

Q: *Can psychotherapy cure alcoholism?*

A: I do not think alcoholism is curable; that is, I don't think the true alcoholic can ever become a moderate drinker. However, alcoholism, like other chronic illnesses (diabetes, food addiction, etc.), can be controlled—and the only way to control alcoholism is through total abstinence. Alcoholics are often people who repress great rage; people who are childish (that is, they lack mature emotional development in many ways); people who feel inadequate and dependent. Psychotherapy can be helpful if the therapist has particular interest in, and experience with, treating alcoholics, but alcoholic patients often lack the sustained motivation that is necessary for success in psychotherapy. I feel that Alcoholics Anonymous is more successful in controlling alcoholism than psychiatric treatment. After the illness is controlled, however, psychiatric treatment can be useful to uncover the problems that led to alcoholism in the first place.

Q: *My husband is a writer and has a growing drinking problem. Psychiatric treatment has been recommended to him by several friends, one of whom is a prominent physician. My husband says that he, too, feels he needs help but is afraid that psychoanalytic treatment might destroy his creative ability. What do you think?*

A: I think that improper treatment can be destructive not only to the creative process but to the patient, whatever his talent or occupation. Treatment by an expertly trained psychiatrist or psychoanalyst is as carefully administered as surgery is by a qualified surgeon or anesthesia by a qualified anesthetist. A psychoanalyst is well aware of the delicacy and sensitivity of the creative instrument and proceeds with ultimate caution. It has been my experience that creative people have become more creative and more productive as their emotional problems have been resolved. This makes sense inasmuch as they are freed from neurotic conflicts and investments that make for vast, destructive expenditures of energy. It also makes sense in terms of their having more self to use and more of their resources to tap as they become reconciled with themselves.

May I point out that a number of people discover their creative possibilities for the first time only after treatment has started. Of course, this is no guarantee that psychoanalysis will produce a creative person. But if the talent is there, therapy can help in its discovery and expression.

There are people, of course, who give up some pursuit as the result of treatment. But this is not because of a loss of talent. It is due to a realization that the original activity was based on a sick need and not born of or contributing to happiness.

It is interesting that your husband fears treatment and not alcohol as a potential death blow to his writing. Yet it is alcohol that may well turn out to be the executioner. He, like so many other people, is not yet ready to change and will rationalize, by whatever means possible, his not getting into treatment. Hopefully, in time his motivation will increase and his resistance will decrease, so that he may seek help.

Q: *My husband is an alcoholic. He is a member of AA, and he hasn't had a drink in two years. He is now seeing a psychiatrist for other problems. Is there a chance that with psychiatric treatment, he could become an ordinary social drinker?*

A: I doubt it. Many experts feel that the alcoholic has a special *physiological* sensitivity and response to alcohol. This has been described as a peculiar kind of allergy, in which any amount of alcohol once ingested sensitizes the tissues, so that an insatiable craving is established. Put simply: One drink establishes an enormous *physical* need for another and another and another. This is not to say that alcoholics do not have emotional difficulties. Most of the people I have seen who had a drinking problem have also had serious emotional problems. The goals in psychotherapy vary with the person in question, but social drinking is certainly not one of them. Psychotherapy with alcoholic patients can be very difficult and unrewarding as far as the giving-up-alcohol goal is concerned. My own feeling is that AA has been much more successful than psychotherapy in this area. Psychotherapy is often very useful for the nonalcoholic spouse of the alcoholic. The relationship between the alcoholic and nonalcoholic is usually a very complicated and disturbed one. It is not unusual for the nonalcoholic woman to have an unconscious need for her husband to sustain his alcoholism, because of serious self-doubt and the desire to be needed. Psychotherapy with the nonalcoholic partner is often more rewarding for both partners than treatment of the one who is alcoholic.

Q: *Why do some doctors say that fat people should try to eat bland foods?*

A: Some researchers feel that the neurological mechanism that tells people when they are "full" does not work in fat people. They simply do not "know" when to stop eating. They mainly eat and keep eating because of pleasant taste sensations. Some doctors feel that removal of heightened mouth sensations (eating bland foods) will result in loss of eating interest. This will substitute for the lack of "knowing" when one has had enough to eat.

Q: *I know from your* Thin Book by a Formerly Fat Psychiatrist *that you see fatness as an emotional disturbance that leads to overeating. But I recently read about studies that indicate there is a large hereditary factor. What do you think about this?*

A: Studies in hereditary fatness will surely contribute much useful information. To date, however, information in this regard is still inconclusive. However, as far as I'm concerned, the following is conclusive:

1. A very small fraction of chronically fat people suffer from any known metabolic or glandular disturbance.
2. The vast majority of fat people overeat—that is, they take in more calories than they use.
3. The vast majority of fat people overeat compulsively.

Broadly stated: They do this to allay anxiety. This means that they suffer from an emotional disturbance. If they cannot cope with this disturbance themselves, then psychiatric help is indicated.

Q: *I have several friends who have all confided to me that at one time or another they have experienced either severe depression, anxiety, irrational fear, or psychosomatic illness. Is this normal?*

A: There are very few people who do not at least once suffer a period of severe emotional distress that affects to some degree their ability to function. Some people are not even aware that they have gone through such a rough emotional time. Many harbor the erroneous belief that their difficulty was physical. Others only vaguely remember feeling weak, funny, moody, different, etc. In any case, human beings are sensitive and vulnerable creatures, and the world is pressure-filled and often downright difficult. None of us, therefore, is immune to emotional disturbances. These disturbances, whatever form they take, simply show that we are human. If they become too frequent, then perhaps we must consider the possibility that a problem exists.

Q: *For years, I have been getting heart palpitations off and on. I have had many checkups, but my doctor finds nothing physically wrong. He recently told me that being anxious and nervous may be what causes my symptoms. Is this true?*

A: Yes, anxiety often produces heart palpitations, plus all kinds of other physical symptoms. But you are very wise to have had thorough physical checkups, since organic illness should always be ruled out first when there are prolonged physical symptoms.

Let me list just a few symptoms of anxiety that may exist alone or in various combinations:
1. Rapid heartbeat
2. Missed heartbeats
3. Strange sensations under the sternum
4. A heavy feeling in the chest
5. Hot and cold flashes
6. Transitory rashes of all kinds
7. A pins-and-needles feeling anywhere on the body
8. Gastric upset, including diarrhea, constipation, heartburn, and flatulence
9. Headache
10. Visual and hearing difficulty
11. Great difficulty swallowing
12. Speech difficulties of all kinds
13. Memory loss
14. Vague, indescribable pains almost anywhere at all.

Q: *I have a friend who periodically threatens to commit suicide. I'm sure she has never made an actual attempt to do this, but she does seem pretty depressed at times. How can you tell if somebody really means it or not? What about threats of murder? How can you tell if they are real threats or not?*

A: Nearly all cases of suicide and murder are due to enormous self-hate. This self-hate is often activated by hurt pride. In suicide, the hate is usually directed inward (a desire to annihilate oneself). In murder, it is directed outward—toward someone on whom one projects a hatred of oneself. People who are severely depressed may commit suicide to rid themselves of themselves. Hysterical people may do it to get even with a supposed wrongdoer ("Then he will be sorry"). A paranoid person may strike out and kill the person felt as his oppressor, who really is the symbol of his own inner oppression and self-contempt.

The dynamics of suicide and murder are always extremely intricate and highly individual. One must have a complete understanding of the various syndromes in which these acts occur. This takes much experience, training and skill.

All people who threaten either suicide or murder (as well as many who make no overt threats) must be taken with utmost seriousness. *But* evaluating the seriousness of such threats is intricate, highly technical and should never be left to amateurs. By all means, try to persuade your friend to get professional help.

Q: *Our twenty-two-year-old son has a long history of lying, stealing cars, forging checks, trouble with girls. We have been in and out of court with him half a dozen times. He is very bright, but he never finished high school. Actually, he never finishes anything. He constantly talks about "big deals," but has never stayed on any job more than a week. He is very charming and gets what he wants from almost everyone, but at times we feel sure he does not know the difference between right and wrong. Will you please tell us what you know about this kind of problem and what can be done to help a person like this?*

A: The behavior you describe, unfortunately, respresents a rather common sickness. Its victims seem to have little ability to link cause and effect (the outcome of their acts). They are impulsive, easily influenced in destructive directions, do not generate normal anxiety in dangerous situations, have almost no tolerance for frustration or concern for the effect of their actions on others. Some therapists think that people suffering from this illness (known sometimes as sociopathy or psychopathy) have no conscience at all. Others think that they have a terrible, overburdening, castigating conscience, which they must rebel against in order to feel free.

In any case, the sociopathic person acts as if he had no feelings of guilt whatsoever, let alone any sense of responsibility for his antisocial behavior. Some psychiatrists feel that these people have an organic brain defect. This has never been substantiated, however. Others feel that the illness is due to early environmental conditions. Clearly, much more research is necessary to trace and understand the cause of this sickness. Unfortunately, as the law is usually more concerned with "justice" and "punishment" than with research and treatment, prisons are full of these people.

Treatment is at best difficult. Sociopathic people do not think they are sick and certainly don't think they need treatment. Therefore, that most important ingredient, motivation, is lacking. When they *are* available for treatment, it is usually as captive patients in prisons. Sometimes they go to psychiatrists as part of a bargain made with relatives, who won't support them unless they see a doctor. In treatment, their concern is usually with how to stay out of jail and how to become better con artists and manipulators.

Parents of children of any age with problems like this are best advised to set and keep absolute limits. They must not allow themselves to be charmed, bribed, or conned. They must be steadfast in refusing money, etc., for work not done. *Without being vindictive or punishing*, they must refuse to become a party to antisocial behavior. This, of course, is very difficult, and parents often need therapy themselves in order to act effectively.

Sometimes, when sociopathic charm, bullying, and manipulation do not work, the sociopathic individual becomes deeply depressed. And this is one of the rare occasions when he may be ready for constructive treatment.

Q: *I recently read about a woman who killed her three small children. I read so often about people who seem perfectly normal*

to their friends and neighbors and then suddenly do insane things.
Is it because terrible pressures build up?

A: While irrational acts, especially violent ones, seem to happen suddenly, abruptly, with no warning, they have, in fact, almost always been in the making for a very long time. People who commit these acts are severely disturbed emotionally. The kinds of disturbance that make such acts possible always develop over a period of years and are usually marked by a chronic, progressive deterioration. The underlying causes are deep-seated, complicated, long-standing and far more significant than the immediate pressure that seems to explain an irrational action. The fact that neighbors and even friends consider a person mentally healthy is not too meaningful. Many people have considerable ability in masking emotional turmoil and even in functioning fairly well despite serious disturbance. I dare say that many people don't look much below surface smiles and so have no awareness of hidden turmoil and suffering.

Q: *Is there any truth to the statement that severely disturbed*
people look much younger than mentally healthy people?

A: Maybe. The theory behind this statement is that certain emotional disturbances severely blunt the emotions; that is, the individual lacks full consciousness of deep feelings. This "flattening out" of emotions results in a lack of facial expressions and fewer lines and wrinkles. Emotionally healthy people consciously experience and feel a great deal. This depth of feeling is reflected in their faces by lines—which are signs of richly lived outer and inner lives.

Q: *I have had severe headaches for years. I've been to all kinds*
of specialists (all reputable) and to a big-city-hospital headache
clinic. They found nothing physically wrong with me that could ac-
count for the headaches. Recently, several doctors, including the
man at the clinic, suggested that I see a psychiatrist.
Of course I have problems, and I do not doubt that psychiatry
would be beneficial in many ways. But I just can't believe that head-
aches as severe and real as these I get can be psychosomatic. What
do you think?

A: Many people seem to be confused about the term "psycho-somatic." They see it as meaning a kind of imagined illness or symptom caused by psychological problems. They also confuse psychosomatic with hypochondriacal (obsessive fear of being sick). The word psychosomatic refers to illnesses or groups of symptoms caused or aggravated by anxiety stemming from psychological prob-lems. *But*—and this is a very important but—these symptoms come from very definite physical disturbances, which often can be demon-strated by physical examination of one kind or another. The physi-cal lesion or disturbance that justifies the soma (meaning body) part of the word is very real indeed, even if it does not show up on X-ray, lab tests, etc. The man with gastric ulcers, for example, is not suffering from an imagined symptom. While the illness may be due to an improper handling of conflicts and ensuing anxiety, which cause an oversecretion of gastric juice, the ulcerated area is very real indeed and more often than not can be seen on X-ray. Once an individual has physical symptoms, these, too, have a bad effect psychologically, thus compounding the problem. If there is a psychosomatic component in an illness, the patient is best treated psychiatrically as well as physically.

This is a good opportunity to say that I've seen many people who just can't believe that emotional disturbance can have so much physical effect. Yet how can it be otherwise when our thinking and feeling apparatus—our nervous system—and all our other bodily parts are in fact contained in one body? The nervous system is highly sensitive to the emotional state and very quick to send mes-sages to various parts of the body, since it is the major body coordi-nator and communicator. The nervous system regulates rate of heartbeat, glandular output, opening and closing of blood vessels, intestinal activity, etc. You can readily see how a poorly handled emotional upset can be transferred to an organ or a gland.

About headaches: You were very wise to check out all physical aspects first. It is always imperative to do just that. At the risk of oversimplifying, let me say that many clinicians feel that the basis for certain kinds of acute headache is an inability to handle anger. Repressed anger causes temporary closure of a small vessel of the brain, which results in blood deprivation and headache. I myself have seen patients whose headaches disappear immediately after an angry outburst. Of course, the ultimate solution to the problem on a lasting basis entails long-term treatment and a better general emotional economy, including the handling of anger.

Q: *My ten-year-old daughter recently took a classroom IQ test. We inadvertently found out that her score was 100, which we have learned is only a low, average score. This is something of a shock, since we've always thought she was quite a bright child. She reads well and seems to do somewhat better than average work in school. She's also very pretty and vivacious. How seriously do you think we should take her IQ score?*

A: IQ tests are at best imperfect aids to evaluating intelligence. Their potential value depends entirely on the following: The experience and skill of the examiner; the appropriateness of the particular test for the particular subject; the emotional state of the subject during the test situation. Also, the IQ test is nearly valueless unless it is part of a complete battery of emotional studies through tests and interviews. A person's emotional state directly affects his intellectual performance. I have known severely emotionally disturbed children who were misdiagnosed as being mentally defective and after treatment tested over 140.

Group IQ examinations are the most primitive type of psychological test given. They are about as reliable as the shape of the small left toe would be in making a complete physical diagnosis. At best, this kind of "test" may indicate a need for further expert testing. At worst, its destructive possibilities are nearly unlimited. Time and again, I have seen it misinform, confuse, and create inferiority feelings and panic.

The fact that your daughter is pretty, vivacious, bright, and a good reader is infinitely more significant than her IQ score.

Q: *My mood seems to depend a great deal on the weather. Is this abnormal, or does weather commonly affect people this way?*

A: I believe that it does, but have no conclusive evidence pro or con. There are studies going on concerning atmospheric pressure and people's moods, but I think they have not been finished. I do know any number of people who are sensitive to changes in weather, and this is reflected in their dispositions. I have worked in hospitals with highly disturbed patients and felt that they were particularly sensitive to weather changes. People who are very anxious and depressed are usually highly suggestible. A cloudy day often adds to their feelings of hopelessness, while a sunny one has an uplifting effect.

Q: *I was told that it is a known fact that people in "certain" jobs tend to be more disturbed than people in other occupations. I resented the statement because postal employees were included in the list of those "certain" jobs—and I work in a post office. What's your opinion?*

A: Each person must be evaluated separately insofar as his or her mental health status and job are concerned. Therefore, I cannot agree with an overall statement that people in certain jobs tend to be more disturbed than usual. However, we do know that people do not get jobs accidentally—they choose them. Some people choose jobs confidently, but even those who merely cling to a particular job out of fear and resignation to the inevitable also choose—they choose to remain in that job. While there are men and women who are driven to jobs beyond their capacity because of deep-seated insecurity and lack of self-esteem ("If I work hard everyone will admire me")—there are also people who work below their capacity, in menial jobs, because they are too scared to use any creative ability they might have. ("If I fail I'll get fired.") The post office may have been spoken about in this latter regard, because it might have been considered a haven for people who feel too insecure to take jobs that are less predictable in terms of work problems and economic security. However, such mention in no way means that everyone employed by the postal system is working below his or her capacity, or that every man or woman who works in the postal system is disturbed. Such statements are irresponsible and without psychological basis.

Q: *Do men (and women, too) become surgeons because they are repressed sadists who secretly like to cut up people?*

A: No. Such generalizations fit into the same category as: all psychiatrists are *voyeurs;* all pilots have a death wish; all male gynecologists hate women. Such generalizations are oversimplistic and erroneous. However, sadistic surgeons *do* exist, and if you have encountered one, I am sorry. Such surgeons are in the minority, however. People choose their field of work for highly individual and complicated reasons. Their reasons are based on complex psychological needs as well as the intricacies of situations in which they find themselves: economic needs, opportunity or lack of it, parental influences, educational training, etc.

Q: *Our daughter is determined to be an actress, and I hate to see her do it, since people in the theater are so emotionally unstable. What is your feeling?*

A: I have no statistics on the subject. The actors I have met are neither sicker nor healthier than other people.

Q: *Are creative, highly gifted people more likely to have "breakdowns" and neurotic symptoms than simpler people?*

A: No!

Q: *My fiancé's mother is a schizophrenic who has been institutionalized for years. The daughter of my great uncle is also emotionally disturbed. I've been told that emotional illness is more prevalent than it has ever been—and that it is often inherited. Can you tell me what the possibility might be of my having an emotionally disturbed child?*

A: There are six points to my answer:
1. Schizophrenia is a poorly understood emotional illness. Some psychiatrists feel that "schizophrenia" is a too-general term that includes many different kinds of disturbances with multiple and different origins.
2. There is no overwhelming evidence to support a theory of inheritance to emotional illness.

3. Emotional illness, on some level, is common to all families. What I'm saying is that everyone has a relative somewhere along the line who has suffered from an emotional illness of some kind at one time or another.

4. All of us have emotional problems of varying degrees.

5. Familial environment—the ways in which family members relate to each other—plays an enormously important role in a child's emotional makeup.

6. I don't believe that emotional illness is more prevalent today. We are just more cognizant and accepting of it—and a little less afraid of it—than in years past.

Q: *I have a girl friend who had a severe nervous breakdown about a year ago. She was in the hospital for four months and has since been seeing a psychiatrist twice a week. I recently read in the newspaper that severe emotional disturbance is due to a chemical imbalance in the blood. I also read about drug treatment and the wonderful cures that are taking place. If this is so, then why should she go on spending so much time and so much money on psychotherapy?*

A: Unfortunately, there is simply no solid scientific evidence that substantiates a physical basis for severe emotional disturbance.

Despite newspaper accounts, there have been no miracle psychiatric drug cures for schizophrenia or other serious emotional disturbances. Some of the recent drugs—energizers and tranquilizers—have been helpful in relieving people suffering from depression, great anxiety, and even severe disturbance. But these drugs are adjuncts rather than cures. They do not solve basic personality problems, resolve conflicts, create growth and maturity, or teach us better ways of relating to ourselves or to other people. Hard work as it may be for both patient and doctor, early and sustained psychotherapeutic treatment with a qualified psychiatrist is still the best route to sustained emotional health.

Too many people have the impression that they can be "cured" by hospitalization. While psychiatric hospitalization can be very valuable in relieving symptoms, it, too, generally remains an adjunct treatment. The fact that an individual needs hospitalization is usually sufficient indication in itself that prolonged psychotherapy is necessary. Your friend is fortunate to have found this out.

Q: *A good friend of mine recently lost her job and her boyfriend, one right after the other. She got very upset and depressed. Was this possibly a nervous breakdown?*

A: I'll bet it wasn't—at least not from my professional point of view. You may know people who have had some severe, even incapacitating, psychiatric reaction (depression, phobia, anxiety attack, etc.), but there is nothing broken down or wrong with their nerves. People suffer from all kinds of so-called nervous difficulties, but these occur on an emotional basis without any illness of the nervous system. There are neurological diseases and difficulties that people contract (multiple sclerosis, brain tumors, arteriosclerosis, etc.), but while these illnesses may produce psychological difficulties, they are not related to the temporary emotional difficulties that are erroneously called "nervous breakdowns." There is usually nothing physically wrong with the brains or the nerves of people suffering from even the most serious emotional disorders.

Q. *My wife is a hypochondriac. She imagines that she has every disease she reads about or finds out about on a TV show. She has been to as many as ten doctors in one week because she feels she has this or that disease. I have always let her go to as many doctors as she wishes—I've even accompanied her—but my patience has gone. What can I do to convince my wife that she is a perfectly healthy woman?*

A: Your wife is not a "perfectly healthy woman." She seems to be suffering from considerable emotional anguish and pain. Hypochondriasis is a serious illness; it can prevent a person from functioning properly, destroy happiness, deplete energy, and keep one from fruitfully tapping his or her resources. No amount of reasoning or yelling at your wife will help her condition any more than these actions would help her get over any other illness. Warmth and comfort can help, but they cannot cure. Hypochondriasis, like other emotional disturbances, has deep, complicated roots. The hypochondriacal person uses concentration on illness to avoid unconscious conflicts and problems. Your wife needs a competent doctor—not for her *imagined* illnesses but for her real one. Your wife should see a psychoanalytically trained psychiatrist who can help her to get at the roots of her problem so that she can obtain relief from her obvious emotional distress.

Q: *Before I underwent a hysterectomy, I enjoyed sex a great deal. Now I have lost all desire for it—and find that I don't feel as affectionate toward my husband as I did before. Does a hysterectomy have this effect on all women—or is it just me?*

A: Let me list a number of factors that are pertinent to a hysterectomy (surgical removal of the uterus). These facts will, I hope, answer your question:

1. Removal of the uterus has no profound physiological effect. The uterus does not secrete hormones of any kind and its removal does not deprive a woman of her female hormones.

2. If the patient retains one ovary or even part of an ovary, this is usually sufficient to produce the female hormones necessary to her physiological well-being.

3. If a hysterectomy includes the removal of both ovaries, replacement hormones can be taken orally. These hormones usually compensate adequately for the loss of hormone production due to ovarian removal. Replacement therapy also displaces the symptoms of natural menopause.

4. Many women suffer emotionally from the knowledge that they have had a hysterectomy. These women are traumatized for a variety of reasons: they suffer from the knowledge that their female organs have been removed, from the fact that they can no longer have children, from the cessation of menses, etc. Often women feel "damaged" in their own feminine concept of themselves, and project these feelings to their husbands. As a result, a woman can mistakenly feel that her husband no longer thinks of her as feminine. It is not uncommon, either, for a woman to unconsciously blame her husband for her operation; the resulting hostility toward him can block or paralyze feelings of affection.

5. It is very useful if, before a hysterectomy is performed, doctor and patient candidly discuss the sexual implications of the operation and any fears the woman has in this regard.

6. In 99 percent of cases in which a woman loses sexual interest after her hysterectomy, the cause is psychological maladjustment to the operation. The surgery has awakened old feelings of sexual inadequacy, fears, taboos, and problems—all of which were present long before the surgical condition developed. Since there is no physiological basis for any of these difficulties, the treatment choice is almost always psychotherapy.

7. Many women lead more satisfactory sex lives following a hysterectomy. Some are relieved to no longer suffer premenstrual tension or painful periods. Others are delighted that contraception is no longer needed; they feel freer about sex, secure in the knowledge that they are safe from unwanted pregnancies.

Q: *My friend had a hysterectomy five years ago and is still talking about it. Why do women (and men, too) go on and on about their operations?*

A: Unfortunately, surgery marks the highest, most dramatic point in some people's lives. They were center stage; they had attention, care, empathy, sympathy, pity, etc., and they just don't want to let go of all that. So they hang on by talking about it. For others, their survival seems like a miracle and must be discussed and shared with all. For still others, the enormous anxiety generated by surgery can only be relieved by talking about, and thus reliving, the events. For many women, removal of the uterus is a particularly traumatic event. Sadly, a hysterectomy is often viewed as an attack on a woman's femininity. Sudden cessation of the menstrual cycle through surgery (rather than naturally, through menopause) can result in a loss of self-esteem, which creates great anxiety. To relieve this anxiety, it may be necessary to talk about the operation.

Q: *I know this is not a pleasant topic, but can constipation be psychosomatic? I've suffered from it for years, and the symptoms seem related to the particular mood I am in.*

A: First let me say that nonmedical people sometimes have a distorted idea of the importance of regular bowel movements. Many who think they are constipated are not. Therefore, it is important to let your own physician decide whether you are indeed constipated. Most doctors agree that for most people great regularity is not very important. A sudden and persistent change in bowel habits should, however, be investigated by a competent medical authority. If indeed there is constipation, a physician should be consulted for possible treatment. Taking laxatives and going on special diets without expert advice can be harmful.

But getting back to your original question, constipation can certainly have a relationship to emotional states or moods. I have seen constipation sufferers for whom psychotherapy has produced considerable relief. This was linked to a freer expression of feelings and emotions and a less stringent attitude toward oneself and others. In short, a higher degree of spontaneity in lieu of compulsiveness.

Q: *A friend of mine claims that deep breathing of clean, fresh air clears the head and helps one to think more perceptively. Is this an old wives' tale, or is there any truth to it?*

A: Some European researchers claim this is true. They say that deep breathing has helped older people to regain memory and clear thinking ability. This is based on the fact that the brain requires oyxgen which is more apt to be carried to it by the blood if good oxygenation of the lungs takes place. However, deep breathing that takes place too rapidly and for too long (called hyperventilation) can produce headiness and even fainting. I would suggest that anyone who attempts to exercise deeper than usual breathing check out the air for pollution first!

Q: *Is there any such thing as actually dying of a broken heart? Can great disappointment or tragedy kill someone through some kind of heart attack?*

A: Not directly. Yet, severe enough emotional reactions can cause sudden rise in blood pressure, very rapid heart beat as well as other physiological responses. These, coupled with an already pre-existing weakened condition may contribute to heart attacks, strokes (cerebral hemorrhage), and even death itself. Of course death sometimes occurs in people who are despondent enough to take their own lives.

Actually all emotional reactions have physiological counterparts and vice versa. It cannot be otherwise since both physical and emotional response occur in the same human being and therefore are intimately connected and must influence one another. However, most physical responses to emotional difficulty are not dramatic and often too subtle to be detected without proper intruments and close examination.

Q: *Is there any kind of food I can eat to make me smarter? When I was a child, my mother always told me that fish was "brain food."*

A: I doubt that fish or any other food can make you smarter, but a well-balanced diet can help you feel fit and alert. Protein is particularly important to general well-being and growth. And fish *is* high in protein.

Q: *Is it true that skin eruptions can be caused by emotional upsets?*

A: Yes, some skin conditions have an emotional origin. Emotional difficulty can also have adverse effects on any pre-existing physical difficulty. This is especially true of the skin. Interestingly, the skin and nervous tissue are both derived from the same primitive embryonic tissue—ectoderm. The skin is loaded with particularly rich blood, glands, and nerves—all of which are highly susceptible and responsive to emotional distress. "Goose flesh," blushing, excessive perspiring, etc., are evidences of response to emotional stimulation.

Q: *My friend's husband will eat nothing but bland foods. There's absolutely nothing wrong with him physically, but he claims that even the sight of fancy food nauseates him. His wife is a marvelous* *cook and feels frustrated by his pure steak and potato tastes. What makes a man so narrow in his eating outlook?*

A: Some people say that "we are what we eat." Childhood training plays an important role in eating patterns, and particular food tastes are highly revealing in particular personalities or character structures. We would have to know much more about your friend's husband to understand his particular eating habits. In any case, let me describe some random possibilities that may or may not be applicable to the man in question:

1. Some constricted, inwardly frightened people who abhor adventure or confrontation with the unfamiliar also shy away from hitherto untasted food and especially exotic food.

2. Some husbands will refuse superior cooking as an unconscious way of expressing hostility to their wives. In effect they say, "You are powerless to make me happy since plain hamburger is all I want and therefore your efforts are wasted."

3. Some men have been traumatized by overbearing mothers who stuffed them as children. They see enjoying "special dishes" as giving in to potential female manipulations. Keeping food tastes simple is equated with keeping free.

4. Some people prefer soft foods that do not require any special effort to eat. Chewing, tearing, and cutting are unconsciously felt as hostile acts that put them in touch with their own repressed anger, which they fear.

5. While some very bland people eat only bland foods, others eat the most highly spiced, fiery foods in an attempt to make themselves more spicy and interesting.

6. Some men stick to steak and potatoes as a confused gesture of masculinity. These men (sometimes unconsciously) see the taste for exotic French or gourmet cooking as a feminine trait. Men who are very frightened of femininity and who make it a point to be manly and strong in all ways may even get nauseated at the idea of eating what they unconsciously regard as feminine food. They unconsciously feel that eating this kind of food will deplete their masculine strength.

7. There are many kinds of food fetishes and phobias. There are people who are repelled by ordinary foods and attracted to inedible and sometimes "dangerous" foods. This is often an indication of severe emotional disturbance.

CHAPTER 6

Will Psychotherapy Help Me?

WHAT IS THERAPY?

A great many people are fascinated, curious, repelled by, or merely interested in psychotherapy. In recent years, there has been a proliferation of books dealing with every facet of the subject, yet many people are still in the dark about how therapy works, how to get help if they need it and want it, and what much of the vocabulary of therapy actually means. If you have ever wondered what the doctor-patient relationship is like, or *ought* to be like, if you want to know something of what happens during the therapeutic process, or if you want to start treatment and don't know how, the following questions and answers will be useful to you.

Q: *I feel that I have a difficult emotional problem and I am considering seeking psychiatric consultation. Is this a good idea?*

A: It certainly is a good idea. Most people attempt to muddle through somehow, no matter how painful or even incapacitating the problem becomes. Too many people wait until they are seriously depressed, severely anxious, irrationally fearful, and unable to function before they seek professional help.

People foolishly equate seeking psychiatric help with feelings of weakness, craziness, stupidity, etc. Such an attitude is self-defeating. Therapy not only relieves pain; it often prevents complications. In spite of this, many family doctors are reluctant to refer patients to psychiatrists when necessary for fear of antagonizing them. This is a great pity because it often inflicts unnecessary pain on people who need assistance.

Q: *My daughter is considering treatment with a psychiatrist who does not have a similar ethnic or religious background to hers.*

Do you think such a similarity is important in selecting the proper therapist?

A: No, I do not think it is vital that a patient and doctor have the same ethnic or religious background. But I do think it important that the therapist understands the background, customs, and value of the culture from which his patient comes. Such understanding helps the patient and doctor to communicate better with one another.

Q: *I am in my third year of high school, and I think I want to become a psychiatrist. How long does it take to become one? Are women psychiatrists discriminated against?*

A: It will take from ten to thirteen years to become a psychiatrist after you finish high school. The time will be spent as follows:

College: four years (if a general education leading to a bachelor's degree is desired).

Medical school: four years (there are, however, combined premedical and medical courses that take six years).

Internship: one year, but this is now optional. You may go into residency (specialty) training directly from medical school, serving no internship at all.

Psychiatric residency: three years.

Psychoanalytic training: usually four years, and taken concurrently with psychiatric residency.

There are many women psychiatrists, and I do not think they are discriminated against by psychiatrists, psychiatric residency programs, or psychoanalytic training institutes. Some patients, often women themselves, do refuse to see women therapists. Other patients, however, want only a woman therapist. As far as I know, women psychiatrists have no difficulty at all getting teaching positions, making hospital affiliations, or establishing full practices.

Q: *I am a fifteen-year-old high-school student. I read quite a lot, and I'm very interested in psychiatry. Can you tell me if there's a place in this field for women and how I could go about becoming a psychiatrist?*

A: Yes, there are women who do excellent work in psychiatry, just as they do in all other branches of medicine.

After high school, go to a good liberal-arts college for your bachelor's degree. Be sure to complete all your premedical requirements. Also, try to get as wide an education as you can in cultural subjects. You may consider either a major or minor in psychology. Then go on to medical school for your general medical education and your M.D. degree.

After medical school, you may intern for a year in an accredited hospital. I suggest a rotating internship, one in which you will work on all the services of the hospital—surgery, internal medicine, obstetrics, etc. Then you will go on to do three years of residency training in psychiatry. At this point, you will be in a good position to evaluate the teaching programs of the various psychiatric institutions. Perhaps you will choose the Psychiatric Service of Bellevue Hospital or Mount Sinai Hospital in New York City, or the Menninger Clinic, in Topeka, Kansas.

If you choose to become a psychoanalyst, you will need further training in a psychoanalytic institute recognized by the American Psychoanalytic Association or by the American Academy of Psychoanalysis. This training takes place either concurrently with your last year of residency or following residency training. Analytic training takes from three to six years, depending on the institute and on you.

Q: *Is it true that everyone who undergoes psychoanalytic treatment winds up hating their parents?*

A: Absolutely not. Psychoanalytic treatment helps a person get in touch with feelings she (or he) may have been repressing and hiding from herself for years. These feelings may or may not include hostility toward parents. Becoming fully conscious and aware of these hidden hostile feelings helps to dissipate rage and guilt and may contribute to great relief and a sense of well being. Exploration and insight into the origin of these feelings results in greater compassion and understanding of oneself and one's parents, and makes for more constructive, fruitful communication with everyone. In many cases, human beings can have a fruitful relationship with their parents only after undergoing analytic treatment.

Q: *I have a nineteen-year-old daughter who has been seeing a psychiatrist for the past six months. He refuses to speak to us unless our daughter is present. Since she refuses to have such a meeting, we have not been able to consult with him. Can you tell me if this is common practice?*

A: Yes, it is. However, sometimes in treating teen-age children who still live at home, psychiatrists prearrange periodic meetings with parents—thus seeing parents and children in intermittent treatment sessions. Most psychiatrists, though, particularly in treating young people in their late teens, do not do this and, further, take special pains to avoid contact with parents. This is not a capricious act on the psychiatrist's part. The fact is that all people, young and old alike, are entitled to privacy. Any breach of privacy can complicate and destroy the treatment relationship between patient and doctor. This is particularly true of young people, who are especially aware of the value of dignity and privacy as part of the process of maturing. Most young people highly treasure things and relationships they can call their own. This certainly includes a psychiatrist, who will be not only a special confidant, but also someone to whom they tell everything. Everything includes all kinds of feelings (socially acceptable and otherwise) about parents. Parent-psychiatrist contact can be destructive, because the young person considers it an invasion of privacy as well as an attack on an exclusive relationship. As such, it has an extremely inhibiting effect, which slows treatment and can even paralyze it.

Q: *Is mental illness as prevalent in other parts of the world as it seems to me to be in the United States?*

A: As far as I know from colleagues and from medical reports, *yes.*

Q: *How much does the problem of mental illness vary from country to country?*

A: Psychiatric observers seem to agree that no country has a priority on mental health or emotional disturbance. Particular problems and symptoms may vary (one thinks, offhand, of such symptoms as violence in the United States, alcoholism in France, melancholia in Sweden); but mental hospitals continue to be overcrowded throughout the world.

Q: *My psychiatrist recently changed what he calls my psychoanalytic "hour" from fifty minutes to forty-five minutes. Can you tell me the length of the average psychoanalytic session? Is it longer?*

A: Many fifty-minute "hours" have been changed to forty-five minutes. However, you ought to take up any feelings you have about the change with your therapist. The clarification of how you feel may give you valuable insights. How the patient feels about his or her therapist concerning any issue is particularly important.

Q: *Is it possible to go through a psychoanalytic treatment successfully talking about everything except one very sensitive area?*

A: No! But you may feel differently and free to talk about that "sensitive area" after your treatment has gone on for a while.

Q: *I have a girl friend who has been in psychoanalysis for years and has recently finally "graduated." But she is still very moody and has lots of problems. Isn't analysis supposed to clear up things like that?*

A: No! To be problem-free and free of moods is the condition of being a vegetable. The human condition is inevitably filled with problems and moods. It would be inappropriate not to respond with laughter in funny situations and tears in sad ones. It is the very antithesis of psychoanalysis—or any psychiatric treatment—to make people automatonlike, vegetablelike, and "always happy." If anything, the purpose of treatment is to free a person to know what he really does feel and to respond appropriately.

Q: *I'm studying psychology in school and object to Freud's completely male-oriented point of view. Is there any psychiatrist you know of who better understands the modern female?*

A: Psychoanalyst Karen Horney was probably one of the first serious workers for women's liberation. Unlike Freud, Mrs. Horney, who died in 1952, did not feel that female psychology was an offshoot of male psychology, or that women were anatomically inferior to men. She felt that any inferiority ascribed to women or men was generated by environment and not by one's sex. Mrs. Horney early realized that much of Freud's thinking was influenced by the Victorian times he lived in. She theorized that the impact of time and place—the culture in which we live—is extremely important in shaping personality and ways of relating to each other. You might want to read Mrs. Horney's *New Ways in Psychoanalysis.*

Q: *I keep hearing people use terms like "personality problems," "character structure," "neurosis," etc. Is there any one book that might give me a clearer feeling about what these terms really mean?*

A: *The Neurotic Personality of Our Time,* by Karen Horney.

Q: *I read a book that contained Sigmund Freud's psychoanalysis of Woodrow Wilson, whom Freud never had as a patient. In fact, Freud had never even met Wilson. Isn't long-distance analysis like this very wrong? Can a psychoanalyst draw valid conclusions about someone he has never met except through newspapers, letters, books, etc.?*

A: Anything and everything a person produces—letters, speeches, books, papers—will in some way reflect his inner workings. A skilled analyst who is particularly good at observation and detective work can come up with a surprising amount of valid information. However, this is no substitute for personal observation. How an individual reacts and relates to the analyst is the most revealing area of all, for it provides information about how the patient relates to other people—and particularly about how he related to his parents. Freud was the discoverer of this phenomenon; he called it "transference." He himself recognized it as one of the most important tools in psychoanalysis. An analysis of an individual without direct contact and the opportunity to examine the transference phenomenon may be very interesting, but it is also very limited.

Q: *I have heard the term "shockiatrist" used several times. I think I know what a psychiatrist and psychologist are, but what is a shockiatrist?*

A: I, too, have heard the word used, but usually in professional circles. This is a derisive term applied to doctors who are believed to be using electroshock (also known as electroconvulsive) treatment indiscriminately. ECT has a place in medicine, but it is a severe treatment that ought to be applied only when absolutely indicated and only when psychotherapy or treatment with drugs is definitely ineffectual. In other words, I regard ECT much as I would surgery, which obviously should be undertaken only when other less stringent methods are not possible.

Unfortunately, there are abuses in medicine as in all other areas of human behavior. I feel that "shockiatry" is a very serious abuse and is best avoided by proper consultation with an expert. An expert is a specialist recommended by a physician with whom one has had a long-standing, satisfactory professional relationship. I hope he makes his choice for psychiatric consultation from that group of men who are certified psychoanalysts. These are psychiatrists who have been graduated from psychoanalytic institutes recognized by either the American Academy of Psychoanalysis or the American Psychoanalytic Association. These men are trained for a long time and most thoroughly. Ninety-nine percent of them do not use electroshock treatment and have no vested interest in its usage. They are very conservative in recommending it and do so only when absolutely necessary. At that time, they send the patient to a psychiatrist who is an expert in administering the treatment and who understands its limitations. ECT at best is helpful, but it should not be misconstrued as any kind of "cure," since it solves no basic personality or human-relating problems. May I say that, in a rather active consultation practice, I have referred only one patient for ECT in the past ten years.

Q: *I keep hearing how hypnosis can cure people of various symptoms. Yet of all of the people I know who are seeing psychiatrists, none is being hypnotized. Why isn't this treatment used more?*

A: First, let me say that hypnosis is a potentially dangerous instrument when used by bogus "experts" and when played with carelessly. It can be a very valuable therapeutic adjunct when used properly and only by real experts. As with all other therapeutic modalities, much depends on the patient's condition and on his particular difficulty. I feel that hypnosis should be limited to selected cases. Determination for its use must be made *only* by a qualified psychiatrist.

Psychotherapy has a much broader application than is possible with hypnosis alone. In psychotherapy, the patient's awake and active participation and the insight that ensues are absolutely crucial to the process. The patient's very awake and active involvement in the psychotherapeutic process is what makes for sustained improvement and continued growth. Psychotherapy is one of the few areas of treatment in which the patient is required to do at least as much work as the doctor. This is no different from any other area of human endeavor in which satisfaction usually requires a high degree of conscious personal participation and hard work.

Q: *Is it harder for a man to ask for psychiatric help than it is for a woman? My husband was severely depressed but refused to seek help until he was practically at rock bottom. When I discuss this with my friends, they admit that their husbands and male friends do seem to procrastinate when it comes to getting any kind of help. Is this typical?*

A: Yes, men are more reluctant than women to seek help. This reluctance stems largely from a fear of helplessness. To most males, being helpless means being unmasculine. Men also feel that having emotional problems signifies that they are weak. (In reality, having problems only means that a man is human.) This fear of being unmanly often keeps men from getting psychiatric help or medical help until it is almost too late. Some men also deprive themselves of help, support, and understanding from their wives because they feel that getting warmth and comfort from a woman is degrading and unmasculine. In some cases, such feelings lead to marital coldness—and the more the man needs help, the colder he becomes. Such behavior not only aggravates the man's problems but also leads to a communication breakdown between him and his wife at a time when closeness is most needed.

Regardless of their sex, people are people—and people have problems. People need people to help them—professionally or otherwise—during hard times. Needing help is neither antimasculine, antifeminine, or antimature. Depriving oneself of needed human contact is antihuman, however, and constitutes important evidence that a person is confused about what being a human being—male or female—is all about.

Q: *I know that I have "problems" and need help. My husband understands and doesn't mind the expense. What scares me—and I guess stops me—is that everybody says that once you become dependent on a psychiatrist, you're stuck for life. Do you think this is likely?*

A: No! But first, please don't listen to "everybody." "Everybody" is not an expert in these matters and is only too often quite destructive. "Everybody" usually has a vested interest in keeping everything status quo and familiar. This includes keeping you "problem-loaded." "Everybody" is often afraid to face up to his or her own problems and projects his-her hopelessness and inertia to you.

Now on to the essence of your question—dependency. I call this very common fear of becoming chronically dependent on a psychiatrist the "crutch phenomenon." Let me say that the psychiatrist will not be a crutch unless you need one, and he will cease being a crutch when you no longer need one. Dependency (on a neurotic level—really overdependency or morbid dependency) is not suddenly generated by entering into psychiatric treatment. Nor does it slowly develop as treatment progresses. An individual who is neurotically dependent has probably been that way for years. Closely examined, this will be reflected in all her close relationships. If she becomes very dependent on her psychiatrist, this is not an indication of new dependency. It is the transfer of old dependency from one person to another.

The psychiatrist has no interest whatsoever in prolonging this dependency. He is interested in exposing it and amply demonstrating it to the patient. This includes getting at its source, its way of operating and the disturbances it creates. His ultimate goal, unlike what has happened in the patient's sick relationships, is to get rid of the need to overdepend and to be free of all crutches. When this happens, the patient will be more interested in her own feeling and good sense than in the advice of "everybody."

Q: *My friend and I live in a small town. Can you tell us how we can find out where there is a mental health clinic in our area?*

A: You may try social service agencies such as the Jewish Family Service or Catholic Charities. If you prefer, you may contact the closest branch of the National Mental Health Association, the American Psychiatric Association, or your local county medical society. You may also write the National Institute of Mental Health in Washington, D.C. In addition, some of the larger community hospitals maintain mental health clinics as part of their services.

Q: *I have serious personal problems, but how can I go to a psychiatrist when I know that they are against religion?*

A: This is not true! Psychiatrists are not against religion or any philosophical belief. They are not interested in "talking you into" or "out of" an old or a new religion, and they are certainly not interested in making you over into their image (or images). There are many psychiatrists who are religious themselves. In fact, I know psychiatrists of all religious faiths.

Psychiatrists are against any compulsions or tyrannies or coercions that you may suffer from (inner or outer). They are against lack of choice. There are people who confuse emotional sickness with genuine religious experience. Some very sick people, for example, delude themselves that they have special God-like powers, derived from long-standing "deep religious observance."

Psychiatrists want their patients to be free to make a choice in the establishment of their own individual values, beliefs and identities. If a patient freely (without compulsion) chooses a particular belief, religious or otherwise, as his own, the qualified psychiatrist would in most cases regard this as evidence of successful treatment.

Q: *I keep hearing about psychiatrists who have severe personal problems or whose children have all kinds of difficulties. Can people like this really help other people? Also, aren't all psychiatrists supposed to be psychoanalyzed? If so, why do they still have problems? Can this treatment help anybody else more than it helped them?*

A: You've asked several questions; let me answer them in several parts.

1. Be careful about hearsay and misinformation. Many people who discredit psychiatrists and psychiatry are really projecting their own fears of emotional problems and of seeking help.

2. Psychiatrists—and other doctors, too—are not psychic, employ no magic, and have no special powers. Hopefully, they are talented and well trained, have a liking for people, are compassionate and sensitive. But psychiatrists are people, and people have problems and children and limitations. People with problems *can* help other people, and this includes psychiatrists, especially those who have resolved their problems. Having been there themselves, they may be particularly helpful to others.

3. You are wrong about all psychiatrists' being analyzed. Only those training to be psychoanalysts (about 10 percent) are *required* to be psychoanalyzed.

Q: *My husband and I were recently forced to put an elderly uncle in a mental hospital. How can you tell whether or not a hospital is really good? We are paying one hundred dollars a week.*

A: Let me list twelve important characteristics of good hospitals:

1. The physical plant. Emotionally sick people need at least the minimum comfort requirements that healthy people do. This includes: proper heat, ventilation, beds, linens, clothes, cleanliness, cheerful surroundings, adequate room, grounds to walk in, entertainment facilities, good food, etc. Contrary to misinformed opinion, emotionally sick people are not oblivious to physical surroundings and requirements.

2. A director who has the highest professional qualifications and who chooses his staff accordingly.

3. A good ratio of doctor, nurse, attendant, psychologist and

social worker to patients. There are, unfortunately, huge state institutions with ratios as bad as one doctor per five hundred patients.

4. A hospital in which patients, however sick, regressed, out of contact, etc., are seen by a doctor at least once a day and whenever necessary.

5. A hospital run on a nonprofit basis is usually safest. This is especially true of those that have medical-school or university affiliations and teaching programs. There are some good profit-making hospitals; but do make sure that the one of your choice is licensed by the state in which it is located.

6. A hospital in which some form of psychotherapy and occupational therapy takes place for every patient, regardless of his or her condition. A good hospital never functions in a purely custodial capacity.

7. A hospital that does not ever use physical restraints—straitjackets, manacles, etc.—and where a patient is never physically subdued.

8. A hospital where socializing, visits (when appropriate) and a permissive, nonclinical, warm, friendly atmosphere prevail.

9. A hospital in which gratuities, tipping, and bribing play absolutely no role.

10. A hospital that is interested in and geared to the possibility of the patient's returning to a nonhospital, active existence, keeps patients as active and productive as possible, and encourages home visits on a more and more frequent basis.

11. A hospital that encourages psychotherapy after the patient leaves the hospital and orients him accordingly.

12. A hospital in which the personnel at all times respects the dignity, individuality, preferences, and needs of each patient, as they would those of any nonpatient.

Go over the above criteria, but do something else, as well. Although you are not a trained psychiatrist, you are entitled to a talk with the man in charge, a nurse, an attendant, and your relative's doctor. Do that! Have the talk, and trust your feelings. Do you like these people? Do they seem like interested, good human beings? If they seem right to you and if the hospital pretty well measures up according to our list, then your patient is probably in good hands. May I suggest, however, that you reevaluate every few months and that you visit the patient and demonstrate your interest frequently.

Q: *Do you feel that self-help books for mental health and sexual problems are ever helpful?*

A: I think the buyer should beware. Expertise is all-important in these vital areas. Books by experts (as opposed to books by would-be experts) can help in some cases where problems are not too intense. I feel that these books are most helpful not in "curing," but in helping a reader to realize that his or her problem is not so unique that he should be afraid or embarrassed to talk it over with the family doctor, or to seek psychiatric help.

Q: *Can music be a form of emotional therapy?*

A: Music can set a mood, bring back memories, and start thought patterns and associations. Music can have a soothing or a stimulating effect: it can allay anxiety and depression and make people receptive to psychotherapy. Sometimes, music can reach those who cannot be reached by words; it can reach deep down into the core of one's being to stir up feelings that have long been dormant. This stirring up of emotions can be the beginning of the road back to emotional well-being. More and more research is being done on music therapy; its potential may be greater than we realize.

Q: *If you could select ten famous historical figures to be your psychoanalytic patients, whom would you choose?*

A: Fame is no guarantee of an interesting analysis. The people I am going to list might have thought it presumptuous of me to select them as patients, but since they are no longer living, here goes: Abraham Lincoln, D.H. Lawrence, George Bernard Shaw, Albert Camus, Rembrandt, Beethoven, Elizabeth Barrett Browning, Edgar Allan Poe, Marie Curie, and Mary Cassatt.

Q: *Do you think a psychiatric examination should be mandatory for all Presidential and Vice-Presidential candidates?*

A: No, no more so than for any other people. Everyone has problems—there is no such thing as a "normal" person, a person without any emotional conflicts or problems. I am sure that at least 90 percent of all people who have occupied the White House have had problems, and many have made fine Presidents. If we had eliminated these people as possible candidates with so-called psychiatric examinations, we would have eliminated such Presidents as Abraham Lincoln (severe spells of depression), Woodrow Wilson (psychosomatic illnesses), and John Adams (bouts of paranoia).

Having problems does not mean that a person cannot handle a job. Having undergone psychiatric treatment or therapy also does not mean a person can't handle a job. Very often people who have had therapy can cope with other people and situations better than those who have not undergone such treatment.

If you had asked me if I thought Presidents and Vice-Presidents should have some psychotherapy, then my answer would be yes. I think anyone who must deal with people can benefit tremendously from psychotherapy. This applies to teachers, doctors, and lawyers, as well as politicians and heads of state.

Q: *Why do patients always have to lie on a couch when they visit a psychoanalyst?*

A: Patients do not always have to lie on a couch. Today, most patients are given the choice of a couch or a chair. For some patients a couch symbolizes a place of withdrawal, enclosure or sleep. Others feel that lying on a couch is a sign of passivity, resignation, and loss of control. To men, lying on a couch might also suggest a loss of masculinity. For these patients, therefore, the use of a couch during treatment would be too threatening and may produce enough anxiety so that it would not be an asset. Patients who prefer not to look at the analyst find the couch helps them to relax and speak with unembarrassed freedom, so that they can relate thoughts and feelings without inner censorship. Because this freedom is so essential in therapy, the patient is allowed to use either the chair or the couch, depending on which allows him the greater ability to speak his thoughts.

Q: *I have a friend who is squeamish about being examined by her family doctor who is a general practitioner. Do doctors ever feel squeamish about examining naked patients?*

A: This depends on the doctor's personal history, character structure, ways of relating to people, level of maturity, and professional experience. However, if a doctor is squeamish about examining a patient, these feelings are so controlled that the patient will probably never know. To most doctors, examining patients—naked or clothed—is purely professional; in other words, part of their job.

Q: *I know people are embarrassed by what they have to tell their psychoanalysts, but are psychoanalysts ever embarrassed by what patients tell them?*

A: Since analysts are human it is possible for them to become embarrassed on occasion. Usually this has more to do with the analyst's own life and psyche than with that of the patient. It is, however, difficult to startle or embarrass most therapists who have been in practice for any length of time. Seasoned analysts feel, as Sigmund Freud did, that "Nothing that is human is foreign to me." It is important to remember that the well-trained psychoanalyst (a graduate of one of the schools recognized by either the American Academy of Psychoanalysis or the American Psychoanalytic Association) does not sit in judgment. He has undergone his own treatment and hopefully accepts himself enough to accept his patient and whatever that patient has to say.

Q: *I have a friend who has problems she ought to discuss with a psychiatrist, but she is afraid he might reveal her private thoughts. How discreet are psychiatrists about what patients tell them? Do psychiatrists discuss their patients with their wives, friends, or other psychiatrists? Would they ever testify in court and reveal a patient's private thoughts and information?*

A: No! No! No! and No! Information disclosed to a psychiatrist (and, for that matter, to any doctor) is inviolate. This privileged information is never treated frivolously or carelessly. It is heard with as much respect for complete privacy as a priest hears a confession. If a psychiatrist ever alludes to a case history in a psychiatric lecture, paper, or a clinical discussion, the facts are handled with extreme care and discretion so that personal identification and embarrassment can never take place. Psychiatrists feel so strongly about this privacy that they will risk a jail sentence rather than disclose information in court. In fact, as I write this, a psychiatrist in California is facing a jail term because he has refused to take the stand and reveal facts about a patient currently involved in a lawsuit. (Please do not confuse this issue with the testimony given by a psychiatrist when he is brought into a legal issue as an "expert." An "expert" is brought in with a patient's knowledge that this testimony will take place.) I would also like to point out that psychiatrists believe in the need for secrecy because those that have been analyzed reveal their own thoughts in their own personal analysis.

I have found that many people who seem to be overly concerned with a psychiatrist's ability to keep a secret are really using this issue to sidestep needed treatment. They are also afraid that the psychiatrist may judge them harshly for desires, wishes, thoughts, feelings, which they themselves find unacceptable. But the psychiatrist does not sit in judgment. He is there to help people free themselves from the fear and tyranny of skeletons in the closet so that they can live in greater peace and harmony with themselves and others.

Q: *I have just read a book called* The Love Treatment, *which is a collection of case histories of sexual affairs between analysts and their patients. (The book was written by a psychiatrist.) Does this sort of thing go on often? Does the psychiatrist believe that such treatment is beneficial to the patient?*

A: No. Most doctors don't have the time, energy, or motivation to have affairs with their patients, and most certainly do not believe in the therapeutic effect of the so-called love treatment. Many times reports of analyst-patient affairs are pure fantasy on the part of the patient. It would be prudent on the part of a patient to ascertain both the credentials and motivations of any therapist who suggests any kind of sexual interplay.

Q: *My husband and I have marital difficulties and have been told that each of us needs psychotherapy. I am afraid to see an analyst for fear he will advise me to terminate my marriage. Is he likely to do that?*

A: Psychiatrists, especially those who are trained as psycho-analysts, have no interest in promoting divorce. Quite the contrary. Qualified therapists do their best to improve their patients' ability to relate—and, in so doing, contribute to improved relationships and better marriages. Some people, however, cling compulsively to very destructive, hopeless relationships. Therapy sometimes helps them to extricate themselves from these disastrous liaisons, for the good of all concerned. Furthermore, a well-trained psychoanalyst does not advise his patients. He attempts to help the individual to better understand herself so that she makes her own healthy decisions.

Q: *What is the best way to find a competent psychotherapist?*

A: Psychoanalytically trained psychiatrists are best trained to do therapy. Most psychiatrists who have been trained in psycho-therapy and graduated by a psychoanalytic institute usually belong to either the American Psychoanalytic Association (Freudian) or the American Academy of Psychoanalysis (Neo-Freudian). These organizations can tell you who their members are in your city.

Q: *I saw a psychiatrist recently for several sessions. He has the highest qualifications and seems nice enough, but I don't feel that we hit it off. Do you think it is possible to do better with one psychiatrist than with another?*

A: Absolutely! Psychiatric treatment, more than any other form of medical therapy, depends on the doctor-patient relationship. Relationships on any level are never simple. Some are better than others; some are impossible. This is particularly true for psychiatrist and patient. This is why an appointment first with a "consulting" psychiatrist may be valuable. Such a meeting allows a "consulting" psychiatrist to learn about your problems and personality and then refer you to a compatible therapist with whom constructive treatment can take place. Most analysts will realize after a few sessions whether or not the patient should continue seeing him (or her)— or be referred to another doctor. If you are not comfortable with your present psychiatrist, I suggest a change. And you should not feel any embarrassment about switching. Your psychiatrist will understand.

Q: *Can you tell me why I keep dreaming the same dream over and over again?*

A: Dreams are often unconscious attempts to resolve emotional problems that the dreamer prefers not to face up to when he or she is awake. However, unless the problem is resolved on a conscious (awake) level, the dreams usually continue. The problem may be so deeply buried that a dreamer is not even aware of it. For example, rage at a parent, a son, daughter, or mate is often repressed because we feel guilty about feeling anger toward someone we love. Dreams may also represent a yearning or a wish for someone—or something—and the frequency of the dream would be some indication of the depth of desire of the wish-fulfillment. Regardless of why you dream, if your dreams reach the point where they interfere with your sleep and, consequently, your health, I would suggest you seek competent psychological help.

Q: *My aunt is confined in a state hospital where she was diagnosed as psychotic. She is allowed visitors, but I have never visited her. However, my sister has and reports that though my aunt hears "voices" and has strange ideas, she is fairly logical in conversation. I have always been afraid to visit my aunt because I thought that psychotic meant "crazy" in the berserk, ranting, raving sense. Does it?*

A: Very few people suffering from a psychosis exhibit wild, crazy, berserk behavior. If they do, such behavior is infrequent and lasts only a short time. "Berserk" behavior is actually more common among so-called "normal neurotics," who may go through short hysterical periods of ranting and raving. These periods invariably subside without mishap. Psychotic people are often logical, even too logical. They are cut off from their true feelings and, as a result, their feelings often take on an autonomy that produces imaginary worlds, voices, visions, and roles. Your aunt sounds fairly typical of people afflicted with this emotional disorder—which, though serious, does not preclude logical conversation. If you feel up to it, you should visit her. Seeing you may be helpful to her.

Q: *Can bigotry and prejudice be changed by psychoanalytic treatment?*

A: Psychoanalysis is the appropriate treatment, I think, but very few bigots would admit that they are emotionally disturbed. Also, their prejudices are likely to include psychiatry! I have never had a patient come to me specifically because he was bigoted or prejudiced. But most people who have undertaken psychoanalytic treatment for other problems discover prejudices of which they were unaware. With motivation and much work, they can be freed of these prejudices, just as they can resolve other serious problems.

Part II
Dealing with Others

CHAPTER 7
Sexual Identity and Relationships

A sexual relationship between two affectionate partners may be the closest tie human beings ever establish with each other. Sex, however, is still a difficult and often unexplored area between two participants: what *is* permissible, what *is* enjoyable, what *is* yet unknown and frightening? A great deal of sexual difficulty and inability to communicate between a couple stems from the individual's insufficient knowledge and early fears about this subject. Being relatively open and vulnerable with another person requires a great deal of self-esteem, of security about one's own sexuality and attractiveness, and a firmly anchored sense of being a separate individual from one's partner. Two people do not become one during the sexual act, after all—they just become as close as they possibly can.

Women and men often have problems in appreciating their partners' perspective; it has often been said that the sexes will never truly understand each other or glimpse the secrets of each other's psyches, but in a close relationship it is always easier to bridge the distance. Our sex fantasies tell a lot about our picture of the opposite sex; many women see men as aggressive and domineering, while men imagine their mates as alternately pure, sexually challenging, or nurturing.

Sex education, at no matter what age, can help to clear up gross misconceptions and fears about topics such as homosexuality, impotence, orgasm, and sexual harmony with a mate, but a strong feeling of one's own physical and emotional identity is the most important factor in the establishment of a healthy, fulfilling sexual relationship.

Why Men Don't Understand Women

One of the questions I'm asked most frequently in psychiatric practice as well as in private life is: "Why don't men understand women?"

Many women feel that men just cannot figure out who women are, what women want, and where women are going. And these women are right; most men do *not* understand women. And to compound the problem, men have absolutely no idea why they can't understand them.

Of course, some men readily boast that they understand women completely. However, when questioned in depth about their rare insight, these men will respond with a hodgepodge of ridiculous, erroneous, cliché expertise. A woman should be wary of any man who claims he understands her completely. Most likely he is a man who is "completely" ignorant about women and "completely" prejudiced against them. The chances are that this man is confusing understanding a woman with affection for her. There is a vast difference between the two.

To understand women, a man must first admit that he doesn't understand them at all. Only then can he come to grips with the fear and hostility that he may be harboring against women. When this fear and hostility come out into the open, a man can then relate to a woman on a one-to-one basis. Only then can he get to know a woman's thoughts, feelings, desires and interests—all the things that one person (male or female) must know about another in order to understand him or her to a reasonable degree.

The ready knowledge that men have about women usually consists of muddled infantile and adolescent fears, fantasies, prejudices, and exaggerations. One of the most ludicrous of these masculine prejudices is that "all women are alike." Men will openly admit that they are attracted to certain types of women, but then these same men refuse to see women as individuals.

Male prejudice against women (like female prejudice against men) can have disastrous consequences to society as a whole. Any breakdown of male-female communications, or any so-called war between the sexes, whether subtle or blatant, usually produces misery. The only way to prevent this breakdown is to increase mutual understanding.

Few men, unfortunately, are mature enough or open enough to make the effort to understand or even get to know women. They don't realize that this knowledge will increase their satisfaction on nearly all levels of living. As I have pointed out many times before, women in our society are not as plagued by immaturity or burdened by the inability to understand as our men are. Our culture has a way of producing mature women, but for some reason too many men remain little boys—with all their insecurities and false male pride. And it is these immature men who must handle a man's responsibility in our world today.

Men take great pride in those attributes that they consider the exclusive property of the male sex. These attributes include: strength, control of emotions, courage, complete absence of helplessness, logic, constant youth, physical prowess, sexual potency, deprecation of artistic aspirations, and glory through competition and aggression. Too many men feel that it is essential to possess every one of these attributes if they are to be considered masculine. They feel "unmanly" if they fall short of these goals. Such an unrealistic attitude can damage and even destroy a man's ability to undertake adult responsibilities or to relate to himself, to other men, to children—and especially to women.

When you ask young men, "What are you?" most will answer, "I am a boy." Later in life, the answer to the same question is: "I am a man." How much better off the world would be if everyone answered that question: "I am a human being." Seeing oneself primarily as a human being, with all the faults and understanding that the word "human" implies, is more constructive to the human condition than seeing oneself as masculine or feminine. This insight also leads to self-acceptance, which in turn leads to mutual acceptance. To understand a woman, a man must accept what she is. But men find this extremely difficult because they refuse to admit that they share characteristics with women. For example, men think all men are strong and all women are weak. The male mind refuses to believe that the "male" characteristic of strength can be found in women. On the other hand, men find it difficult to believe that women are different. For example, it is hard for men—who require orgasm for sexual satisfaction—to believe that women can at times find sex enjoyable or satisfying without orgasm.

Depression, cowardice, envy, jealousy, love, sexual interest, artistic talent, involvement with children, shyness, greed, generosity—these and hundreds of other traits are neither masculine nor feminine. They are *human* traits. The extent to which a man (or a woman) recognizes these traits as human (instead of male or female) will determine in large part the success or failure of that man's (or woman's) male-female relationships.

Certainly important and interesting biological and psychological differences exist between men and women. But these differences do not account for that wide variance in male vs. female thinking in which our upbringing has led us to believe. Actually, men and women are more alike than they are unalike. Heterosexual men have almost as much in common with heterosexual women as they do with other men.

In other words, human beings—if permitted and encouraged to do so—can have deep human friendships on a nonsexual basis, regardless of what sex they happen to be. *Men and women can be friends.* This sounds simple enough, but in our culture, nonsexual man-woman friendships are rare. After marriage, friendships between men and woman on a nonsexual, nonbusiness, noncouple level are virtually nonexistent. Women are supposed to have women friends, and men, men friends—and there the line is drawn.

This separation of men from women is a throwback to the social separation of the sexes that takes place from birth through adolescence. A boy is branded a sissy if he demonstrates any interest in girls before the age of sexual awakening. As a result, boys (who become men) experience little involvement or information-sharing with girls (who become women). This failure to exchange information—often perpetuated by a boy's or girl's family—causes a breakdown in man-woman communications right from the beginning. This male-female communications gap is widened by the fact that the American male has a deep-rooted fear of his own femininity, and worries that deep down he may have homosexual tendencies. Thus it is easy to see why men, consciously and unconsciously, do little to open avenues that will permit them to understand women. In rejecting traits that men consider feminine, men also reject women, who are the bearers of these feared characteristics.

Women can help men understand females—and in doing so, can learn to understand themselves better. But let me warn any woman who undertakes the task of helping a man to understand women: the job requires patience in large amounts, because men—like the little boys that they are—do not listen readily. Compassion is also necessary—in large doses—in order to overcome long-held, deep-seated male prejudices. Prejudice is born of fear, and I have already pointed out why men fear women.

Men must give up their false, masculine, infantile pride before they can realize that women are capable of understanding business, checking accounts, politics, plumbing, electricity, football—and all those areas that many men now consider "for men only." Women can help to create areas of mutual interest as well as areas of potential mutual concern. To convey real feelings, people must talk to each other, but talk is meaningless unless the words convey real feelings. By words that convey feelings, I do not mean words of judgment, blame or recrimination—such words are conversation stoppers and do not promote understanding.

Women can do much to mitigate the masculine behavior pattern that prevents so many men from understanding women by stopping that masculine pattern where and when it starts—in a boy's early years. Women can teach their children—particularly their sons —to accept themselves as human beings. Women can teach their youngsters that it is much more important to be human than to be masculine, feminine, black, white, American, or European. A mother has primary and sustained contact with her infant sons, and she should try to transmit the concept that softer feelings, human sensibilities, human limitations, frailties, and compassion are not the exclusive province of either sex. Parental acceptance of both sexes on an equal basis, including the particular aspirations of both sons and daughters, leads to a child's self-acceptance and will help him or her relate better to the opposite sex. Mutual respect of parents for each other also makes a considerable impact on children and on their future relations with other members of the species.

What Women Don't Understand About Men

Women often understand men better than men understand women —and better than men understand themselves. This is because most women are basically more open than men, more in touch with deep feelings, and more accepting of human limitations. Women tend to be less prideful than men, so it is easier for them to ask for help when they need it. Women seem to enjoy life more than men do because they do not feel threatened by as many of the things that life has to offer, nor do they feel that they have to continually prove that they belong to the superior sex. "Women's lib" seeks equality, but men, unfortunately, seek superiority. Women usually mature earlier in life than men do, and many remain more mature throughout life.

Despite their differences, men and women together have more in common than they have apart. So-called male-female differences are largely illusions fostered by our culture, illusions that pressure men to sustain these differences and to maintain an apartness from women.

There are a number of factors or attributes common to most men in our society. These characteristics are not completely understood by women—nor, in many cases, by men themselves. Most misunderstandings exist in the area of sex, an especially important area because it deeply affects marriage and family.

Here, then, are those male factors that I think it is important for women to understand if they want better male-female relations.

1. I've said it before but it is worth repeating: throughout life, men retain more of the "little boy" in themselves than women do the "little girl." Men may transfer their interests from marbles to money, but they never rid themselves of the "little boy" qualities of poor tolerance for frustration, inner conflict, responsibility, and anxiety.

2. Unlike women, men do not like to admit they are dependent. However, men *are* dependent on fixed and predictable routines, on admiration from others—and on their wives.

3. Many men do not like women. They need and use women, but they do not trust them and are fearful, jealous, and contemptuous of them. The degree to which a man feels this way depends on how his mother related to him and to his father. Overprotective mothers often prejudice sons against "other women."

4. Many men fear homosexuality, and consequently draw a rigid line between what they consider weak (feminine) and strong (masculine). They will not admit to soft, warm feelings, which they consider feminine. This lack of emotional display can have an adverse effect in their relationship to their families.

5. Fear of homosexuality also prevents some men from having good relationships with other men. Men feel they must be strong (meaning stubborn, competitive, etc.). These characteristics, which men erroneously label masculine, often put masculine friendships on a childlike, competitive basis.

6. Men often have trouble relating to children because they are children themselves. They see their own children as competitors for their wives' affection, time, and energy. In a sense, men often

transfer competition with their own sisters and brothers to their own children.

7. Men are much more prone to self-hate than are women. Men have built up such great illusions about the "masculine ideals" (courage, strength, independence) that it is almost impossible for any human being to fulfill them. Failure to reach these masculine ideals produces self-hate and depression, which are then magnified because men consider failure to be feminine.

8. Consciously, many men view their wives as sex partners, but unconsciously they regard them as mothers. This combination causes conflict and confusion and can result in the man's having problems relating to his wife—or other women.

9. Men see their wives and children as extensions of themselves rather than as separate human beings. As a result, some men demand absolute authority and loyalty. When his family does not meet these demands the man will become enraged and depressed because he feels that his family is disloyal!

10. Men cling to childhood values and fantasies. Two examples are: putting undue importance on a son's athletic prowess and viewing war experiences as the highlight of life..

11. Men won't admit it but they crave affection and, in times of stress, want to be fussed over, coddled, and presented with gifts.

12. Men are as vulnerable to the youth cult (looking young) as women are. They also have as much vanity and are as concerned with being sexually appealing.

13. Men fear impotence. The degree of this fear is related to a man's fear of inadequacy or lack of self-esteem in other areas. Because men in our society measure self-esteem in terms of money and power—or "net worth"—a business setback can cause temporary impotence. The importance of a man's "net worth" can lead him to be stingy (in order to increase his bank account) or to spend money lavishly (to convince others that he does have a bank account). Whichever game of "net worth" the man plays, it can sometimes have sexual repercussions.

14. Men fear loneliness even more than women. They are afraid of not "being with the boys," afraid of leisure time, and of vacations. Most men do very poorly when they retire, since their energies and feelings of self-esteem have been invested in and derived from work. As a result, many men are psychologically unprepared for

retirement and suffer severe emotional depression, and even heart attacks, because they no longer feel useful.

15. Men are as intelligent, altruistic, naïve, sophisticated, foolish, and as capable or incapable as women. They are also as possessive, envious, jealous, gossipy, and vindictive as women.

16. Men are terrified by the possibility of rejection by women. They equate such a rejection with lack of masculinity, which in turn leads to self-hate and depression.

17. Most men fear that their sex organs are too small. A woman's reassurance seldom helps to allay these fears, but business success sometimes helps. By the same token, business reverses can lead to renewed concern about the size of their genitalia. Fathers will often be overly concerned about the size of their son's sex organs and masculinity. Men view any of their son's inadequacies as their own, even though a son's condition may have a much different, more complex basis.

18. Sexual rejection by a wife is, for most men, the most total rejection he can receive. Such rejection is almost always followed by rage, which may be suppressed or expressed. Sexually, men have a much lower threshold of frustration than women do.

19. Men are concerned about the adequacy of their sexual performance and have exaggerated ideas about other men's ability to sustain erection without ejaculation. Many men measure their sexual ability in terms of a wife's orgasms. Husbands feel that a wife's failure to achieve orgasm signifies an inadequacy on his part. It is difficult for most men to understand that a wife may, at times, prefer intercourse or lovemaking without orgasm. Wives also feel that their husbands only care about orgasms—to the exclusion of showing affection. I have received letters from wives stating that they would regard embracing and petting without male orgasm as a sign of affection. However, some men become excited rapidly, and affection quickly leads to orgasm. Such action is no indication of lack of affection, but usually the result of combined affection and physical need. (Premature ejaculation is something else entirely—and that can also be helped.)

20. A man's sexual response is usually simpler than that of most women. For both men and women, desire is linked to romance and feelings of affection, but most men are more easily excited than women and are ready for sex with minimal stimulation. These stimuli include sight, sound, smell, or suggestion. The sight of an

attractive woman is often sufficient to initiate sexual feeling in a man. Men can be excited by women they don't know, or have any feelings for. These actions in no way indicate that the man does not love his wife. Women who equate love with exclusiveness of attraction are unrealistic. Many men choose to have sex only with their wives, but all are stimulated by other women.

21. Men love to experiment in sex, yet they have inhibitions and need their wives' help to break through to free sexual attitudes.

22. Though men like their wives to initiate sex some of the time, they can also feel threatened by a wife's assertiveness. It may be helpful for husbands and wives to discuss their feelings about initiating sex.

23. Sexual attraction is the biggest force in starting a man-woman relationship. This is based largely on how a woman looks. Few men will initiate a relationship, however, unless the woman indicates that she will not reject his approach.

24. Men do have their own form of menopause. It is a very painful, sometimes devastating middle-age crisis. While a wife's understanding and warmth can help a husband through male menopause, some men must seek professional help as well.

25. Women tend to idealize men. Idealization does not leave room for human limitations, and when the man turns out to have human faults, disappointment follows.

Any misunderstanding—regardless of what it is—can be helped by an open, honest discussion. A discussion means listening as well as talking. And talking means open communication and mutual respect for the other person's needs and aspirations as well as compassion for problems. This applies to all human beings, regardless of sex.

Women's Sex Fantasies

For me the human mind is much more than the brain and the spinal cord. The mind is the sum total of an entire human being. This includes all of the internal organs and glands, the bones and muscles, blood vessels and nerves, eyes, ears, nose, skin—absolutely everything that comprises a human being. The mind is still the most magnificent and complicated structure ever devised on earth.

The brain and spinal cord transmit messages and directions to the rest of the body, which in turn directs enormous quantities of information to the brain. This in turn leads to choices and decisions in a vast number of matters, which in turn lead to actions and a countless variety of human experiences. I think of it *all* as the human mind and I sometimes also think of the mind as a kind of passionate tape recorder. This particular instrument, the finest and most intricate ever conceived, distills, records, and transmits enormous quantities of information and feelings or passions. The mind (a passionate tape recorder) begins its enormous work at birth and never ceases to grow until death. Unlike any other tape recorder or electronic computer, the mind is capable of enormous flights of fancy, and the ingenious passionate tape recorder can produce fantasies in the form of thoughts and ideas, sounds, visions, feelings or all of the former combined and all it thought of, heard, seen, and felt only by the mind's owner. Of course, an instrument so sensitive to inner working, even able to perceive itself, and so rich in its storehouse of experiences and diverse information, has much to draw on in creating fantasy. As a result, the mind has an ability to produce an almost endless variety and infinite number of combinations of fantasy —many of which are indeed fantastic compared to the relatively prosaic world and modes of living in which most people find themselves.

Just about all people with normal brain function fantasize and they do so a great deal of the time, very often in fleeting bits and fragments and often as they go about other and even very complicated activities. Producing fantasies is, in fact, so common and spontaneous that, like our very breathing and heartbeat, we are often unaware that we are doing it. This is true of both men and women, people of all ages and personality types, and people in all walks of life. Fantasies may involve people, places, things or ourselves exclusively, and they may come in fragmented showers or long, continuous sequences. Some people have a life-long ongoing fantasy to which they return again and again, much like a continuous soap opera on television. Some fantasies are almost purely intellectual; others are full of color; still others full of emotions. Some fantasies are well thought out and indulged in logically as one would study a difficult text. Others burst on the scene and into awareness, seemingly out of context with whatever may be going on in the individual's personal life at the moment and seemingly divorced from whatever the person consciously knows about himself or herself. Some serve an anesthetizing, deadening function, while others produce overt feelings, including outbursts of laughter, tears, rage and even hysteria.

Since all fantasies are born of a particular person's experiences, feelings, desires, and frustrations, fantasies, like dreams, always have meaning and usually serve some important function. But understanding either the meaning or the function of a dream is impossible unless one knows a great deal about the inner life of the person in question. We human beings are highly symbolic creatures, and fantasies and dreams are filled with symbolic meaning. While many of us share similar symbols that represent the same or similar objects or functions, we each of us still develop a highly individual symbol language. Psychoanalysts spend literally years getting to know and understand the symbol language of patients. Only when these are known in the context of a person's entire life can a fantasy or dream give much valuable personal information and insight. Thus, to one individual a fantasy of fighting and yelling may be symbolic hostility and a function of repressed or hidden rage, while to another it may be linked with a desire for contact and healthy emotional friction and involvement. To one individual, a fantasy of flowers and bees may represent a return to nature, simplicity, and a world lacking in pretense, while to another, this may represent sexual need and desire. Listening to an individual's associations relative to the elements in a fantasy and knowing much about their person's personal history and way of relating to herself or himself and to other people tells us much about the symbols and the meaning of a fantasy.

The same applies to the dynamics of a fantasy, which usually serves one or multiple functions. These may include an attempt to escape unpleasantness in one's current environment, an attempt to resolve a problem or conflict, an attempt at stimulation, an attempt to repress and avoid some feeling emerging in one's self, a way of exploring and testing one's desires and feelings, a way of expressing emotions that a person may be afraid to express overtly, or a preparation for rehearsal or participation in some activity. It must be remembered that a fantasy is not an action, and very few fantasies are translated into overt action.

Many people are terrified by fantasies, largely because they apply the same standards, values, and judgments to fantasies as they do to real life and to actual actions. This invariably leads to terror, self-hate, and further inability to understand one's fantasies. Given the extraordinary richness of the human mind, it is no wonder at all that just about any perfectly normal human being can produce the most bizarre, distorted, obscure, confused, cruel, kind, terrible, wonderful, unique, commonplace fantasy. This is particularly true of fantasies born of attempts at repression of strong feelings. Trying to hold feelings down results in fantasies that seem most bizarre and utterly divorced from the feelings that generate them. This very often applies to sexual feelings and fantasies, but again it must be remembered that understanding a fantasy's deeper meaning takes considerable expertise as well as experience with the passionate tape recorder in question.

Sexual fantasies are particularly prevalent, and many workers in the field believe that people have an almost innumerable number of sexual fantasies on any uneventful average day. This applies equally to both men and women. Perhaps this is a way nature has of keeping us highly sensual and in constant readiness for sexual reception, since the most primitive, primary, and most important function of sex is procreation and perpetuation of the species.

Generally, there are three broad categories of sexual fantasies:

1. Sexual fantasies that are overtly sexual in nature and truly born of sexual feelings, needs, and desires.

2. Fantasies that on the surface overtly demonstrate no sexual content at all but which are truly sexual on a deeper level. These often occur in people who attempt to repress their sexual feelings. Thus, a woman may constantly picture men walking into deep tunnels, houses, etc., as an expression of sexual intercourse.

3. Fantasies that are overtly sexual but which are used to obfuscate hidden and unwanted nonsexual feelings. Thus, a woman may have sadistic sexual fantasies if in fact she harbors repressed feelings of rage and desire for vindictive triumph. This kind of conversion of nonsexual material to sexual expression is not unusual if we realize that we express much of ourselves and how we relate by the manner and ways we prefer sex. Sex itself is highly symbolic of how we encounter life generally. Very gentle men who are aggressive, indifferent to their partners' needs and even cruel and selfish in bed often may be consciously unaware that they harbor much repressed hatred and fear of women.

Given the privacy of one's own fantasy world, without the impingement of civilization's rules and conventions and without the judgments that decide what constitutes acceptable and nonacceptable sex practice, a vast number of women have a vast number of fantasies, many of which would be considered perverse in most cultures. This is not unusual when one considers the high degree of repression that exists in our society, even today. Nice but healthy women do have healthy desires and when these are ignored or put down out of awareness, they often result in highly exaggerated fantasy productions. The very society that insists on maximum repression ultimately produces fantasies that are laden with substance most tabooed by that society. Sexual feelings and needs are extremely powerful, as well they should be, to insure continuance of the species, and they will have expression even if only in fantasy, despite the embroidery and complications of a particular environment. But I must point out that oversimplification can lead to misunderstanding. Again, one must know the person in question to understand the fantasy life of that person. Some very sensual, happy, and sexually satisfied women have a great number of very exotic sexual fantasies and some don't. The same applies to women who are overtly lacking in great sensuality (even in their own conscious feelings) and who are almost completely lacking in actual sexual satisfaction.

Let me briefly list and describe some common characteristics and functions of women's sexual fantasies. These may exist singly or in combinations and their originators are usually unaware of their purpose.

1. Women's sex fantasies are usually more intricate and imaginative than those of men. This may be due in part to a culture that fosters more sexual repression in women than men. But I believe that this is mainly due to the fact that women's sexual lives are more closely interwoven with their relating processes generally. This kind of integration of sex relatedness and love makes for fantasies often full of romance and complicated plots. Men tend to have simpler fantasies, direct and involved with the physical mechanics of sex.

2. Narcissistic fantasies involving desire and admiration by multiple lovers are exceedingly common and are sometimes connected to need of proof of lovability and sexual appeal.

3. Some women repress all feelings to an unusual degree and use sexual fantasy, and sometimes sexual activity as well, to generate feelings generally. Since sexual feelings are among the strongest, they are used as igniters of other feelings in order to increase a general sense of aliveness.

4. Some highly romantic fantasies are used to compensate for actual sexual lives that are relatively boring, mundane, and lacking in desired expressions of warmth and affection. They are also used as a form of revenge against seemingly uncaring husbands and as a substitute for actual extramarital activity.

5. Fantasies of great personal degradation are often used to remove and dilute inhibiting and even paralyzing feelings of purity. Some girls have been overwhelmed and inundated with the necessity of being nice, clean, and pure. In fantasy they sometimes must wallow in symbolic or literal filth to come down to human levels in order to free and to experience sexual feelings.

6. Sexual fantasies that are particularly anticonventional are often used to express rebellion against internalized parental authority or powerful and paralyzing religious scruples.

7. Both hetero- and homosexual fantasies are experienced by women who are afraid to feel warmth and to express closeness to either sex.

8. Sadomasochistic sexual fantasies are used to express repressed feelings of hostility, a need to be manipulated and told what to do because of undue feelings of dependency and aggressive feelings and desire to dominate and manipulate others. Creating pain in one's self and in others can be an attempt to mitigate otherwise deadened feelings. The combination of pain and sex produces very strong stimulation in direct proportion to the degree of paralysis of feelings. I do not believe in the theory that masochistic fantasies are due to women's inherent passivity. There are many healthy women who are assertive and not nearly as passive as a great many men in the population.

9. Many continuous, evolving serial-like fantasies are characteristic of extremely lonely women who actually have no relationship with any men.

10. Stimulating fantasies can be used to satisfy yearnings for forbidden childhood incestuous desires.

11. Fantasies of sex with complete strangers can be used as an expression of resentment and rebellion against familial responsibility, work, and boredom.

12. Fantasies of sex with much younger men can produce feelings of youth and stimulate early memories of actual past encounters.

Variations are enormous. Meaning is seldom immediately apparent. Fantasies are only "crazy," "awful," "evil," and "bizarre" if we apply conventional value judgments to them. Fantasies are almost always harmless and often function as necessary outlets that help people feel better. As with all psychological phenomena, constructive understanding is possible only if we mix observation with human compassion.

Q: *I often have sex fantasies. Is this normal?*

A: If you have such fantasies, you are not alone. Nearly all men and women, married or unmarried, from early adolescence on fantasize about sex. Sex fantasies take many forms, depending on the imagination of the individual involved. They can be as quick as a flash or as long as a novel. Some continue from day to day, much like a TV soap opera. Sex fantasies may or may not involve one's own mate. Sometimes they involve people we don't know, but few sex fantasies are acted out in real life; they are just that—fantasies.

Q: *I am aware that people suffer from a great many sexual problems and difficulties. But have you found any single factor that seems to be most prevalent in this area?*

A: You are right—sexual problems abound, and they are inevitably the complicated results of difficulties in relating generally. But there is a single factor that is particularly "prevalent" and destructive. I refer to the inhibition and inability of sexual partners to discuss their sexual feelings. The refusal to exchange information about sexual likes, dislikes, preferences, and feelings results in a breakdown in sexual communication. Too many people remain sealed off, encapsulated and sulking (instead of loving) and forever waiting for their lovers to understand, to catch on, to guess, and to do the "right thing." These people look on the actual exchange of information—in words—as a hurt to one's pride and as something that one "should know" and "should not have to talk about." Some people regard sexual discussion as crass, mechanical, and unromantic. While making love is not the time for discussion, there are plenty of other times that are opportune. However much in love lovers may be, they are not telepathic. Telling each other about likes and dislikes can be valuable and is not evidence of lack of love or romance.

Q: *Do all psychiatric problems have a sexual origin?*

A: No. There are psychiatrists who might say yes, but I say no! However, psychiatric problems always affect the way we relate to people. Since sex is a human-relating experience and potentially the closest one of all, it nearly always reflects problems that exist in one way or another. This could be said as follows: People who have personality problems will have problems with people and particularly with people in a sexual relationship, which will further contribute to the original problem. Thus, most sexual difficulties are symptoms of general relating difficulties and personality problems. These personality and relating problems must be resolved, to make for a better and sustained sexual adjustment.

Q: *A man friend of mine insists that women who are somewhat sexually promiscuous are more sophisticated, liberated people than those who aren't. What is your opinion?*

A: Psychiatrically speaking, if they were sexually liberated, they would not be promiscuous—somewhat or otherwise. I think that your friend is confusing sexual freedom and promiscuity. Sexual freedom involves a choice as to when, where, and with whom an individual wants to have a sexual relationship. Promiscuity is a function of anxiety. It is a symptom. The sexually promiscuous person is choicelessly driven from one partner to another, in an effort to feel less anxious. I say choicelessly because she in fact has *no choice*. She is suffering from a compulsion to "act out" sexually. Sex for her often has little to do with relatedness and invariably proves to be disappointing. The promiscuous people I have seen in treatment were usually anything but sophisticated or liberated. These terms are hardly suitable to describe what is really an effort to rationalize unresolved infantile yearnings; a strong need to rebel against authority and an overpowering and very conventional conscience; an extremely immature sexual outlook; and a marked inability to sustain a mature relationship on any level—especially the sexual level.

In my opinion, a woman must be capable of an exclusive, sustained, involved (investing emotions, and caring about) heterosexual relationship, to be liberated and sophisticated sexually.

Q: *My nineteen-year-old-friend worries constantly because she is a virgin. She thinks all men will reject her because she doesn't believe in the more permissive "new morality." Does every male need to make love to a woman before he marries her? I'd also like to know if you think all virgins are really prudes?*

A: If all virgins are prudes, then there are a great number of prudes. I don't know how new the new morality is, or how prevalent it is, but I'm sure that there are still a vast number of nineteen-year-old virgins of both sexes. There are probably just as many people—male and female—who insist on virginity up to the time of marriage as there are people who feel that premarital sex is all right.

Your friend should be more concerned with establishing her own personal, individual values and sense of identity. Compulsive conformity to other people's conventions will invariably have a demoralizing effect on her and will destroy her self-esteem.

Q: *My son is fourteen years old. He seems perfectly happy and well adjusted. Cleaning his room, I recently found several magazines hidden away in his closet. They were of the nude- and semi-nude-girl variety. My husband doesn't feel I should be too concerned, but I am, and I would like to know what your opinion is.*

A: Your son sounds like a lot of men and most boys. There is a difference between compulsive involvement with nude-girl pictures and curiosity. Unfortunately, there are people for whom "looking" is a substitute for actual relating. This does not seem to be the case with your son. Like most boys his age, he is curious about sex and about girls and what they look like. When he is older, he will doubtless transfer this interest to real girls.

May I point out that most psychiatrists see no correlation between looking at sexually stimulating pictures and destructive sexual acting out. The problems of sexual offenders are usually rooted in very profound and complicated early family relationships.

I *would* be concerned about boys who are stimulated by pictures of "muscle men." This can be an indication of difficulty with sexual identification, and here a psychiatric consultation might be in order.

Q: *My husband wants to know how you feel about men who like to cook? A few days ago he got into a discussion with a friend who fancies himself an amateur psychologist, and this man insists that men who like to cook have hidden feminine traits. What do you think?*

A: Beware the amateur psychologist—especially when he is giving vent to hidden hostility or projecting aspects of his own problems. Many of the world's most famous chefs are men, while some of the finest bacteriologists, engineers and business administrators are women. Some utterly feminine women have no interest in either cooking or knitting, but are experts at finance. No feelings other than heterosexual attractions are either feminine or masculine. It is a great pity when men and women have to blot out aspects of themselves or deny themselves enjoyable activities because they harbor confused ideas about masculinity and femininity. This usually leads to stunted creative possibilities that might otherwise flourish. Secure men and women will do what comes naturally because they know their feelings, interests and activities are neither masculine nor feminine—but simply human.

Q: *My fifteen-year-old son is an excellent student, yet he does very poorly in his French conversation class. When I asked him why, he told me that he "feels like a sissy" saying the French words. I know that in later life he will be delighted to be able to speak fluent French, but how do I handle the problem now?*

A: Unfortunately, too many things in our culture have been labeled masculine or feminine. Children inadvertently learn about these "differences" early in life and tend to cling to them forever. Wanting to cook, being sensitive, playing chess, wanting to become a violinist, etc., are neither masculine nor feminine feelings. They are *human* feelings and aspirations. Having these feelings or aspirations does not make people any more or any less masculine or feminine. Boys consider being good in foreign languages to be feminine, along with liking poetry, classical music, or fine art. Pronouncing French words correctly might also be added to this list. I think it would be a good idea for you to have a serious discussion with your son. Point out that feelings, intellectual and artistic taste, speaking French, etc., are in no way characteristic of either sex. Remind him that Frenchmen are as masculine and as attractive to women as Americans, Germans, Norwegians—or men of any other nationality.

Q: *I am twenty-four. I have been seeing a very charming, interesting man who is twenty-eight, but he does have one habit that is beginning to get on my nerves. Wherever we go, he always points out effeminate-looking men and tells me how much he hates homosexuals. He seems to be very masculine, but I find myself wondering what all this protesting really means.*

A: I can't say with any degree of certainty whatsoever, since I don't have enough facts about your young man's history, feelings, way of life, and so on.

Some people who "hate" homosexuals or men they think look homosexual are really attracted to them. These people are terribly threatened by their feelings of attraction and attempt to nullify them by covering up with reverse feelings of revulsion and hate. Other men hate homosexuals because they are afraid of characteristics and feelings in themselves that they consider feminine. Their hatred of homosexuals is an attempt to destroy these unwanted characteristics and feelings. Some of these men do, in fact, have unresolved problems involving hidden homosexual yearnings. Others are much confused about sexuality and have come to regard many things about themselves as effeminate and possibly homosexual that are not this at all. I have seen men in consultation who felt that a love of cooking or music, a show of tears or kindness were feminine and a threat to masculinity.

Your friend's preoccupation and inordinate reaction undoubtedly spring from some kind of problem and considerable sexual confusion. However, it is impossible to know just what is going on without knowing much more about him.

Q: *My husband finds it very difficult to assert himself. He is a wonderful man, but he just can't stand up to his boss or other domineering men. Could this possibly mean that my husband has homosexual tendencies or that he has trouble with his masculinity?*

A: Your husband's actions have nothing to do with homosexual tendencies or with his masculinity. Difficulty with self-assertion is common to both men and women and is often linked to poor self-esteem. Men (and women) who do not have a high regard for themselves and their ideas will usually back down before a more self-assured adversary. Many homosexuals, by the way, are very self-assertive, and many decidedly heterosexual men are self-effacing and compliant.

Q: *My husband had a vasectomy several years ago. He was then fifty-two. Before his operation we had a very active sex life, but he now tells me that since undergoing sterilization, he has not enjoyed sex and has lost all desire for it.*

A: Since a vasectomy does not affect hormone balance or sexual stimulation, I see no physiological reason why the operation itself should cause your husband's present condition. Some men are not emotionally prepared for a vasectomy and tend to think of the operation as castration. That's why I advise any man who is thinking of having a vasectomy to be psychologically prepared before undergoing it.

There are two things you and your husband can do. I would advise him to have a thorough physical examination. If all physiological difficulties are ruled out, then I would suggest that he see a psychiatrist. Loss of sexual desire usually stems from emotional problems. Some men irrationally convince themselves that they are old and "sexually finished" when they reach a certain age. The age depends on the man—some feel "old" at forty, some at fifty, some at sixty. Your husband may be one of these men. If he is, he would probably tend to blame his lack of sex drive on something concrete like a vasectomy rather than on his subconscious feelings of being old. Competent psychotherapy would be helpful in this case.

Q: *My husband goes through increasingly long periods when he is impotent. It makes us both nervous, but my main concern is that it has a terribly depressing effect on him. Our family doctor has sent him to two different urologists. But there has been no improvement. Is this kind of problem really physical, or is it emotional?*

A: The vast majority of cases of impotence or transient impotence stem from emotional problems. That your husband was checked out physically was very wise. It is now time to have a psychiatric consultation.

The Impotent Husband

Medically speaking, the term impotence is used only to describe the male's inability to function sexually. Some doctors consider frigidity the female equivalent of impotence, but, from a physiological point of view, this is not true. Since the anatomy of a male is so different from that of the female, I feel that equating frigidity with impotence only creates confusion.

The psychology of men and women is similar, however; so women who are frigid and men who are impotent may have similar reactions to sex; both can be interested or not interested in it; both can or can't become excited. Here again, there is one great male-female difference: a frigid woman can have intercourse; an impotent man cannot, because he cannot sustain an erection long enough to complete the sexual act.

Impotence is more common than most men believe, and causes both husband and wife to suffer. For these reasons, impotence should not be ignored or considered a taboo subject.

Many women misinterpret impotence as a sign that their mate is rejecting them. Other women feel that they themselves are responsible for their husband's impotence—because they are not attractive enough, or because they lack the sexual know-how to enable their man to perform sexually. Men fear impotence because they equate it with old age, approaching death, lack of masculinity, and homosexuality. These mistaken male and female fears result in self-hate and mutual loathing of the other person—all of which are destructive to a relationship that is already precarious because of the husband's impotence.

Physiological causes: Few cases of impotence are caused by physiological problems. The rare cases may be connected to one or several serious physical illnesses such as advanced arteriosclerosis (hardening of the arteries), endocrine or hormonal problems, severe urological diseases, advanced venereal disease, neurological disorders or accidents (such as paraplegia—paralysis and loss of function from the waist down due to spinal cord injury).

Physical causes: Physical conditions that produce impotence are rare and are relatively easy to diagnose. The most common physical basis for impotence is over-indulgence in alcohol or drugs. Severe fatigue and/or physical debilitation (starvation, overexposure, etc.) can also cause impotence. In all these physically induced cases, the impotence is usually temporary and will vanish when the physical problem is eliminated. Even though physically caused impotence is rare, every man suffering from impotence deserves a thorough physical examination.

Emotional causes: Emotional problems cause impotence in the majority of afflicted men. There are two kinds of emotionally caused impotence: chronic and temporary.

Chronic impotence is a very serious and difficult problem. Some men suffering from it have never functioned sexually, not even once. The causes are often there from as far back as birth. These causes are woven into the pattern of a man's personality and character; they deeply affect the way he views himself and how he relates to others.

I believe it is valuable for men and women—as sex partners and parents—to understand the causes of chronic impotence. Here are some of the principal factors—they may exist alone or in combination. And, as with many emotional problems, they will probably exist on a subconscious level—meaning that the impotent man will not be able to connect the real causes to his problem.

1. Overprotecting parents. They can emotionally stifle a son and make him unable to think of himself as an individual able to get along on his own.

2. Cruel, emotionally castrating, and inhuman parents. Upbringing by such parents leads to a son's chronic poor self-esteem, self-hate, distrust, and repressed rage—especially at his mother. This rage and distrust is then displaced to other women.

3. An exploitative mother who uses her son for her own benefit. She is overinvolved with him, too close emotionally—and sometimes physically. She overconfides in her young son, sometimes telling him about her sex life (particularly her sexual dissatisfactions). She may be consciously or unconsciously seductive to him. She may take him into bed with her and sleep with him, even though there may be no overt sexual encounter. She may use him as a surrogate husband and dissuade him from relating to girls his age.

This mother nearly always disapproves of any girl her son has anything to do with, often stating that she is "not good enough" for him. This kind of background produces two kinds of sexual guilt: first, an encounter with another woman is unconsciously felt as an infidelity to mother. Second, attempts at intercourse result in tremendous guilt because of the son's incestuous sexual feelings for his mother, generated by her seductive maneuvers. His resulting impotence effectively removes the anxiety and guilt that would follow intercourse.

4. A clinging mother, coupled with a father who is passive and fails to participate in bringing up his son. These parents can cause the son to have sexual misidentification, fear and hatred of women, and sometimes to become a homosexual. Homosexuality may result in impotence. (I must point out that not all homosexual men are impotent, and the vast majority of impotent men are not homosexual.)

5. An overly strict, puritanical, antisexual, and antipleasure-oriented upbringing. Such households view any kind of pleasurable activity as sinful. There may be a history of terrible parental recriminations following discovery of the boy's masturbation or sexual interest.

6. A household that is an emotional vacuum, devoid of any exchange of feelings. In such a home, there is little or no opportunity for a child to learn to make emotional exchanges, to communicate, and to relate. This can lead to asexuality or to an anesthetizing of sexual feelings.

7. Sex education that is prejudiced against women, together with frequent warnings about the danger of sex and women.

8. Inadequate parents who pass on to their son their own feelings of near-total incompetence. As a result, the son feels inadequate and is incapable of self-esteem in any endeavor. He sees sexual performance as a test situation in which he will surely fail. While most men may feel concerned about their sexual ability (especially in initial encounters), they do not have the all-consuming fear of inadequacy characteristic of men with this background.

9. Men who have been brought up to "be perfect in every way" suffer self-hate following any less-than-perfect performance. The fear of resulting self-hate can be devastating to sexual performance.

10. Castrating fathers who constantly put down their sons. They tell the boy that he is too small, weak, shy, intellectual, not athletic

enough, etc. Such fathers are very competitive with their sons, and often arrange competitions in which their sons must lose. These men also project their own inadequate feelings and demand that their sons fulfill Dad's own unfulfilled expectations.

11. Traumatic sexual experiences at a very early age that can be destructive in adult life. These experiences can include contact with prostitutes and older women who mock, castigate, and put down a young boy's initial sexual overtures. Some boys were told as youngsters that their genitals are inadequate and that they will never be able to satisfy a woman. (Traumatic though the experience may have been, this problem is not as hard to treat as the others listed here.)

12. A background of emotional disturbance. Chronic disturbance can result in impotence as well as other sexual problems. But some very disturbed people who hardly function in any other area, may be fairly competent on a sexual level.

Temporary impotence can strike nearly anybody, and often has as much to do with a man's immediate life situation as with his personal, emotional, and sexual history. Transient impotence can become chronic if the situation leading to it is not corrected, or if help is not provided. The following is a list of common factors that can lead to temporary impotence on an emotional level:

1. Impotence itself. Any small sexual mishap may make a perfectionistic man extraordinarily self-conscious. This concentration on self and on performance can lead to continuing attacks of impotence.

2. Misinformation and fear regarding the process of aging.

3. Misinformation and fear regarding diseases of the genitourinary system—especially prostate or genital surgery or hernia repair.

4. Serious emotional depression.

5. Any blow to self-esteem, especially in the business area.

6. A change in the long-standing status quo situation, such as moving from a house to an apartment.

7. A change in family status quo. For example: marriage of a child, sickness or death of a parent, mate or child, etc.

8. Fear of a real or imagined illness.

9. Change in economic status.

10. Any change in his marital relationship that leads to related problems and possible hostility. For example: a wife's going back to work or school, or her feeling different about herself because of psychoanalytic treatment. Change in a wife's attitude toward sex—

she may be sexually demanding for the first time—can also cause impotence.

11. Guilt following a man's extramarital affair, or his rage and fear following his wife's disclosure of her interest in another man.

12. A newlywed may become temporarily impotent because of fear of his inability to perform or fear of inexperience.

Most men need a wife's help to overcome the embarrassment of admitting to impotence, and in seeking competent help to overcome the problem. Wifely rage, recrimination, or demands will only make matters worse. Patience, warmth, and friendly, even loving talk and demonstrations of concern and affection can be quite helpful. In chronic impotence, deep and prolonged psychoanalysis is necessary. In temporary impotence, a combination of psychotherapy and treatment by experts in the field (such as Masters and Johnson in St. Louis, or Dr. Harold Lief in Philadelphia) can be helpful.

Q: *Should a husband or wife ever fake sexual response? Doesn't the "little lie" do more good for a spouse's ego than the harm of telling the lie?*

A: Lies, however well meant, often promote frustration, resentment, and hostility. The energy used to fake a sexual response should be used more constructively in honest response. (Remember, for sex to be pleasurable, sexual responses need not be total or equal, for both partners.) "Ego building" based on a lie rarely has significant value. Furthermore, the person doing the faking usually does it to avoid his or her own problems rather than to bolster a spouse's ego. I also feel that truth will inevitably out. While people may fib to convince themselves or someone else of something, deep down they usually know (or soon learn) the truth.

Sex Lives that Lack Fun and Warmth

For too many men and women, love, warmth, and fun have vanished from sex. Too many sex lives have become arenas where performance is all important. Technique, style, duration of the sex act, response, and frequency have all become more important than the whole being of sex—a sharing of intimacy and fun. Unfortunately, the sex act has become a test, a standard for measuring masculinity or feminity, a test of a partner's ability to relate, ability to care, and ability to please. Sex has also become a bad way of measuring self-esteem.

Many men and women do not realize they are using sex to test themselves. They only know that they are not enjoying sex very much and at times it has even become a burdensome and depressing activity. Many confused and unhappy men and women read and reread how-to sex books and think, "Well, I do everything right, why doesn't it work for me? Why don't I enjoy it more?"

Very often the answer is: "it" did not work because subconsciously the man or woman is primarily concerned with sexual tests and standards rather than with love, warmth, or fun.

Any self-imposed standards that are not met generate self-hate, which in turn is destructive to sex. Sexual standards kill spontaneity, produce inhibitions, and have been known virtually to paralyze sex partners. Fun, warmth, and humanity, so vital in sex, are replaced by anxiety, depression, and fear.

In these days of supposed sexual freedom and enlightenment, I see many men and women in psychiatric consultation who are sexual cripples. They have become victims of self-imposed tyrannical sex standards, often further reinforced and exaggerated with the help of so-called experts. I use the word *tyrannical* because, once started, sexual tests and standards become extremely demanding and cruel. Little that I know produces as much self-hate and cruelty as misguided notions about one's own sexual inadequacy. This cruelty can take various forms; it may produce anxiety, depression, or phobias—all of which can lead to sexual symptoms, including impotence, frigidity, premature ejaculation, and genital pain. If the individual has other emotional problems (as invariably we all do), these difficulties are compounded and self-hate and cruelty increase, destroying much needed self-esteem.

Millions of words have been written—some for fun, some for education, and most for profit—all purporting to educate adults sexually. While these words may or may not educate, they almost invariably convey all kinds of ideas about sexual etiquette, protocol, standards, norms, and expectations. Who initiates sex and how it is initiated becomes all important. Who refuses sex and how it is refused takes on all the confused protocol of high-level diplomatic maneuvers at the United Nations. How-to manuals convey the feeling of opportunistic manipulations between strangers or enemies who are being taught to trick themselves and each other into having successful sex. These books seem to forget that sex is between two people who know each other as friends and lovers.

The areas in which many books inadvertently create the most fear are: *foreplay* (rigid definitions abound as to what constitutes good foreplay, including time, technique, and expected effects); *positions* (importance of variety); *frequency and duration of intercourse* (averages and expectations); *orgasms* (individual, multiple, frequency and intensity); *postcoital techniques* (descriptions of and mutual feelings about); *love as opposed to lust* (virtues of and differences between, etc.). Standards, expectations, and goals are described in all these areas, and unless the zenith is achieved in each area, unless one scores everytime, all is considered lost and is followed by a sense of failure and guilt.

People are not machines. As obvious as this statement is, there are men and women who still try to program themselves into being perfect sexual machines. Human beings do not work that way. When humans demand the inhuman of themselves, the consequences are disastrous.

Machines do not fluctuate, machines do not vary, but humans do. This is why sex can sometimes be great, but not always. Sex can be many things, but it cannot always be the same things. If you expect perfection every time, then you are asking for a machinelike performance that you, a human being, are simply not capable of delivering.

If, then, sex tests and standards are destructive, what can a person do to be a better sex partner, to enjoy sex more by putting fun, warmth, and love into it?

What I am offering here are not rules; they are, hopefully, helpful observations and suggestions.

1. Sex education can help you enjoy sex more, but there really is not that much to know. The mechanics are not that intricate and are easily learned.

2. Sex can become boring and then, just like anything else, it can become good again. It can't always reach the same level of intensity.

3. There is no norm. Individual tastes and appetites vary, responses vary—even within the same individual. No one sex partner, no one couple, ought to be compared with another.

4. Periods of desire fluctuate and usually have more to do with general moods than with mutual attraction or the lack of it. People are generally arrhythmic. Couples don't always have the same desires or needs at the same time. Adjustments and accommodations are always necessary.

5. Women (and men) do get tired, moody, anxious, and depressed now and then and at such times may prefer not to have sexual contact. Pleading fatigue all the time can be evidence of sexual abhorrence and, therefore, should be discussed with a competent therapist.

6. Sex can be loving, lustful, and mechanical at various times—and sex can also be a combination of all three at various times.

7. Few problems men or women have in relating to other people are caused by sexual problems, but relating problems can affect one's sexual life. Relating problems are seldom resolved sexually, but sexual problems are sometimes helped by improving one's general ability to relate to others.

8. Chronic pain, degradation, or constant lack of fun in sex indicates a need for psychiatric help. Serious problems need serious help, and serious help means a trained psychoanalyst.

9. However much in love, turned on, or tuned in you are as a sex partner, you are not psychic—and neither is your mate. He does not automatically know what your tastes, preferences, irritations, or complaints are, just as you do not automatically know his. Experimenting helps, yes, but there is no substitute for direct talking.

People have the strange notion that true love equals automatic and complete sexual understanding and harmony and that the need to talk over sexual feelings is proof of a lack of love or of irreconcilable sexual differences. Rather, talking is proof that we are all individuals with unique differences. It is these very differences that make a relationship interesting. Talk, real talk, is necessary for real sexual communication to take place. Too much talk during sex or vindictive verbal exchanges after sex can have a cooling effect, but lovers talking openly about sexual feelings can add to sexual fun and spontaneity.

10. No matter how good a liar you think you are, sooner or later the masquerade almost always comes to an end. Faking responses often makes for added complications. Whatever you feel (or do not feel) is perfectly okay and need not be exaggerated to manipulate or please yourself or your partner.

11. Moods come and go—that is a human fact of life. Try when

you can to take advantage of a mood and feelings of receptivity. No one lives forever and it is just plain unwise to miss out on the possibility of fun.

12. Rewards and punishments have no place in an adult sex life. Giving gold stars for performances well done and withholding sweets for poor performances are not even recommended for children. Sex as reward or the withholding of sex as punishment can only destroy a relationship.

13. Imagination and creativity help any human endeavor—and sex is a human endeavor.

14. Being a slave to love or sex is ruinous to self-esteem. Whatever you do sexually should be done for pleasure, and not because you think your partner will love you more.

15. Taking part in sexual techniques that repel you will generate self-hate. However much a sexual activity is recommended to you by a friend or so-called expert, if it is not pleasing for you, forget it. But you should explain your feelings to your partner.

There is no simple, magic formula for becoming a better sex partner, but it can be easier if you remember you are a human being, with human faults and human failings—and so is your mate. Relating problems must be resolved through communication and not through sexual manipulation. If sexual partners can't talk about relating problems and sexual problems, then expert marriage counseling may be helpful.

Q: *I always expected to achieve perfect sexual harmony with my mate and after several happy months of marriage, I am very disappointed in this respect. Is there anything I can do?*

A: With impossible expectations, you were bound to be disappointed. Two people, however much they love and are attuned to each other, are still two *separate* individuals. It is impossible for any two people to have a perfectly adjusted relationship in any area, including sex. Everyone has his or her own individual mind and emotions, and though two people may be on the same emotional and sexual wavelength, there will be occasions when their emotional rhythms, moods, and needs may be far apart. It is important to know that perfect sexual harmony is a myth. Understanding this will enable partners to accommodate one another's needs and moods.

Q: *I have a friend who goes out with a man, then invariably finds out that he is either married, has a sexual problem or is a homosexual. Is her constant choice of the "wrong" men accidental, or does it mean that my friend has a problem of her own?*

A: If this has been a consistent pattern it is certainly not "accidental." Your friend may not consciously choose a man with the characteristics you describe, but she is certainly attracted to them and is undoubtedly motivated by unconscious needs. These needs may include one or more of the following:

1. Many women like your friend have much unconscious self-contempt. They do not feel that they can "make it" with a man who is wholly eligible, a man who is not defective in one way or another, sexually or socially. The men your friend has chosen to date certainly fit into this category. They are regarded as "safe" because such men can never force her to face up to her own problems.

2. Many women like your friend are afraid of any sexual encounter because they have little confidence in their sexual ability or, for that matter, in their ability in any area. This will cause them to seek out men with whom a sexual encounter is unlikely.

3. The vast majority of women like your friend are afraid of any kind of sustained involvement. Despite protests to the contrary, they conscientiously resist any relationship that may bloom into sustained emotional involvement. Thay may say they want marriage but they really want a hit-and-run superficial relationship. They see marriage as a trap, a burden, a great loss of freedom. Naturally, they will then gravitate toward married men, men with sexual problems—in fact, any man who is safely ineligible for a long-term, sustained relationship.

Perhaps one day your friend will realize her life pattern (if she has not already done so) and seek the advice of a competent psychiatrist.

Q: *Can you tell me about my husband? We have a fairly good relationship. I know that he needs me in many ways and I need him too and we appreciate each other. But he frequently makes disparaging remarks about me, and often makes hostile remarks about women generally. The fact is, he really seems to have contempt for women.*

A: A great many men need women and some can't do without
them. But many of them don't like or respect women. This usually
stems from childhood familial experiences and the way their parents
related to each other and to girls in the family. Lack of self-respect
in mothers and contempt for women by fathers is perceived by young
boys even though their awareness may not be obvious. A *need* for,
or dependency on, women, especially in men with confused notions
about masculinity, produces self-contempt, which is often projected
onto women since they are the reminders of male dependency.

Q: *My husband refuses to see* I Am Curious (Yellow)—*or any
other explicitly sexy film—although he is not a prude. Can you tell
me why?*

A: There are a number of reasons for your husband's actions—
and they are often present in combination. Here are the most common:

1. Some men idealize their wives. Part of this idealization is to
"protect" their wives and sometimes themselves (*i.e.,* remaining
"clean and pure" for their wives) by staying away from anything
that might be considered sexually degrading. Interestingly, some of
these men will go alone to see what they consider "dirty movies," but
will not take their wives, in order to protect them from this "impure"
experience. These same men will very often separate "nice" girls
from "bad" girls, and "clean" sex from "dirty" sex.

2. Other men are afraid they'll feel inadequate when they compare
their sexual performance to those in the film. Such a man may feel
threatened by what he sees—or what his wife might see and subsequently demand from him.

3. People are sometimes afraid that sexy films will stimulate old,
buried feelings—all of which will make for temptation, conflict, frustration, and anxiety. People are particularly afraid of finding out that
they may like things they are not "supposed" to like. This realization
could detract from a person's desired image of himself. The childish
desire to see others engage in sex (the vestiges of which exist in
nearly all adults) is known as voyeurism; it is particularly applicable
in an overtly sexy film. A movie-goer may envy the players because
he, too, has a secret desire to exhibit himself. Some men stay away
from these films to avoid guilt that would ensue should they feel
sexually stimulated by a woman other than their own wife.

4. Some men may be fighting the urge to engage in all kinds of hitherto untried sexual activity. Seeing a sexy film may be taken as a step in that direction.

5. There are men who feel that sexy films are oversimplified, tasteless, and boring. They feel that they make sex seem mechanical, routine and dull. They prefer to avoid such movies.

6. Finally, many people over the age of eighteen will not try, do, or see anything that is not utterly familiar, true, safe, tested, or conventional. Potential confrontation with anything different is rationalized as "bad" in order to avoid the threat of the unfamiliar.

Q: *I have a friend who has a very unhappy sex life. She and her husband have been married for ten years and have always had sexual difficulties. Would it be helpful for them to seek advice from experts in this area?*

A: Expert sex education can be exceedingly valuable when both parties are willing to consult with real experts. (Of course, it is important to ascertain the credentials of the expert.) Strong motivation to resolve any problem of this nature (indicating maturity and real interest in each other) contributes immeasurably toward success. Sexual education seldom completely eradicates sexual difficulties, however. The way a person expresses himself sexually reflects how he feels about himself and his partner. Some simple sexual problems are the result of ignorance and confusion and are greatly ameliorated by knowledge properly applied. But many problems are the result of difficulties in relating to one's self and others. This is why many sexual difficulties are best treated by psychoanalytic psychotherapy.

Q: *My husband and I are in our early thirties and have been married for eight years. I have never experienced orgasm and sex has become an obligation for me rather than something I want to do. I know I should not set goals for myself, but I want more pleasure from sex. I find it embarrassing to talk to my doctor about this— which is why I'm writing to you.*

A: A person can have pleasurable sex with or without orgasm; however, judging from your letter, this is not so for you. The fact that sex has become increasingly distasteful to you is bound to cause repercussions in your marriage. Remedial steps are indicated in terms of your marriage in general, and specifically for the purpose of making sex more pleasurable for you.

When a husband or wife is having sexual problems, more often than not both partners contribute to the difficulties. Sometimes simple sex education will solve the problem. At other times, a husband and wife might have a problem in relating to one another. This problem of "relating" must be solved before any sexual problems can be solved. It is also possible that some hidden fears are causing your sexual problems. In any case, expert help is certainly indicated. If you can't talk to your family physician (and while he may not be the best person to handle this problem, at least he is a start), I would suggest you seek out a psychiatrist. You might also consider consulting the Masters and Johnson Clinic in St. Louis, Missouri, or another reputable sex clinic closer to your home. There may even be such a clinic at a nearby hospital; many hospitals, particularly in large cities, are opening sex clinics. Whatever you do, please believe me when I say that you are not the first woman (or man) to write me because of embarrassment over talking to a doctor about sex problems. It is a common occurrence. But also believe me when I say that the pleasure you will receive and the boost you will give your marriage make it well worth taking the first step toward getting over your embarrassment.

CHAPTER 8
Marriage

People's concept of marriage has changed radically over the past several decades. People just aren't living "happily ever after" and are deeply troubled as to why they are not. And yet, for all the trial marriages, the living together, the communal arrangements that many are experimenting with these days, the basic unit of a couple—man and wife bound together in the state of matrimony—continues to be the foundation for the nuclear family that exists in nearly every society.

Establishing and keeping a marriage together is difficult; it takes time, growth, love, a sense of humor and a great deal of patience. Petty problems mushroom out of all proportion and serious lacks of communication are often overlooked until it is too late. A husband who wants to take a vacation by himself or a wife who is upset when her husband is late for dinner have to learn to understand their mates' objections. A tearful bride or a husband who sees other women may have deep problems that extend beyond the province of marriage itself. The bond between two individuals who have vowed to spend the rest of their lives together is only as strong as the two links of the chain. Mature people who can give and take and who are sure enough of their own strengths to enjoy their mates' successes and to be supportive in mutual failures, contribute valuable ingredients to a marriage. The institution will remain alive and flourishing if newlyweds and old married couples alike approach it with a realistic and less-than-perfect image in mind.

How Good Is Your Marriage?

Many factors are involved in personal relationships, but I consider twenty of them vitally important in marriage—the closest and most important human relationship. It is not necessary, however, for every one of these factors to be present in every marriage. Your marriage, for instance, may lack factors from this list, yet it still can be happy and harmonious. In such marriages other factors are usually present in a greater-than-average degree. Marriage, remember, is the sum of its total parts.

Although each of the dynamics on this checklist is separately numbered, they can overlap. Here, then, is my list of twenty factors present in a good marriage:

1. Both parties come from families with a history of stable, happy marriages.

2. Both spouses have a strong sense of self-esteem and identity. Each is able to recognize his or her own feelings, values, likes, dislikes, goals, assets, and limitations.

3. Mutual sexual attraction has existed from the very beginning of the relationship. I do not agree that sexual attraction can "develop later on." The chemistry of mutual sexual attraction is either there at the start or it is contrived and forced.

4. Each partner has a good sex education and a mature sexual outlook. This means a willingness to learn and to make adjustments. Sexual compatibility requires patience, experimentation and adjustment. A mature couple knows that perfect sexual compatibility does not exist, but good sexual relations do—and they depend on many factors. A couple's sexual life usually reflects the way the partners relate to each other.

5. Similar ethnic and cultural backgrounds are present. This allows husband and wife to speak the same language—literally and figuratively—making it easier for them to understand and communicate in matters of sex, people, community, country, religion, philosophy, and life-style in general. A mid-Victorian woman and a thoroughly modern man may make an interesting combination, but their marriage would probably be disastrous.

6. There is similar intellectual endowment and educational experience. I am talking here about levels of education (high school, college) rather than any kind of specialized training.

7. The husband and wife can laugh at themselves and at each other. They are able to get angry and to express that anger instead of harboring it or bearing a grudge. Happily married couples can talk to each other, listen to each other, and be willing to forgive and forget.

8. They share similar feelings about earning, saving, and spending money. This is very important because money represents time and

energy as well as prestige and power. Partners with separate fortunes and couples who maintain separate bank accounts often find it very difficult to share their lives in other areas. When material outlook varies to a great extent, there is usually marital difficulty.

9. Neither partner expects perfection in anything, and each is willing to struggle if necessary to achieve a common ground. What this means is that each partner has a high frustration tolerance.

10. There are similar ideas and feelings about wanting children and agreement in the way children should be raised. If both partners have happy memories of their own childhoods, then they are way ahead of the game.

11. There are no large gaps in ideas and general outlook. Such gaps are far more important than a difference in age. It is important that the maturation process and the gathering of knowledge, wisdom, and human compassion be similar in both partners.

12. Common likes, dislikes, and interests make for a better marriage because couples can share involvements and pleasures.

13. The partners enjoy each other's company. They should also have friends whose company they can enjoy together.

14. Neither partner has prejudices or animosity toward the opposite sex. The wife should like and respect men and masculinity; the husband should like and respect women and femininity.

15. There is a strong sense of responsibility, jointly and individually. For the welfare of the entire family, each spouse should be willing to undertake tasks for which he or she is better suited than the other. These tasks should be undertaken without feelings of oppression, self-sacrifice, or martyrdom, since they are being done in the family's behalf.

16. Neither partner feels that marriage has deprived him of a career, great freedom, fun, etc. Properly oriented husbands and wives feel that marriage and the formation of a family are primary to their well-being.

17. One partner's personality complements the other's. One spouse may be an igniter, a stimulator, while the other may be more stolid or stabilizing. One may be a dreamer, the other more practical. One may make judgments based on feelings, the other may contribute more logic. As a result, each can help the other grow by charting territories with which the other is unfamiliar.

18. Both partners are mature enough to consider themselves adult and to have successfully separated themselves from the families in

which they grew up. Of course, interest is maintained in parents, brothers, sisters, and other relatives, but the marriage partner's prime concern is his or her own marriage and children. And children are regarded solely as children. There is enough emotional health and clarification of feelings on the parents' part to realize that children should not be used to relive one's own childhood, or to pursue rivalries with one's own sisters and brothers. There is also enough health so that even if the wife feels a little daughterly, motherly, or sisterly toward her husband, she will principally feel like—and be—his wife. A husband, similarly, will also be a husband first and foremost.

19. The happily married couple knew each other well before marriage. There are exceptions to this rule, but they are rare. Getting married without really knowing one another is like playing poker against a stacked deck. Impulsive marriage is a bad start because it indicates that neither partner takes the other one—or marriage —seriously.

20. Love. Feeling lovable. Having the ability to love one's mate. This is almost the sum total of all twenty factors. When I say that good marriage partners love each other, I mean that they are concerned about each other's welfare and happiness as much—and even more—than they are concerned about their own. Happily married partners are a team, and they do not compete with one another. It takes two to make a marriage and these two people must always remain two distinct individuals, bringing their own unique, creative aspects to the marriage rather than trying to meld into one—like a two-headed monster, isolated, encapsulated, and separated from the rest of the world.

In summation, it is important to remember that perfect marriages, like perfect human beings, do not exist. But good marriages can and do exist—on a deeply mature level. These marriages offer the unique satisfactions and fulfillments that come from being grown-up and alive—and from communicating on the highest possible level with a grown-up of the opposite sex. Good marriages, happy marriages are never stagnant. Partners grow and help each other to grow, and their relating becomes more fun and more interesting as they open up and explore new facets of each other. These twenty basic ingredients help immeasurably. They provide the seeds for future growth.

How Wives Can Help Their Husbands Live Longer

Even mature men sometimes act like little boys—particularly when it comes to taking care of themselves. Men may be capable in many areas—including business—but they often show poor judgment about their own health and welfare. This is particularly true of husbands who are devoted to their families, for in their pursuit of success and security, these men often neglect their own health to a remarkably self-destructive degree. They do not seem to recognize their own physical and emotional limitations. They don't eat, sleep, or rest properly; they don't relax, and they often suffer physical and emotional breakdowns.

Men who drive themselves so relentlessly have confused ideas about masculinity. They think that to be manly they must have unlimited energy, resourcefulness, and control, that they must face adversity with a minimum of emotional response. These unrealistic ideas generate such enormous stresses and strains that many of these men walk around like emotional time bombs—ready to explode. Some eventually do "explode"—mentally and physically—in depressions, anxiety attacks, heart attacks, strokes, ulcers, etc. These conditions cause impaired functions, which the man in turn views as unmanly, setting up a vicious cycle that frequently ends in death at a far too early age.

It's my belief that a wife is potentially the strongest and most immediately available force in relieving such a situation. There are very positive and practical steps that a wife can initiate to help her husband live longer. They are a combination of dos and don'ts—and, of course, some of them overlap. It also goes without saying that marriage is a two-way street; a husband would do well, too, to be considerate of his wife. But that is a point I will take up another time. Here is what a wife can do:

1. Be very careful with criticism. When people have a good relationship, constructive criticism can be valuable, but timing is very important. Constructive criticism is best delivered when a man (or woman) has first had an opportunity to rest and regain physical and emotional strength and energy. Even then the criticism should be given with understanding and compassion, not vindictively. The first way is life affirming and life saving; the second is ego shattering and potentially life destroying.

2. Don't Nag. Nagging destroys morale and produces fatigue in all concerned. Making unrealistic demands is equally destructive, especially to a man who is already making unrealistic demands of himself. Such a man should not be goaded into doing a bigger or better job. If anything, he should be encouraged, with emotional support, to work toward realistic goals. This can be done by helping him feel a sense of gratification and accomplishment in the work he has already done and in goals he has already reached. Expressing appreciation for what he has already provided can be most supportive of his efforts to tap the energy and personal resources he needs to attain further goals.

As with criticism, timing is also important in the making of requests. A woman should know her man; she should be sensitive to the emotional wavelength he operates on so that she knows when he is under minimal pressure and is most receptive to a new challenge. At such times she should encourage him toward goals that are realistically attainable, not toward far-out goals that must end in failure and increased feelings of helplessness, self-hate and resignation.

3. Don't be an armchair general. A wife should not chastise her husband with such statements as: "If you had only listened to me." or "I told you so." Instead, she should help her husband absorb any failures that occur by sharing responsibility for bad times as well as good. A life-preserving wife tries not to engage in the production of destructive energy-draining guilt and mutual hate. She helps her man realistically appraise failures so that he can learn not to make the same mistakes in future ventures. She should indicate to him verbally that her acceptance and love are not based on his material success but rather on his human value.

4. Do teach him to relax. Try to share interesting and relaxing interests with your man. There are times, however, when he'd rather be with members of his own sex (particularly for sports events)— but then there are times when a wife would rather be with other women. When a husband spends time "with the boys," it is important that a wife not make him feel guilty for not including her in everything he does.

5. Do help your husband to be a good father. Try not to chastise him for lack of perfection in this area, either. Much of a man's life goes on outside of the home—in order to support the home—so he cannot be expected to be as tuned in to his children's needs as his

wife is. She can help him to understand and enjoy the children and to relax with them. She must not make him the sole agent of their punishment when he comes home after work. This destroys the possibility of a good and relaxing relationship with his family.

6. Do encourage him to take a vacation. Vacations are important and many men never take them without a push from their wives. It is pointless and it neutralizes potentially good medicine, however, for a wife to urge her husband to take the kind of vacation he cannot afford. But, within their means, it is valuable for a couple to vacation periodically, and also to go off together alone, without the children, to enjoy adult privacy and do adult things. Even a day alone in the country or an evening of dinner and the theater can be very valuable.

7. Do learn your husband's tastes and needs. These include sex, food, drinks, home décor, etc. If a wife takes proper care of herself and makes herself attractive, a husband often interprets this as caring for him. In caring about herself, her health and welfare, etc., she gives both her husband and her children a constructive example to identify with—and she also adds to family morale. A smart wife sees to it that her home is a place in which to be comfortable and relaxed—not a museum or showplace but a bulwark against the pressures of the outside world. Small things count in a home. If a husband has a favorite chair, a wife should see that it is empty and waiting for him when he comes home. He will feel appreciated if his favorite drink is waiting, too. If he is very hungry when he comes in, have his meal ready as soon as you can. Frustration at home following frustration at work is not easy to tolerate.

8. Do urge your husband to go to the doctor when necessary. It is extremely important that men, especially when they reach middle age, eat the right foods. Most doctors agree that it is very important not to overeat and to eat foods that are low in cholesterol. I have known women who feel insulted and hurt if their husbands don't eat huge, rich meals. These women do their husbands—and themselves—an enormous disservice. It may take courage and fortitude in the beginning to keep the house free of these rich "poison foods," but this is important in prolonging life.

9. Do permit your husband to feel tired. A wife should realize that there are times when working hard all day makes it impossible to be a romantic cavalier at night. Also, confronting him with household problems and chores as soon as he enters the house is destruc-

tive both to a marriage and to emotional health. A man cannot view his home as a haven if every time he enters it he is immediately confronted with broken appliances, family problems, and bad news.

10. Be a good listener. Encourage your husband to talk, to share his responsibilities, struggles, and daily burdens. It is also important to allow a husband (or a wife) to be moody, irritated—even angry. A good marriage can take this in its stride.

11. Do put him first. In nearly everything she does and says, the life-preserving wife will indicate that her man has top priority. Knowing that his wife is on his side will dilute problems and difficulties to a greater extent than most wives think possible.

People who are in love, who are genuinely tuned in to each other, who operate on the same emotional frequency, will genuinely be concerned about each other's welfare. A wife who loves her husband will not view these measures to save his life as demeaning to her. Preserving a husband's health and life will be considered an enhancement of her femininity and will elevate her own self-esteem. Aside from the obvious values involved, a life-saving wife will also reap the benefits of increased family communication and emotional security. The steps she takes to ease her husband's life will almost always ease her own by alleviating family tension and improving family morale. People who help others to function better always benefit personally. They develop realistic values rather than glory-seeking, self-destructive ones. A marriage that is people oriented, a marriage that puts an emphasis on "him" and "her" rather than "things," "accomplishments" or "possessions," is invariably a life-affirming relationship. The dos and don'ts given here merely make it more so.

Why Won't Some Husbands Talk to Their Wives?

Most wives—particularly those who have been married for several years—complain that their husbands won't talk to them. "No matter how I try to get my husband to talk," said one wife, "he just grunts and buries his head in a newspaper." Another wife revealed, "My husband tells his friends all kinds of interesting and important things, but he never lets me in on anything. He treats me like the village idiot." Still another wife told me, "My husband comes home from the office, eats, turns on the television set, and falls asleep. We haven't talked in years."

The statements vary but the complaints all suggest a serious breakdown in husband-wife communication.

What causes such breakdowns? Though each marriage is different, there are certain factors involved that are common to many marriages. I will list the most prevalent. It is important to remember, however, that more than one of these factors can be involved.

1. Couples who married even though they had very little in common and, in fact, never had anything to talk about.

2. Couples who started married life with common interests but who have taken radically divergent routes. As a result, one partner has grown intellectually and emotionally, while the other has remained stagnant.

3. Men who have enormous emotional and intellectual investments in their jobs. These men feel that their wives don't share their all-important interest. Some of these men remain preoccupied with business after they arrive home at night. Since they feel that sharing their preoccupation with business would bore their wives, they'll think silently about business matters instead of talking them over with their wives.

4. Men (and women) who impose and sustain silence to frustrate, irritate or punish their spouse for some supposed hurt.

5. Men who feel that their wives don't really care about what they have to say. The attitude of these men is, "My wife doesn't really listen to what I say, so why bother to say it?"

6. Couples who suffer from "pride deadlocks" in which they feel that the first one to break the silence and talk will be the first one to lose face.

7. Men who believe that women "don't really understand" politics, business, economics, etc., and do not feel that these subjects can be discussed with women.

8. Men who feel that it is unmanly to share difficulties, anxieties, and worries with their wives. These men feel compelled to sit in silent desperation rather than talk and seek reassurance and comfort from their wives.

9. Men who won't talk because on previous occasions talking has led to emotional outbursts. Some men feel that tears and emotional displays on their part are evidence of weakness. These men are also

afraid of wives who scream or weep as a result of a conversation or argument.

10. Men who feel chronic resentment toward their wives because they view a wife as a symbol of adult responsibility and lack of bachelor freedom. These feelings may exist only on a subconscious level, but they still can produce hostility and chronic silence.

11. Men who come home too drained and exhausted to talk. When they face a wife who insists on talking about daily household or child problems, these men resent it and become silent.

12. Men who use silence and withdrawal as prime defenses against anxiety and depression. Some of these men (and women), find it most difficult to talk at the very times that talking would lead to emotional release, support, and relief. In these instances, some spouses will assume that they are responsible for their partner's silence when, in truth, they are not.

What is the best way to deal with an uncommunicative husband?

As with most difficulties in relating, it is best to recognize the symptoms and to treat lack of communication before it becomes a real problem. Young couples must make a conscious effort to communicate in the widest possible areas from the very beginning of their relationship.

They should realize, however, that there will be individual interests that they do not share, but this gap must not be widened by labeling these disparate interests "male" or "female." Sharing information on a level that includes both sexes is most valuable. A wife who excludes herself from her husband's professional or business interests is courting future difficulties. While she may never be as expert as he is in his particular line of work, she may still become sufficiently knowledgeable to be able to conduct a conversation on the subject.

Couples must converse from the very beginning of their relationship if they are to have a common communicating language. By that I mean a language that includes common interests, emotional investment, and understanding. It is important that they have a language that easily conveys hostilities, fears, problems, worries, loves, appetites, etc. I feel that this kind of common language cannot happen or develop without practice. This vital practice cannot take place if a couple is constantly preoccupied with television, entertaining other people, etc. A couple must be alone together to practice talking together about their interests in and away from the home.

Early attacks of silence by either partner must be breached immediately. These silences must not be permitted to deteriorate into "pride deadlocks," where both persons become too proud to break the ice and talk. Early silences must also be discussed so that the silent partner immediately sees the destructive potential of his refusal to talk. If early intervention does not take place there is danger of establishing a chronic pattern of a "battle of the sexes" that can lead to future marriage problems.

When I speak of husband and wife communication, I am not talking about, nor do I recommend, idle chatter. I am talking about a husband and a wife communicating important things to each other. Some can do it in a few words, others need more words to say what they feel. The important thing here is not the number of words but the meaning those words express.

If a wife feels that her husband is not talking, that he is not conveying how he feels about things that are important to her and to him, she must tell him. This is the only way remedial action can take place. If the wife is too proud to tell her husband or interprets his failure to communicate as a rejection of her, she may be missing an opportunity for genuine closeness. If she can help him to talk— that is, to break through his silence and verbal inhibition—she will be helping him, and her marriage, immeasurably.

This kind of assistance will be enormously relieving to the would-be "silent partner" and will help to establish lifelong loyalty, friendship, and interest between both relating partners.

Breaking through a husband's silence is particularly important if his reason for not talking is because he feels it is unmanly to share problems with a wife. A husband who feels this way has usually been confused by the pressures of society about what is masculine and what is not. The husband obviously feels it is masculine to sit and suffer in silence, but that is it not masculine to talk over problems with a woman.

In truth, all human beings have problems and pressures and all human beings need to seek support, sympathy and relief from their problems through talking with other people. Advice is neither masculine nor feminine—nor is the act of seeking advice masculine or feminine.

Such silence on the husband's part is a form of "pride deadlock."

It is important that the wife break through the deadlock and help her husband to relieve his pressures through talk. In addition to feeling relief, the husband will also come to realize that a wife's advice is invaluable. He will view her as a true helpmate and realize that together they are a team. He will see that they are working for the same goals (mutual happiness), that they are two people traveling on the same track rather than two individuals on two parallel tracks never interfering with each other, but never "touching" each other (communicating with each other), either. When a husband and wife travel on the same track, they *must* communicate; when they take separate tracks, they cannot—they become "silent partners."

Unfortunately, many couples have been silent partners for too many years. In these cases, the communicating process has been permitted to deteriorate. Often these silences thinly cover chronic cynicism, suspicion, and hostility. But here, too, the only "cure" is talking—and developing (or reactivating) the habit of mutual communication of feelings. Such reactivation is possible, but first the couple must honestly and openly discuss their differences, complaints, hurts, and misunderstandings. Sometimes such complete airings are possible only through the intervention of a psychotherapist.

Cases of long-standing chronic silence need mediation by a third party to break emotional freeze-ups or long-standing "pride deadlocks." Sometimes an objective mutual friend can be very helpful. Very often, however, regular visits to a psychiatrist trained in family therapy may be necessary to reestablish a constructive, verbal communicating process. If two people still retain common interests and a basis for relating, remedial intervention can be very helpful and, logically, the sooner the better. However, for even professional intervention to help, it is vital that both partners have some minimal interest and motivation in each other's well-being and happiness.

Q: *Do all new brides cry a lot? I got married only three months ago, and since then I've had tears in my eyes at least four or five times a week. I should be very happy. I was poor and I married a law student whose family is very wealthy—his father just gave us a beautiful new luxury apartment. I have everything a girl could possibly want, including a sweet, handsome, understanding husband. Am I crazy?*

A: You certainly are not crazy. Your excellent assessment of the merits of your current situation, as well as your recognition of feelings that something is amiss, are ample evidence of that.

Changes in status always require personal adjustments and adaptation. These adjustments take time, patience, and compassion—with ourselves and others. While a change "for the better" may well be appreciated, it is nevertheless a change, and we must understand that it takes time to shift one's emotional center of gravity.

Marriage always involves major changes that have a traumatic effect—no matter how loving and compatible the people involved are. For serious and sensitive women, marriage has great symbolic value. It signals the beginning of real adulthood and the surrender of many cherished childhood fantasies. Marriage also entails the beginning of greater responsibility—and this realization often creates new emotional pressures. Learning to live with another person in closer proximity than ever before is never easy. It involves social, economic, and sexual adjustments on every level. Your marrying into a wealthy family has obvious assets, but this too requires all kinds of adjustments. Until these adjustments are made, there will be periods of self-doubt, anxiety, and guilt. Tears and moodiness are very often a natural, healthy outlet for, and response to, all these new strains. When adjustments to new situations, especially marriage, are particularly long and difficult, psychotherapy may be very helpful.

Q: *My husband is more involved with his parents, brothers, and sisters than he is with his own family. He is a fine husband and a good father to our children, but he is a better son and brother. I am irritated by his constant visits and attention to his "other" family. I don't want him to ignore his parents, but I feel that the majority of his time and efforts should go to me and our children. Am I right?*

A: Many men and women never quite make the emotional break with their parents. These sons and daughters have an unconscious need to continue to be children rather than a need to be adult—even though they may seem to be adults because they have wives and children of their own. In a sense, each husband (or wife) has two families: spouse and children comprise one family; parents and brothers and sisters comprise the other. I feel that very few men and women are capable of simultaneously maintaining equal involvement with both groups. One "family" has to take second place. Mature people will be primarily interested in their own spouse and children first; parents, sisters, and brothers will be put in second place. Neither "family" will be ignored in the life of a well-adjusted person. Complete involvement with one's wife and family—to the total exclusion of one's parents and siblings—also indicates immaturity.

Q: *My husband and I are worried about the man our twenty-two-year-old daughter has chosen to marry. His faults are obvious to us, yet our daughter is very happy and going ahead with her wedding plans. Should my husband and I speak our mind, or should we keep quiet?*

A: You must use your own judgment here. However, if you do decide to voice your objections, do so in such a way that you do not break off all communication with your daughter. As parents, you should be able to tell her what you think—and at twenty-two, she should be mature enough to understand this. She should listen to your objections, think them over, then come to her own conclusion. And when you "speak your mind," be sure you don't do it so vehemently that you close forever the door between you and your daughter. Such action can only lead to heartache for everyone.

Q: *My twenty-three-year-old daughter is living with a young man. They are very much involved with each other and say they are having a "trial marriage." My husband thinks the arrangement is very constructive, but I'm appalled by what my daughter is doing. What do you think of trial marriage?*

A: I think much depends on the two people involved. If they do not feel as stigmatized, immoral, etc., as you obviously feel, then less harm will come from this trial marriage than from a disastrous legal marriage. If, however, the two young people secretly harbor moralistic feelings about sex without marriage, then the arrangement can engender considerable self-hate and depression at a later date in their lives. Living together in a sustained, mutually responsible, mutually caring and concerned relationship results in greater gratification and growth than a series of fleeting, nonrelating liaisons. Living together is the ultimate test of a relationship. This arrangement inevitably reveals much to all concerned as to the advisability of "making it legal."

Interestingly, some people can relate successfully only if they are not legally married. Legalizing their relationship—signing a marriage contract and telling the world about it—produces intolerable coercive feelings and generates such fear and anxiety that the marriage fails.

Q: *Why would a young, attractive woman who literally "has everything" marry a man twenty-five years older than herself?*

A: To understand her motivations, we would have to know something about the young woman's personal history. Details, for example, concerning her childhood family life and emotional development. Much would depend on her early relationship with her parents and siblings, her fantasies, and the image she has of herself. Let me list a few theoretical possibilities. One or a combination might shed light on the question.

1. Some highly intellectualized young women are minimally affected by chronological age. They view adults of all ages equally and are chiefly concerned with areas of common interest. Such young women will marry a man of any age, so long as there seems to be sufficient common ground to sustain an interesting intellectual relationship. This is often a marriage between teacher and student, virtuoso and protégé.

2. Some people regard marriage as a secure socioeconomic base, which frees them to explore and experiment with other partners. For these women, economic and social standing are more important than age or physical attraction in choosing a husband.

3. Some very cynical, world-weary young women marry an older man in a spirit of surrender and resignation.

4. Young women with powerful unconscious residuals of unrequited and unresolved childhood yearnings for their fathers often seek father substitutes. They sometimes confuse age with fatherliness.

5. A very dependent, self-effacing, insecure young woman may seek an older man as a mate—here confusing age with dependability, strength, and security.

6. The young woman who seeks the most inappropriate mate possible as a vindictive act, in order to shock, hurt, and dismay her parents, may choose an older man. Inevitably she suffers from much self-hate.

7. A highly narcissistic, expansive woman with insatiable yearnings (hidden or apparent) for power and position may marry a man of any age who can fulfill her childhood fantasy. This woman (unconsciously) sees herself as queen of the world, and her prime ambition is to marry the king. Age is no barrier. She identifies with and marries the man who most represents prestige and power.

Q: *My five-foot, two-inch daughter is marrying a man who is a full foot taller than she is. My grandmother always used to say that ideal marriage partners should be the same size. Is there any truth to this idea?*

A: Absolutely none.

Q: *My husband looks at other women all the time. He doesn't do more than that. He just looks. I'm not even sure it upsets me. I would like to know the significance. We've been married over fifteen years, have two lovely children, and we are very happy. He is a devoted husband, but he just can't resist looking at attractive women. What do you think?*

A: I think you ought to count your blessings. Your husband apparently reacts as most of the normal male population does. He enjoys looking at attractive women. This makes it possible for him to have a very happy relationship with you, too. He "looks" with your complete awareness. He has nothing to hide. Neither marriage nor love precludes curiosity, a response to attractiveness, and an appreciation of beauty. His "looking" is not evidence of impending infidelity, lack of love, or lack of attraction to you. It demonstrates a healthy reaction to the opposite sex, of which you apparently continue to be his favorite representative. Please remember that "looking" is a relatively superficial activity. You clearly have a great deal in common, including two children and mutual happiness. You have obviously lived up to his expectations of what a deep relationship with a woman would be like. His gratitude enhances his esteem for all women (you included), and he continues to look at and admire them.

Q: *My husband sees other women. He says he loves me, but just can't help himself. Maybe I'm a fool, but I believe him. We've been married twenty years, and there have been fights and separations, all based on this. I always take him back, because he is otherwise a good husband, a wonderful father, and really a great guy. I guess I love him. He tells me that other women don't mean anything to him, but he can't say no. Why is this? Are most men this way? Do you think a doctor could help him?*

A: Most men are not this way. Since people are not saints, nearly all people, men and women alike, will have all kinds of temptations and "opportunities." Some will resist temptation; others will not. This depends on the individual person's history, values, levels of maturity, and health.

As with nearly all human behavior, promiscuity, too, can be understood only in terms of the individual in question. A few of the dynamics we find, separately and often in combination, in "compulsive sexual acting out" are as follows:

1. Men who had an unfortunate relationship with the first woman in their lives—namely, their mothers.

2. Men who have great contempt for women and see them as objects to be used and discarded. Some of these men cannot have a satisfactory sexual encounter with a woman whom they respect.

3. Men who have great feelings of inadequacy and doubts regarding their masculinity.

4. Men who fear close, sustained involvements and relationships and to whom many affairs represent a continued state of "freedom."

5. Men who are very immature—who cannot say no to any potential offer of momentary pleasure—who are looking for a better mother again and again and again.

A psychiatrist can help, *but* he can help only if the patient wants help. Motivation is all important. People who have been promiscuous for a lifetime seldom want help for this condition alone. If they seek help, it is usually because of severe anxiety or depression. This sometimes happens when they can no longer attract members of the opposite sex or when their wives carry out the threat to abandon them.

I am not suggesting that you leave your husband. Many people have compromised and live in less than perfect harmony. But professional help has sometimes been very helpful to the *mate* of the compulsively promiscuous person.

Q: *I have a friend whose husband beats her when he's had too much to drink. The woman is quite pleasant, but I think she must be a little "sick" (if I may use that word) to put up with this abuse. I have witnessed the beatings as well as the mornings after, when both of them walk around as if nothing had happened. I know it is usually unwise to interfere in other people's lives, but I want to help. What can you say on this subject that will help my friend— and me?*

A: The relationships between abusive alcoholics and their wives —or alcoholic wives and their husbands—are very common neurotic situations. Some complain bitterly to friends, but, at the same time, do everything possible to maintain a sick status quo. I know a woman who has married three times and "somehow" she has always managed to marry an abusive alcoholic. While the underlying motivation may well be unconscious, the choice of a sick mate and a subsequent sick marriage was certainly intentional and not "accidental." Some unfortunate people can only feel "useful and acceptable" in the role of martyr. Some can only assuage guilt feelings and self-hate by choosing a partner who will inflict verbal and even physical abuse on them. Some can have sex only after being "stimulated" by such abuse.

Your friend may well be using you as an audience to further effect stimulation and excitement. If you interfere, you may find your friend resentful; she may even attack you and defend her husband. Should your friend openly ask for help, you may refer her to Alcoholics Anonymous, which maintains an organization for helping spouses of people suffering from alcoholism. A.A. members recognize the need for help on all levels and are well acquainted with the fact that sick people attract each other and maintain sick relationships. Until your friend asks, however, you would be wise to extricate yourself from audience participation. Your refusal to be exploited in this exhibitionistic activity may give your friend confidence in your wisdom so that she may ask you for advice.

Q:　*My husband died eight years ago. I'm remarried and fairly happy, but I periodically think of my first husband and sometimes feel a longing for him. In view of my present happiness, is this longing abnormal? Shouldn't I have gotten over my first husband by now?*

A:　Being human, we never completely "get over" anyone or anything meaningful in our lives. It is completely human to recall meaningful moments and important relationships. Though we go on with our lives, there is no reason for us to eradicate past emotionally laden areas of our lives. To try to do so would be an imposition on the human condition.

Q:　*I have a friend—my husband—who can't understand why vacations are so important to me. I just feel so much better about us, and the kids too, when we go off for a few days alone. Is this such a crazy way to feel?*

A:　Absolutely not! It is exceedingly important for adults to get off by themselves, particularly if they can go away to a different environment. There is little as relaxing as leaving cares and kids at home periodically. It helps romance and morale and also makes for better mothers and fathers. It invariably makes *home*, wherever it may be, that much more appealing.

Q:　*After fifteen years of marriage, by husband has decided to take a vacation alone. He is going back to Europe for two weeks. He has not been there since he left before we were married. He says the trip will be strictly a visit with family and old friends, and that I'd be bored since I don't speak the language. I don't mind*

staying home—since he obviously doesn't want me to go—but don't
you think his behavior odd?

A: No, I don't think it is odd. Sometimes, when resuming old
relationships and tapping nostalgic feelings from the past, a person
prefers to be alone. You should not interpret your husband's wish
to be alone at this time as a lack of love for you. Also, you should
not feel that he is ashamed of you or doesn't want to introduce you
to his friends and family. It will obviously be a difficult emotional
time for him and for reasons he probably doesn't even understand
himself, he prefers to face this situation alone.

Q: *We were terribly shocked when we heard that our best friends*
are getting divorced. They've been married for twelve years, and
there's been no outward sign of any great difficulty. The husband
met another woman about six months ago, and away he goes, even
though they have two lovely young children. This is about the
tenth time I've heard such a story, only it's never been so close.
I just don't understand how a man can suddenly break up a family
for this kind of thing.

A: Some very immature men and women do not relate on anything that even resembles a more than superficial level. They flit
in and out of relationships and often find marriage a burdensome,
contractual arrangement. However, your friends have been married
for twelve years, so we can assume their relationship was, at least
at one time, stronger than the relationships very immature people
can establish. Then why did the husband break up his family for
another woman? Again, this did not happen suddenly. The other
woman may have been the catalyst; but chances are your friends'
marriage had been in difficult straits for many years, despite no
outward manifestations of "great difficulty." Had there been a firmer
relationship and a relatively satisfying marriage, the affair with the
other woman probably would never have reached serious proportions and might never have begun at all.

Q: *I can always tell when my husband has had a bad day at*
the office because he comes home grumpy and angry and gives me

a difficult time. I know when he's had a bad day, but why does he take it out on me?

A: Your husband is obviously displacing his emotional reaction from an area where he feels threatened (the office) to an area where he feels safe enough to open up and let go (his home). While this is unfair to you, it is an indication of his trust and faith in your relationship. All men cannot cry or ask for help when they are frightened or "down." These men displace their feelings and turn them into outbursts of anger, rage, or vindictiveness. Men do this in order to get rid of the feelings of self-hate they have generated because they feel helpless and vulnerable. Most of us find it easy to comfort a person in tears, but many of us shy away from a person who is angry. Unfortunately, many an angry person is "crying inside" and is in need of comfort and warmth.

Q: *My husband and I would be very happy if you could solve a problem. Whenever I lie down on my living room sofa at night— regardless of whether I'm reading a book, watching TV or listening to music—I fall off into a wonderful, sound sleep. When my husband awakens me at about 12:30 A.M., to go to bed, I can't fall back asleep. I toss and turn until daybreak, and only manage to go to sleep just before I have to get up again. Is there an explanation for my behavior?*

A: There are several possibilities for your rather common behavior.

1. Falling asleep on the sofa is a relaxed, spontaneous act. It is secondary to another act (in this case, to listening to records, watching TV, or reading) that automatically removes the pressure of your having to go to sleep. This lack of pressure also provides a lack of self-consciousness about falling asleep. Once you are undressed and in bed, this self-consciousness returns. Getting to sleep then becomes of prime importance—a test, a fight, a burden. How long will it take? How deep a sleep will you fall into? All of these anxiety-provoking matters destroy the possibility of natural sleep. What would help here is for you to stop fighting your inability to sleep and to adopt a casual attitude about it ("So what if I can't sleep? I've had other sleepless nights and I'll have them again.")

2. Your ability to fall asleep is dissipated on the sofa instead of in your bed. After you awake from your sofa sleep, you must get up, undress, get in bed, and test your ability to fall asleep all over again. Falling asleep once a night is enough for anyone who suffers from insomnia. Therefore, it is a good idea to forego sofa sleeping and go directly to bed. It is best not to wait for overwhelming fatigue, which can cause enough pain and stimulation to keep you awake.

3. Some women (and men) don't like to go to sleep in a bed with their mate, so they fall asleep alone on a sofa. These marital-sexual problems require resolution before sofa sleeping can be cured.

4. Many people sleep better in their clothes because being dressed and ready for any eventuality gives them a greater sense of security and, therefore, increases the possibility of relaxation. Books and music are helpful sedatives—as is TV, which also functions as a hypnotic.

5. Some people feel safer and easier at daybreak, when everything seems lighter and brighter. These people will fool themselves into believing that they are using the sofa as a place to nap or rest a while, when in reality they are using it for the night sleeping they fear. Once dawn approaches, these people can dare to face their beds for what they call "real sleep."

Q: *My wife gets terribly hurt if I don't get home to dinner on time. I think her hurt is all out of proportion. If I am late, the food is cold. But I do not complain. So why should she?*

A: Many women go to great pains to prepare a proper meal to please their husbands. For most women, cooking represents considerable creative effort as well as feeling of involvement and concern for their family. The act of sitting down to dinner together represents family unity, interest, and involvement. Coming late to dinner, therefore, is often felt as contempt for the wife's creative efforts as well as for her position as a homemaker. Men who have a hidden need to thwart and frustrate their wives manifest this by being constantly late for meals. Men who cannot accept wifely efforts made in their behalf—unconsciously feeling that this makes for too much closeness and the feeling of being possessed and smothered—are also chronically late to the table.

Your own "need" to wait for a warm dinner to become cold before you come home may be an attempt to cool your wife's feelings. Your wife's irritation may be entirely appropriate to the real feelings going on between you, symbolized by your seemingly careless but perhaps carefully calculated attitude toward the food (her symbol of love) she prepares.

Q: *My husband is totally preoccupied with baseball. It is really one of his great passions. I am, in fact, a "baseball widow." Any cure? I mean, for him?*

A: This is a well-known condition, endemic to North America. It can provide the kind of relaxation that follows total involvement, absorption, and enjoyment. The hours this costs you each week may well be worth it in terms of mitigating daily tension and real illness. This can also help make your husband an easier and pleasanter fellow to live with. All this *if* you don't nag and make him feel guilty for neglecting you in favor of baseball. It could help if you would learn about the game and would participate with him occasionally in his "great passion."

Q: *My husband absolutely refuses to wear a wedding band. He says he doesn't know why, but that he just feels degraded by it. He claims that it has nothing to do with me. He doesn't flirt with other women, etc., and I'm sure that he does not attempt to give the impression that he is single. I'm not really adamant on the subject, but I can't help wondering why he feels this way.*

A: Some men see a wedding band as a symbol of being too conventional, of being caught or trapped, or of being old. In short, it hurts their masculine pride to wear one. Others simply see it as a type of uniform, since everybody else wears one. As such, they experience it as a blow to their individuality.

There are other men who feel that marriage and the closeness and responsibility it brings are too burdensome and constricting for them. They love their wives and children, but want no extra reminders of their marital status.

It is possible that your husband does not want to wear the ring because he unconsciously does not want to connect you (his loved one) with conventional symbols that he dislikes.

Q: *Why can women tolerate more pain, inconvenience, problems, etc., than men can? My husband had a small operation recently (hernia repair), and like all men I have known, he was a fussy, generally awful patient.*

A: This is probably a myth created by shrewd women. I have seen ample evidence of low and high levels of tolerance—for pain, etc.—in both sexes. *But* women have the advantage of many years of tolerance acclimatization. Think of the years of wearing tight girdles, high heels, uncomfortable and unseasonable clothes, to which they subject themselves. Men do not have the advantage of pain dished out in small packages throughout their lives.

Seriously, though, you will find that men are often more afraid of helplessness than of pain, etc. Our peculiar culture allows and even condones helplessness in women. But men are persuaded that they must never under any circumstances permit such feelings.

P.S. The postoperative days following a hernia repair can be quite uncomfortable. Also, some men unconsciously regard any surgical procedure close to the genital area as threatening.

Q: *You keep saying that a wife shouldn't nag, but what else can a woman do about a husband who puts off doing everything until he is nagged into it? My husband handles his job well, but at home he just wants to sit and read while bills go unpaid, our checkbook isn't balanced, and correspondence is neglected. Once I tried not to nag him about paying our auto insurance premium. He forgot—and our coverage lapsed. He couldn't drive until I had the policy reinstated, but even that didn't cure him. I am more efficient than my husband, which tempts me to take over these chores, but we both feel strongly that the man should handle money matters. What can I do?*

A: Some people can't face certain responsibilities, especially those involving money. Coping with money matters, particularly with unpaid bills, can bring on feelings of insecurity, worry, and anxiety. Nagging may get your husband to do something you want him to do, but it does not resolve the basic problems. Instead, it almost always has an aggravating effect and only serves to break down needed communication between husband and wife.

I certainly see nothing demeaning to either a husband or a wife if the wife handles the family's money matters. I do not categorize these important activities as male or female; I do not think it would reduce either your femininity or your husband's masculinity should you take over these necessary chores. Being efficient, as you put it—that is, being able to handle family business matters with ease and dispatch—is also neither male nor female. Some people are just better suited to this type of work than others. As with any partnership, it is efficient and realistic for each partner to be in charge of those activities for which he or she has talent rather than dislike.

I think it would be helpful for you and your husband to do these chores together; your support may make your husband feel more secure. However, if sharing this responsibility doesn't work out, I think it entirely appropriate for you to become chairwoman of these particular activities.

CHAPTER 9

Child-Rearing

Bringing a child into the world is one of the most fulfilling, exciting, and joyful acts of parenthood. When a child is planned for, eagerly awaited, and encouraged in each step of the growing process, he or she has the best opportunity to mature into a healthy, interesting adult. But parenthood is difficult: it is a huge responsibility and it usually occurs when a man and woman are only just beginning to adapt to each other in married life. The unexpected addition of a child to a family can pose many problems if the parents are ambivalent about the birth.

Allowing one's children to become separate individuals and not forcing them into becoming carbon copies of their parents is an important factor in the growth process of an entire family. Overprotective parents who smother their offspring with too much care and solicitude can cause many problems in a child's later life. Do you, as a parent, know when to "let go?" What about decisions as to how much television is too much, how to start in on sex education, how to explain divorce or adoption?

Parents must also realize that they themselves are separate individuals and that the children must not rule the roost. Taking vacations from the family can be an excellent idea for a couple, and being away from the children for a period of time each day can allow a family to grow closer together rather than farther apart. Parents are, of course, ultimately responsible for their child's wellbeing during the early years, but a good parent-child relationship involves a gradual acceptance of each other's separate lives, identities, and needs.

Allowing Your Children to Leave Home

Children must leave home, just as they must grow up, have children, and then let their own children grow up and leave home. Leaving home is not a sudden thing. Children start to leave home at birth, when the umbilical cord is cut and the baby becomes an individual human being, separate and apart from mother.

There are two stages of leaving home. Leaving home physically (moving out) is the first step; it is important because physical separation teaches children to cope with practical realities. It has a powerful symbolic meaning to all concerned.

Leaving home also means making the enormous transition from being one with mother (as in the womb) to becoming an individual. It is a key step in the development of an utterly dependent infant, who becomes a toddler and makes small, independent choices and decisions. Next he becomes a small child, and then an adolescent, who often plays at leaving home by spending more and more time with friends. Eventually, the child becomes an adult who marries, has children and establishes a separate family unit.

For complete individual and emotional development to occur, a child must leave home. One must leave home in order to develop values, identity, a sense of responsibility, good judgment, the ability to be in emotional conflict and to resolve that conflict. One must leave home in order to make choices and decisions, to relate to, and have sustained relationships with, members of the opposite sex, to invest emotionally in people, activities, and causes, to see reality well enough to fear what is dangerous and enjoy what is enjoyable. In short, one must leave home to become a relatively well-developed, adult human being.

If children have been encouraged to leave home, they will depart free of the debilitating guilt feelings so often generated by smothering parents. Free of guilt, they will always enjoy visits to their old homes. Because they left home freely and without overwhelming pain, visits and departures are not dreaded.

Overprotective or overpossessive parents seldom encourage or train their children to take those vital steps toward leaving home. Their overprotection destroys the self-esteem, self-acceptance, and self-confidence that are necessary to growing up. Overprotection stunts emotional growth and makes for future helplessness and despair. One of the most pitiful sights to see is a grown man or woman —grown up in age, at least—who is terrified of leaving the parents and their nest. Such "children" actually are the result of households in which relationships are severely aberrant and disturbed. Unfortunately, many such children do not come into psychotherapy until the death of their smothering parents, because only then do they realize that they cannot face the future alone. Long-term psychoanalytic treatment is usually necessary in these cases because such development and growth must take place before the patient can stand alone.

Now let's look at those parents who "hang on" to their children, who cannot let go. Such parents usually lack self-confidence and see their children purely as extensions of themselves; they also lack confidence in their children. Parents who "hang on" unwittingly incapacitate their children emotionally, and once the children are thus crippled, they must stay at home, where the parent can do for them what they cannot do for themselves.

Parents, like most people, try to avoid unfamiliar situations. Then, when the unfamiliar can no longer be avoided, there is much anxiety. The way parents avoid the unfamiliar is to do whatever they can to promote the family status quo. Many times parents are unaware of their resistance to change, particularly change in the family's psychological patterns. Some parents go so far as to deny the passage of time so they won't have to face feelings of insecurity. Time and its passing represent aging of all members of the family group, and aging makes for continuous change. This change takes place in our individual emotional lives and in our lives vis-à-vis all members of the family. In a family in which the members are relatively secure emotionally, changes in psychological patterns take place constantly, and required adjustments are made relatively smoothly. In insecure families, however, there is an attempt to magically freeze the status quo and to deny the passage of time and the changes that accordingly take place in relationships. It is sad to see mothers make infants of their children—to dress them in infantile clothing and to treat them as if they were years younger than they actually are. It is just as sad to see mothers dress like their teen-age daughters and attempt to take part in teen-age activities. Some parents feel painfully excluded and rejected when their children insist on healthy and appropriate privacy. Some feel excluded when their children prefer the company of their friends to the company of other family members.

Preparations for change and for leaving home—physically and emotionally—are best made early in a child's life. The family's emotional life must never be viewed as static. Parents should know that change must come—and, in fact, encourage it. The earlier parents accept change, the better it will be for them—and their children. Parents must actively help children to leave home, and help themselves to adjust to that departure. The saddest words I've ever heard are: "Now that the children are off on their own, what do we have to live for?" I have seen too many parents who feel this way—parents whose happiness at a child's wedding fades into sad statements like: "The house is dead and empty. We feel all alone!" Such sadness can lead to serious depression that has an unfortunate effect on both parents and children. This depression generates guilt in the adult children who, quite rightly, went off on their own. Sometimes parents try to use this kind of suffering to manipulate married children into living with them or visiting them with inordinate frequency. Such smothering makes children disgusted with their parents; it causes alienation instead of the desired closeness. When all maneuverings fail, the parents either get "sick" or seem to grow old overnight.

In my practice, I've seen many children who have been smothered by their parents. I almost always discover that the parents' attempt to "hang on" to their children has actually been going on since birth. It is always gratifying and surprising to come across a child who has somehow managed to break away from smothering parents in a healthy way. Unfortunately, many more such children never leave home, or leave in a most self-destructive, rebellious way, producing heartache for everyone.

Making an emotional investment in one's children is desirable. But making the kind of investment that excludes other emotional interests invariably turns out badly for all concerned. Parents must not neglect themselves—and each other—when children are born. What often happens in such cases is that husband and wife become disinterested in each other, with disastrous emotional consequences. As their children grow up, husbands and wives must make it a point to renew interest in each other. They must do more than that, too. Many parents have the awful misapprehension that they should be less and less involved with outside things as they grow older. Quite the contrary. As people get older and as the family keeps changing, parents need more and more mutual interests. It is most important for young couples to realize as soon as they have children that they must also continue to have lives of their own. Yes, devotion to children is important, but it is equally important for parents to make sure that they go off now and then to continue their own private lives and interests. Unless parents do this early in their family lives, they will be ill prepared to do it when their children depart.

It is also especially important for parents to continue to relate to their friends instead of becoming isolated from them once children are born. Generating meaningful friendships in later life is often more difficult and less satisfactory than relationships continued from early life. Too many people are "waiting for the children to grow up" so that they can "go out and do things we've always wanted to do." It is best to go out and do these things from the beginning— and to continue to do them as children take each step away from home.

If the preparation has been open and adequate, the separation that ensues when children leave home will be particularly gratifying. Of course, there may be a bit of anxiety and loneliness, but there will also be the satisfaction of a job well done. There will be the rewards that come from a new and most interesting kind of relationship between adult children and their parents. And there may be still greater involvement between husband and wife, the regeneration of old interests and the exploration of new ones that can bring still more gratification and happiness.

Q: *My wife would like me to be a total pal to our kids. She feels that we all ought to be friends and pretty much on an equal level. I disagree and we decided to ask you what you think.*

A: I agree with you. Friendship is important, but friendship between parents and children must not be forced to the level of friendship between contemporaries. It is important for a sense of reality, happiness, and well-being of all concerned to differentiate between the expertise, authority, maturity, and experience of parents and that of children. Emotional solidity and security suffer a considerable blow in people who feel that while growing up their parents were children themselves.

Q: *We have only one child—a little boy ten years old—who was born twelve years after we were married. I am afraid to let him cross streets alone, and I'm very careful with him generally. My husband feels strongly about my "letting go," and frankly this has*

*become a source of considerable irritation between us. Is it really
so bad to be very protective of a child?*

A: Yes. Too much protection can be just as destructive as
neglect. It destroys a child's potential for individual growth, individual identity, and self-esteem. He grows up feeling fragile and
crippled, inhibited sometimes to the point of paralysis in regard to
many life activities and relationships.

Overprotection is often confused with love. While love may also
be present, it is certainly never love that produces overprotection.
Difficulty in having a child, an only child, likewise has little effect
in this regard. Overprotection is the result of great anxiety in a
mother who sees herself and her child as fragile and vulnerable in an
overwhelmingly junglelike, dangerous world. Recognizing that you
are overprotecting a child is in itself constructive. But it is not
enough. A mother who "must" overprotect her child is in need of
expert help. The sooner this help is instituted, the better for all
concerned.

Q: *I have a friend who is eighteen years old and who was terribly
overprotected as a child. Her parents watched her all the time and
barely let her move without hovering over her and making sure she
was safe. After three months away at college, she had a nervous
breakdown. She is back home now and seems all right but is afraid
to try an out-of-town school again. What do you think?*

A: Your friend's reaction is a very common one, especially in
young people who have a background of overprotection. Parents
rationalize this overprotection or "smothering" by professing great
love for the overprotected child. While love may or may not be
present, overprotection is not born of love. It is the result of parental insecurities and anxieties. It is used in an attempt to allay the
parents' own fears and is ultimately very destructive to the child. In
effect, the child is made to feel that she is not trusted, that she must
not trust herself, that she is vulnerable and fragile in a potentially
hostile world. It destroys the possibility of developing self-confidence and self-esteem. It convinces her that she cannot possibly
make it as a separate, whole individual but must always be de-

pendent upon her parents. Smothering curtails and often prevents the formation of a child's own feelings, values, and opinions. When the victim leaves home, she feels that she is leaving her lifeline since, she thinks, she is only half a person without the immediate presence of her parents.

Fortunately your friend is young. I'd call her reaction a "breakup" rather than a breakdown. It is probably a "breakup" of the old and sick ways of relating to herself and other people. Most importantly, with the right kind of help she can go on to develop her various potentials so that she becomes a truly mature and whole individual, secure in her emotional well being. Consultation with a psychoanalytically trained psychiatrist would be best. There is no point in leaving home precipitously. After she and her doctor have worked together and agree that she is really ready to do so, it will undoubtedly be most beneficial to "make the break."

Q: *I have recently heard that there is an increase in sexual crimes against children. How can a mother tell a seven-year-old daughter to protect herself without making her generally distrustful of people?*

A: Let me list a number of significant facts involved in this problem.

1. Hard as this may be to believe, most "sexual crimes against children" are committed by people they know. Close relatives are often involved, and these acts often take place in the child's home.

2. A seven-year-old child is very much attuned to the sexual atmosphere in his household. His own sexual attitudes, while they may be hidden, will nevertheless reflect much that is going on around him. Many parents are unwittingly stimulating, exhibitionistic, seductive, markedly Victorian and repressed, regard talk about sex as dirty, talk sex constantly, and so on.

3. Many sex crimes are committed against children who are sexually seductive and teasing. Some of these children are in fact acting out the unconscious desires of the adults who are around them.

4. Old-fashioned, honest straight talk about strangers and not going with them or accepting gifts from them or talking to them when no one else is around, is still good and necessary. It is also

important to know where and with whom a young child is, and this includes boys as well as girls. *But* this does not include gratuitous descriptions of frightening sexual details, forced daily lectures, or constant overprotection.

5. Children do not easily become distrustful of people. When they do, this is more often the result of emotional problems in the home than a few practical warnings about strangers. Parental cynicism regarding people, parental insecurity, and poor self-esteem on the part of the child all contribute to his seeing himself as fragile and vulnerable in a world that is primarily hostile.

Q: *Do you believe it's better to give a child sex education at home or in school?*

A: If it is *good* sex education—in both places. Children will learn at home from their parents' attitudes. If their parents have a healthy attitude toward sex and if they have real affection for each other, this will inevitably be conveyed to their children. Stilted, prissy, sadistic, or exhibitionistic parental sexual feelings and actions will also be conveyed and will have destructive effects.

School is an excellent place for providing all kinds of formal learning, and sex is no exception. Here as in other areas education is best conveyed by the educated.

Q: *My wife is constantly worried that she is not a good enough mother. Our three children, aged nine, twelve and fourteen, are perfectly fine and normal in every way. They are really wonderful kids, but should they have any problems whatsoever, my wife chastises herself terribly, feeling that she is a failure as a mother. Would you care to comment on what gives?*

A: Some women are more concerned about their reputations as "good mothers" than they are about the reality of their situations. Sometimes this concern about reputation robs a mother of real interest and insight into what her children are all about. This preoccupation with being a good mother often has little to do with the children at all. It is usually based on guilt feelings—often arising from roots in the mother's own childhood. The ideal of "good mother" is usually based on unrealistically perfectionist demands that cannot possibly be fulfilled. Failure to meet these impossible criteria results in feelings of guilt, attacks of self-hatred, and renewed efforts to mitigate guilt through further impossible strivings. Sadly, this mother will be cut off from spontaneous feelings, which are so valuable in reaching children. Often psychotherapy is necessary so that the woman with this problem can become less *self*-conscious, and tune in to her children's needs. Then, she will be able to enjoy a less-than-perfect but more human relationship with them.

Q: *Our five-year-old son listens to his father, but he simply does not obey me—and it is getting worse. Is there any common rule I can apply? For instance, I had to go shopping the other day and my son simply wouldn't go with me. I had to wait until my husband got home.*

A: Children are quick to observe what is really going on, what people really feel, and they react accordingly. Your son probably identifies with your husband and may be imitating his attitude and behavior toward you. He may also be imitating your own attitude toward yourself. It may be most valuable if your husband does what he can to establish your authority in the house. If he undermines your authority in any way, his attitude will be conveyed to your son. You, too, must have sufficient self-respect to take responsibility for making decisions. Your child must not be allowed to take on the role of surrogate leader in his father's absence. Also, you must not postpone household decisions until your husband comes home. It is urgent that both you and your husband discuss matters and make every effort to establish you as a prime authority in the family.

Q: *My husband and I have been separated for more than a year. Despite my reassurances to the contrary, my seven-year-old daughter believes that her father left because of her. Why do youngsters blame themselves for the breakup of their parents' marriage?*

A: Your daughter's reaction is common. Some of the basic reasons for her behavior are:

1. By blaming herself for the separation, your daughter raises herself to the same level of importance as you in her father's life. Subconsciously, daughters are in competition with their mothers for their father's esteem. While being abandoned by a father brings sadness, it also brings bittersweet feelings of being important enough to have been abandoned in the first place—and often raises hopes of being more important to daddy than mother is.

2. Children equate presence with love and nonpresence with lack of love. Their logic is that if daddy isn't around it is because he doesn't love them enough to be there.

3. A child may feel that if a father left home because he didn't like mother, then he must also dislike that part of his child that is like mother. Daughters have particular difficulty on this score, because, as females, they identify so closely with their mothers. Little girls might also think that their fathers left home because they don't like women, and if fathers don't like women then they don't like daughters.

4. Very young children think in very personal, concrete terms: they see themselves as the world—they are the center of their own universe. (Grown-ups, hopefully, do not think this way!) Therefore, if a father is no longer present in that child's universe, it means he has deserted it—and the offspring—because of lack of love.

Q: *My husband teases all children—including our own. When I point out how annoying this is he just laughs and claims it is all in good fun. I'd like him to read whatever you say about grown-ups teasing children—and what it means.*

A: Teasing is a way of discharging hostility and sadism. Some adults will displace feelings of hostility onto children because they feel less threatened by them. Some grown-ups who tease children do so because it is the only way they know to make contact with the youngsters, or the only way they know to show affection. Many adults, especially men, simply don't know how to relate to children on any basis, and they are too embarrassed to make any ordinary or direct display of affection. Consequently, they take their feelings of affection and turn them into a tease—a process also commonly found among teen-agers who, when they are embarrassed by affectionate feelings toward each other, try to hide—yet express—this affection by mutual teasing.

Q: *My friends and I are shocked when we read about parents who beat, maim and even murder their children. What kind of person would do such a horrible thing?*

A: For years, doctors have been trying to interest the public, legal agencies, and officials in what is called "the battered child syndrome." Even though some parents do not treat their children properly, it is still very difficult legally to separate victimized children from their dangerous parents. To counteract this, new laws are needed. Until then, we should be aware of some common conditions that can lead to "dangerous parents" and battered children:

1. Psychopathic parents. These are people who do not operate with normal "conscience." Often they do not know right from wrong. They usually have a history of lying, stealing, or just getting into trouble. Society terms them "petty criminals." Ordinary judgment is beyond their capacity; their actions are based on "not getting caught" rather than on avoiding feelings of guilt. All psychopaths do not brutalize their children, but cruel, sadistic ones can cause disaster.

2. Psychotic parents. These severely disturbed people are greatly removed from reality and are just as likely to hurt themselves as hurt children. Many, of course, do not hurt anyone, but the very disturbed ones are too sick to have any idea of the consequences of a particular act. They may love children and they can be totally unaware of what they are doing. Some may batter children as part of a delusional religious belief: "to beat the devil out of them."

3. Mentally defective parents. Most mental defectives are not dangerous, but those with severe intellectual deprivation and emotional disturbances are. Occasionally these people can be damaging to themselves, others and especially to young, helpless children.

4. Alcoholic parents. Alcoholics often suffer from severely repressed rage. This rage sometimes unwittingly explodes during an alcoholic stupor. When the person sobers up, the misplaced rage is always regretted, but by then it is often too late.

5. Parents with brain disorders. Rare and peculiar neurological disorders can manifest themselves in uncontrollable temper tantrums.

In some cases, loud or irritating noise (a baby's screaming) can initiate a rage reaction similar to an uncontrollable convulsion. Such people cannot "stop" until they have exhausted themselves, physically. They do not "hate" their children and are often completely surprised to find they have hurt them, since their actions have taken place in a nearly unconscious "dream" state. They usually suffer profound regret after the "attack."

6. Other children. Many youngsters are beaten by other children. Quite "normal" parents may leave their babies in charge of older children or siblings who are not fit for this kind of responsibility. They will act out their confusion, jealousy, or envy by hurting their helpless charges.

Q: *Both my husband and I have careers that keep us quite busy. We have a daughter four years old. We see her evenings and spend our weekends together. But lately I've been feeling very guilty. It's true we have a warm and devoted housekeeper taking care of her. But I wonder if I shouldn't give up my work—even though it is terribly important to me. I know you can't tell me what to do, but do you have any special views on the subject?*

A: Many parents spend a good deal of time with their children but are really not there at all. Some parents spend relatively little time with their children but are really there. Physical presence is not enough. "Being there"—really being there, involved and tuned in—is what children require. Your constant physical presence, under duress, coupled with feelings of resentment would be a poor substitute for shorter periods of really being there and being involved.

Q: *We have two little boys, age seven and nine. We take many vacations with the children, but we also like to go off on a weekend together now and then without them. Friends tell me that this is not good for the children. What do you think?*

A: Provided they are well taken care of by somebody who really cares, I think it is good and necessary for both you and the children to part company now and then. Adults and children do not always share the same interests and activities. Adult couples do need each other's company, exclusive of children, at least once in a while. It makes them better lovers, happier people, and better parents—parents who are *really* there when they *are* with the children. Children, too, need periodic breaks from parental authority, so that they can initiate and practice the feeling of being separate and independent human entities.

Q: *My mother can't understand why I occasionally feel a desperate need to be away from my children for a few hours. My friend's mother was appalled that her daughter was not happy to discover she was pregnant only a few months after the birth of her second child. Can our mothers have forgotten some of the less "joyous" moments in child raising? Or are we currently less dedicated parents than our mothers were?*

A: They either forgot or actually deluded themselves into believing that they fulfilled an inhuman and impossible representation of motherhood. All people get fatigued, impatient, harassed, and fed up, and all people need privacy, time, and energy to be used exclusively for themselves. This includes mothers. Young women who realistically indulge their own needs as well as those of their children make the best mothers. Their own honest, open feelings about their own needs gives their children a strong sense of practical reality as regards human needs and limitations. Their children in turn, will have the ability to enjoy themselves without guilt. Totally self-sacrificing "saintlike," totally dedicated mothers project a sense of martyrdom and are almost invariably manipulative of their children through guilt. These mothers are usually extremely neurotic and are more interested in their reputation as mothers than in good mothering itself. One must be a good friend and parent to oneself before one can be a really worthwhile friend or parent to anyone else.

Q: *My sister and I are always arguing about the fact that she plunks her four-year-old child in front of the TV set all morning while she does her housework. I would feel guilty allowing my child to watch TV all morning. I would prefer an untidy house because I'd be calm in the knowledge that I have been involved with my child and have given him meaningful experience. Which of us is right?*

A: It is interesting to note that you accept your own guilt feelings about not spending time with your child, but you do not accept your sister's guilt feelings about an untidy house. Your sister may find that an untidy house is too anxiety-provoking for her to contend with in any other way than to clean it each day. She may then feel free to play with her child in a relaxed and enjoyable manner.

I do not feel that every moment of a child's day must be filled with meaningful activities. A child must have time to daydream and to be left to his own devices.

Q: *My seven-year-old granddaughter watches television every Saturday at noon. She lies on the couch and watches while my daughter gives her lunch. She eats and watches in a reclining position, not ever getting up to go to the table. Isn't there something awfully decadent about this?*

A: I don't know about decadence, but I do hope the child is careful not to choke, and I am serious.

Not eating at the table with the rest of the family certainly does not enhance family communication or family social harmony. Lying on a couch, eating, and watching television also indicate to me that your seven-year-old granddaughter is being spoon-fed fantasies as well as food. The television set provides ready-made fantasy. This does not enhance her ability to use her own imagination and ultimately will have a damaging effect on her creative spontaneity, her incentive, and her production.

Q: *I realize I've been very hard on my two kids lately whenever they've done anything wrong—harder than I would be on myself. Is it possible that I expect more self-control from my children than from myself?*

A: In their rightful desire to be respected by their children, parents often expect them to show too much self-control. It should be remembered that children are not "little adults." Children, especially young ones, have not yet developed the neurological and emotional mechanisms that enable grown-ups to show self-control. For example, a child's ability to tolerate frustration is much less than that of his or her parents. Remember, too, that children identify with and imitate their parents. Therefore, if you throw temper tantrums or use strong language, you must realistically expect the same behavior from your children. It is important to set limits to what children may and may not do. But it is unrealistic to expect them to exert as much, or more, self-control than you do.

Q: *My friend's husband insists on buying a dog for their two-year-old son. My friend thinks her son is too young for a dog and that the entire burden of taking care of the animal will fall on her. Since I denied my own young son a dog on the very same grounds, I wonder what you have to say on this subject. Are we being too selfish?*

A: There are probably more facets to this problem than you have indicated in your question. Generally, however, I can say that a two-year-old child does not need the companionship of a dog if that child is being properly cared for. This means adequate emotional involvement as well as physical care on the part of both parents. Moreover, the father's insistence on a dog would indicate that he desires a dog and is displacing this desire on to his son. If this is so, then the husband should be a real partner in the care of the puppy and all that it entails. You and your friend may seem selfish in not wanting the dog, but on the other hand you are probably being very realistic. Few women have the energy to care for a youngster and a puppy and still have strength enough to pursue their own interests—let alone the energy to be an interesting wife and homemaker.

Q: *Why does a child four and a half years old suddenly start soiling herself after months of being housebroken? Is there anything I can do about this?*

A: She may be looking for attention, protesting, or demanding help. Don't make a fuss. Do spend more time with her—exclusively, giving her your full undivided, *involved* attention.

Q: *Our four-year-old son is quite precocious. He talked and walked very early and is a warm, happy child. A friend read a book about teaching very young children to read—and she feels our son is an ideal subject, even though he is only in nursery school. My husband and I feel uneasy about pushing young children to read. How do you feel?*

A: I don't like the idea of pushing anyone, especially young children. I also feel that reading is best taught by professionals. Children vary, but all of them take time before their central nervous systems are developed enough to undertake certain activities without undue strain. Some children will ask and even insist on learning early—and this includes reading. To parents who are "tuned in," these children will also demonstrate a pace that is comfortable for them and appropriate to their age limitations (i.e., limited attention span). Other children's development and interest in learning will perk up when they are older. The eventual level of their attainment will have little to do with how *early* they started; it is more closely related to the household in which they are brought up. A love of books and reading is often contagious, especially if there is no early trauma induced by forced learning—which, by the way, is often used to bolster the parents' own neurotic pride.

Q: *In our five years of marriage, we have lived in six different places. We have a son, three years of age. My husband wants to change apartments again. What effect does all this moving have on a child?*

A: A child depends on his environment, more than an adult does, to give him a sense of identity and self. Consistency in place —particularly school—and people (teachers and friends) contributes to a feeling of security and identity. A constant necessity for readjustment to places and to people is difficult for a child and contributes to a sense of insecurity. All other things being equal, the child who was brought up in one place, one school, etc., will have greater security and greater adaptability when he gets older. Thus, changes will be easier for the adult who, as a child, did not have to change too often. Of course, a great deal will depend on the child's relationship to his parents—that is, the sense of acceptance and security he derives from them. Everything, including radical change, is much easier for the child whose parents are consistently tuned in to his individual needs and really care about him.

Q: *We are about to buy a new house. The one we like best would make us very happy, but is it in an old neighborhood with hardly any small children about. How important is it for a six-year-old boy to live where there are other children around to play with?*

A: *Where* a six-year-old lives is not as important as *how* he lives in relation to the people around him. What makes parents happy, particularly the mother of the family, is really significant. However, it is also important that young children have ample contact with boys and girls their own age. With the complications of modern living and with so much less free street playing than there used to be, mothers often have to be more active in seeing that their children have playmates. It doesn't matter so much where friends come from—school, the neighborhood, the local child center, more distant neighborhoods—as long as children are with children (of or around their age level) a good deal of their free (nonschool, nonsupervised) time. Early social contact and intercourse are essential to future relating. There is no substitute for the experience and emotional development that come of contact in childhood with friends of one's own age group.

Q: *I'm in my sixth month of pregnancy. I want a baby very much, and right now I feel fine. But I was quite moody on and off during the first few months. I know there's a theory that the mother's mood during pregnancy can have an effect on the child's personality and mental health. I've also heard that the first year of the child's life is psychologically all-important. How much truth do you feel there is in these ideas?*

A: I know of no scientific evidence to support the mother's-mood-during-pregnancy theory. However, how she feels *after* she has delivered her baby may or may not be a continuation of her attitude and moods during pregnancy. The tiniest infant "knows" and responds inside himself to how his mother feels. He often knows about her feelings before she does. He does not need words or ideas to know in this way. He knows with the totality of all his feelings and through all his conceivable perceptions—in short, with his entire being. Through his skin and his senses of touch and pressure, he will know whether his mother is at ease, warm, enveloping, protective, and loving—or anxious, tense, distant, cold and rejecting. He will know how sensitive she is to his condition by her response to his various tensions—needing food, a change of diaper, a warmer or cooler room, needing to be burped, etc. His earliest attitudes about the world will be largely predicated on these needs and her responses. From the very beginning, the world can seem warm, safe, and wonderful—or cold, harsh, and potentially dangerous. Remember that the microcosm of his mother and himself is to him, in his infancy, the entire universe.

Remember also that the central nervous system (brain and spinal cord) is not fully formed at birth. Since it is in a state of semicompletion and formation following birth, it is extremely impressionable. I believe that during the early days of central-nervous-system completion, whatever is conveyed to the baby becomes part and parcel of his very subsistence. It all registers and is bound to have a profound effect on his personality and emotional life. Please also remember, however, that he will continue to develop and grow in later life. The development of personality is not the sole province of infancy. I have seen relatively early mistakes rectified and difficult problems solved. Generally, most mothers are best able to do what is right when left to their own devices.

Q: *My two children—a daughter, five, and a son, eight—have both known for a long time that they are adopted. A few weeks ago, my son said, "I wonder who my real mother is?" I was so taken by surprise I didn't know what to say. I replied, "I don't know." I know my answer was not sufficient and I wonder what I ought to say if the subject comes up again.*

A: Curiosity about our origins is natural, healthy and human. For the most part, adopted children's curiosity about their biological parents is just a way of asking about themselves and their origins. Your little boy is asking, "Whom did I come from? What kind of people are they? What kind of person am I?" He may also be asking, "Are you a real mother and can I rely on your wanting me and keeping me even if you didn't give birth to me?"

An appropriate response to your son's question might be, "I don't know the mother who gave birth to you, but I am your real mother and you are my real child whom I shall always love and care for. I think the lady who gave birth to you must have been nice because she made it possible for me to be your mother."

No answer you give your child will be absolutely correct, because the human condition is never absolutely correct or perfect. We must deal with difficulties as they arise in life and we can only handle them in our limited, human way. There was nothing wrong in the answer you gave your child; it was your human way of handling the problem when it arose.

I want also to point out that despite your children's self-doubts, and no matter how many questions they ask about their biological mother, 99 percent of their security will be unaffected by this issue. Their relationship with you and the very real love and caring you convey—regardless of spoken words—make you their "real" mother, and makes them your very "real" children.

Q: *Why does my eleven-year-old son hug me one minute and show hostility the next? Is this normal?*

A: Your son is probably torn between his dependency on you and his need—at his age—to begin to be independent of you. His hostility is based on the fact that, inwardly, he feels the need to be independent; his hugs indicate that outwardly he is afraid to make the break. Your son's actions toward you are completely normal and will invariably become more placid as time passes and his adolescent development becomes more solidified in his own mind.

Q: *My daughter is four years old. She is a beautiful child, but she doesn't talk and in many ways seems to be behind in things. Sometimes she acts alert, while at other times she cannot be reached. She often cries for no reason at all and moves her body, swaying up and back in peculiar ways. We've taken her to several doctors, who say she is retarded. Recently a new pediatrician in town said that she probably has normal intelligence but may suffer from schizophrenia—a severe emotional disturbance. Do you think this is possible?*

A: Yes, even very young children can suffer from severe emotional disturbance. Unfortunately, a large number of children suffer from childhood schizophrenia or autism. Very little is known about the etiology or cause of childhood schizophrenia. Some people feel that these children suffer from organic brain damage. Others feel that the illness exists on a purely emotional level, without any kind of neurological disorder. Some of these children respond well to special and expert psychotherapy. It is important to make the right diagnosis. Unfortunately, many disturbed children are diagnosed as being mentally retarded and are given inappropriate treatment. I have known disturbed children misdiagnosed and seen as having very low IQs. Later, with proper treatment and an improved emotional state, the IQ was raised to extremely high levels (very superior).

Obviously, these children were not mentally defective in the first place. When there is any problem whatsoever in this area, the child ought to be examined thoroughly by an expert neurologist, a child psychiatrist, and a psychologist who is an expert in psychological diagnostic testing. One of the best treatment centers for severely disturbed young children is the League School for Seriously Disturbed Children, in Brooklyn, New York.

Q: *On more than one occasion I have caught my fourteen-year-old son torturing bugs and small animals. He is perfectly nice otherwise. Why does he do this? Is this a normal experimental phase that will pass?*

A: Torturing bugs and small animals is often a sign of a person's deep feelings of inadequacy. Mastering and manipulating weaker, helpless creatures provides insecure people with a fleeting and false sense of strength and confidence.

Sadism (cruelty to others) is generally used to compensate for feelings of inner emptiness. The sadistic person lives and feels vicariously. The pain he or she inflicts on others represents an attempt to stimulate his own deadened feelings. Your son is old enough to have gone beyond the experimental stage through which very young children pass. I think it would be a good idea if you and your son consulted a psychiatrist.

Q: *Our twenty-three-year-old son has been seeing a psychiatrist twice a week for two years. He is no longer depressed and seems to be doing better in many ways. My husband and I urge him to continue his treatment, and though he doesn't say much, he seems glad to go. I must say, though, that the trouble now seems to be with me. I feel so guilty about his having got sick in the first place. Is it true that the mother is usually to blame for a child's emotional problems?*

A: Let me answer you in several steps.

1. Blame and guilt are destructive enterprises that rob us of energy, insight, real responsibility, the possibility of growth and happiness. If a child has difficulties because of a parent, then the parent certainly had difficulty because of *her* parent, etc., etc., and so, in a way, we are all the victims of victims.

2. *But*—depression, like all other emotional reactions, has its roots in many complicated sources. It is never due to one event, one person, or one relationship.

3. Some mothers are quick to assume blame and guilt for a child's problems in order to mask enormous grandiosity. What they are in effect saying is: "My child's disturbance, like his happiness, his assets and everything else, is due to *me*, and if he is having difficulty now, it is only because *I* pulled the wrong strings."

4. Many parents become depressed when a child has problems, because this is an enormous blow to their pride. They don't seem to understand that our civilization is complicated and that most people, however well brought up, *will* have problems.

5. Many parents become anxious when a child starts psychiatric treatment, because they fear radical changes in the familial relationships. These changes are almost always good for all concerned.

6. If a mother responds very painfully to a child's "getting sick" and "getting well," it is often useful for her to enter into treatment herself.

7. The fact that your son has responded to treatment is an indication that he has many assets. Some of them at least have undoubtedly come from you and your love.

8. Your encouraging him to continue treatment is further indication of your love, concern, health, and maturity.

Q: *My friend has two teen-age daughters with only a two-year difference between them. They are both pretty and they look somewhat alike, but there all similarity stops. One is a fine student, the other is not; one has great interest in boys, the other ignores them; one likes rock music, the other prefers Mozart; one is moody, the other lighthearted. How can two girls born of the same parents and brought up in the same household under the same rules be so different?*

A: However closely related they are, no two people ever have identical hereditary structures or identical reactions to environmental influences. No two people are ever born with identical genetic structures. Each of us inherits different genes and combinations of genes from different ancestors. No two people have identical family environments or identical family influences or relationships. There are often subtle changes in family conditions that take place as time passes. These changes can affect growing children more than adults. The entire emotional status of a family is greatly changed by the addition of each child. Each child, therefore, has an individual and different relationship with his parents relative to the parents' age and economic status and to the total emotional status of the family and their relationship to each other. In addition, each new child has a different environment, inasmuch as he has more brothers and sisters than the child before him had at the time of his or her birth.

Of course, influences outside the home can also vary with different children and may have different effects. Compliant children tend to be more suggestible and to conform more. Unlike less compliant brothers and sisters, they tend to adopt what is currently "in" or popular and to go along with the crowd.

In some very rare cases, minimal and temporary biochemical brain dysfunction may affect the future development of a child and cause "differences."

Some sisters or brothers may exhibit differences in childhood but, as they grow older, demonstrate that they have much more in common than was initially apparent. In any case, it is constructive and advisable to let each child grow up according to his own instincts. Comparisons sometimes lead to destructive competition, self-hate and hostility between brothers and sisters.

Q: *My fourteen-year-old son is bright, confident and outgoing, but he has absolutely no interest in athletics, either as a spectator or as a participant. He would rather read than play ball. Is there any cause for worry?*

A: That depends on whether or not he has any serious problems. A lack of interest in sports is certainly in itself no indication of this. Some children who act as though they are not interested in sports are really shy about getting up there and letting go. Some feel inadequate and afraid that participation will result in humiliation. This, of course, can deprive them of what could be fun. This probably does not apply to your son, whom you describe as confident and outgoing. I feel that we ought to keep in mind that the main purpose of athletics and interest in sports is *fun*. Many people push their children unnecessarily hard in this direction. Too many men attempt to live vicariously and gloriously through athletic sons. Books will probably be much more important in most children's future adult lives than athletics, since very few children grow up to be professional athletes. Some children have a natural interest in both—without parental pushing and pressure—and this is fine.

Q: *Our eighteen-year-old son is an outgoing boy, who has many friends and does fairly well in school. He is a first-year college student. A few of his friends (boys) wear their hair long. From the little I know of them, they seem all right in other respects. Does the long hair mean they have a sexual problem? They certainly look effeminate.*

A: No! Boys who wear their hair long are no more likely to have sex problems than are those with crew-cuts. Many girls seem to find them attractive, and I believe that many boys wear their hair long in order to please the girls. Every generation has a way of dressing or grooming or acting so as to be antiestablishment and antiauthority. The long-haired boys are often quite assertive, even rebellious, and, in their desire to be different, invariably wind up quite uniform and conforming in their own particular way. As with most young people, growing feelings of adult identification are usually followed by adult changes in behavior and—haircuts.

Q: *My son is entering his last year of high school. He is a fairly good student, but like so many of his friends, he seems to be very vague about what to do after that. Even though our means are very limited, we would like him to go to college, but he seems to have no real goal. A friend of ours suggested a place that gives aptitude tests. What do you think about these tests?*

A: Aptitude tests can be of some value in revealing potential interests, talents and capacities. *But* the cooperation of the subject is very important. A person who is forced to be tested may not achieve the best results. Even more important, it is imperative that the tester or testers be expert at the job. Aptitude testing has become a big business, and unfortunately not everyone in this business is properly qualified. To go to bogus professionals or amateurs can be expensive, misleading, and even dangerous. If there is a university near you that conducts a testing service, I suggest you try that.

Remember, however, that while aptitude testing may reveal potential interests, assets, and possibilities, it does not appreciably enhance motivation. Any increased knowledge of self and especially of one's abilities can have constructive and motivating effects. But young people who lack motivation, who are drifting aimlessly, usually need more than aptitude testing. They often suffer from apathy born of self-doubt, fear of responsible involvement, and gross immaturity. I have seen too many thirty-five-year-olds who are still "trying to find themselves"—some of whom have taken numerous aptitude tests. A psychiatric consultation and full psychological testing may be of value.

Q: *Our twenty-one-year-old daughter has moved into an apartment which she shares with two other girls. It is small, uncomfortable, impractical, and she will spend nearly all her earnings on it. She has a perfectly beautiful room at home, with complete freedom, since we don't bother her in any way. She explains that she just has to be on her own by herself and doesn't want to hurt us. We are trying to be very modern about all this, but what really does hurt is the feeling both my husband and I have had, for several years now, that she has been growing away from us. I spoke to her girl friends' parents, and they feel exactly the same way. Is this the normal thing, for children to want to separate themselves from their parents as soon as possible?*

A: Today, healthy children, even teen-agers, usually want to leave home. This is an indication of considerable self-esteem, security, and optimism, much of which is a credit to their parents. Also, in our affluent times, it has become possible for young people to have jobs and the money necessary to leave home. Additionally, the role of women, particularly of young adults, has changed considerably. Victorian home-bound, double-standard ties are no longer the order of the day. Young adults have a need to explore and to test themselves and their ability to adapt to the world outside the bosom of the family, in preparation for future responsibility. The urge to test and to grow is very strong and, if thwarted, usually results in great frustration and bitterness.

It is important to stand by and to be of help when needed and, above all, never to succumb to making statements like "I told you so," let alone judgments, moralizing or vindictive tirades. It is important to keep the lines of communication open, so that your daughter can "talk" to you when she is ready to. True, she does not have much to say to you now; but this is largely because her world and its values are different from yours, as they must be from generation to generation. But if you have not been overly antagonistic or vindictive, if you have sustained the openness and the possibility of communication, she will come back and talk. This will happen when she has satisfied her yearnings for stretching, growing and exploring, when she has settled down and has a more solid feeling of who she is and what she stands for, at which time she will have much more in common with you.

Please do try not to view her leaving your home as a blow to your pride. Her leaving is an intitial step in eventually establishing a home of her own.

Q: *Our twenty-two-year-old son has been seeing a girl his own age for over a year now. She seems nice enough, but he told us recently that she has been getting psychoanalyzed for three years. We don't like the sound of this. Do you think we are right to try to persuade him to get interested in a more normal girl?*

A: I can't say, because I know nothing about your son or the girl he is seeing. The fact that she is seeing a psychiatrist on a regular basis is no indication that she is any sicker than the general population. Many people who need help are not in treatment. This is no measure of their degree of health. By the same token, I can tell you that I consider a fair percentage of my patients healthier than many people out of treatment. The fact that your son's girl friend is in treatment is an indication that she knows she has problems and is doing something constructive about solving them. In this respect, she—and perhaps your son, too—are well ahead of the game.

Q: *Why do some mothers act so peculiarly about their daughters and marriage? I have a friend who keeps saying she wants her twenty-five-year-old daughter to get married, yet this woman never fails to tear down any boy her daughter brings home. I've met some of the boys, and they seem to be nice, eligible young men. Why does my friend reject them? Is she well on her way to becoming a terrible mother-in-law?*

A: There are several possible reasons for your friend's actions. Let me describe some of the most common possibilities:

1. Some women say one thing and mean another. The more they talk about one side of an issue, the more they feel, want, and mean the reverse. Often, these people are not aware of what they are doing; they don't even realize they are keeping their true feelings hidden from themselves. Some women say what they think others want to hear, what convention demands, and use this to cover up what they really feel. There is a good chance that your friend doesn't really want her daughter to marry. She may say that she does, but her actions toward a potential son-in-law speak louder than her words —and they indicate that she has a greater desire for her daughter to remain single than for her to get married.

2. Some parents (often without being aware of it) do not want to share their children. They are extremely possessive and often very dependent—emotionally, financially, or even just for services—and feel that marriage would deprive them of filial love, devotion, or material support. In effect, they say and feel, "How dare you take my child away from me? I struggled all these years to bring her up as my very own, for my own exclusive use, and then you, a stranger, want to snatch her away? Never!"

3. Some parents see their children as living projections of God-like ideal images that they themselves secretly wanted to attain. These

parents feel very self-important as parents of God-like offspring. They unrealistically see their children as perfect, angelic, and ideal, and come to believe that nobody can possibly be good enough for them. In addition, a daughter's marriage to a mere mortal might destroy the God-like image her mother has desperately manufactured over a period of years. If children of such parents should somehow manage to get married, some of these parents will unconsciously continue to see them as single. I know one woman who, despite her daughter's marriage, kept dreaming that her daughter was a teen-ager who never dated. When her daughter had a baby, "Grandma" said that she felt the baby was really only her daughter's, and that her son-in-law had played little or no role in its conception. "Grandma" simply had to go on denying the marriage of her "angel child" to an "ordinary man."

4. Some mothers whose emotional balance is precarious will resist any change of family status quo that they feel is a threat to their stability. The marriage of a child represents an enormous family change, and however much they may protest to the contrary, these mothers will somehow try to sabotage a child's effort to get married.

5. Some mothers, though they will vigorously deny this to themselves as well as to others, are in competition with their daughters. These women have ambivalent feelings toward their daughters and are quite torn apart emotionally. On one hand such mothers want the best of everything for their girls, but they also see any achievement or attainment by their daughters as a threat to their own prestige and importance in the family and the world. These women say they want their daughters to have happy marriages, but at the same time they must destroy this possibility since the daughter's potentially enhanced status represents a great threat to the mother.

6. Unfortunately, many mothers refuse to let their daughters grow up. "Mary is not mature enough or ready to leave home," a mother will say. When asked how old Mary is, it turns out that Mary is forty years old. These parents are unaware of a powerful, unconscious need on their part for their daughter Mary to remain a baby. This can be due to the factors I have already discussed above as well as a new one: the need to own and control Mary. In order to deny the reality of their own aging, some of these mothers fantasize their children as magically remaining young and immature. In her unconscious delusion, this type of mother remains the eternally young matron as her daughter gets younger and younger and increasingly incompetent. Sometimes when a son or daughter manages to go off and get

married regardless of mother's feelings, mother may develop severe anxiety, depression, imagined physical illness, and/or psychosomatic illnesses. These mothers need professional help. Psychotherapy is the most effective way of preventing the "mother-in-law sickness." Destructive mothers-in-law are, of course, advanced forms of destructive mothers. Children caught in this kind of mother trap sometimes need psychoanalytic psychotherapy in order to escape.

Q: *My thirty-one-year-old daughter has been married for seven years—and is childless by choice. She says that for the time being she and her husband don't want any children in their lives. I feel that a family is not a family without children. I also think that a couple that feels as my daughter and son-in-law do might have serious problems that should be looked into. Whenever I bring up the subject —and I think it's perfectly normal for me to have it on my mind— my daughter angrily tells me to tend to my own business. Who is right?*

A: At the age of thirty-one, I think any woman has the right to live her life as she pleases. Despite the obvious desire on your part to have grandchildren, your daughter has no obligation to comply with your wish on this score. I feel that it is extremely important to respect the desire of people who choose not to have children. Couples who are coerced into having children against their will often develop serious emotional problems that are passed on to the unwanted children. There are many styles and ways to live life—and one is not necessarily any more or less "normal" than the other. Some couples derive more individual and mutual satisfaction from a childless marriage. With others, the opposite is true. Neither way of life—of itself —is an indication of profound emotional disturbance. In those cases where emotional or marital problems exist, having children is no remedy. Quite the contrary, having children will usually bring on added pressures—and possibly cause even greater difficulty in the marriage.

Part III
Dealing with
Society

CHAPTER 10

Coping with Leisure Time:
Boredom and Stimulation, Violence in
Our Everyday Lives

As man's life becomes easier, as he requires less time for work and has more time for relaxation, many difficult problems make themselves felt. One is boredom. What can we do, fruitfully, enjoyably with our leisure time? Why is it so hard to make use of the time we have, to get something out of doing what we really have fun doing?

BOREDOM and STIMULATION

Our society has gone out of its way to fill every available moment. Television and magazines provide stimulation to fill the empty hours, and many can escape into fantasy worlds through the media and its exploitation of artificial excitement. Sex and violence, made palatable enough for the average viewing audience, are attempted cures for boredom, which inevitably fail. Drugs are another attempted avenue of escape; young people who have discovered the pleasure of a marijuana high, and older people who have resorted to tranquilizers and alcohol to get through a day can relieve the agony of boredom, but only for so long. Money, too, is a form of stimulation. Many people spend their lives acquiring riches and shape their life-styles around acquisition of wealth and material goods. None of these forms of stimulation leads to even relatively sustained happiness, of course. Tapping our individual resources and expending energy in the service of growth of self is the only real antidote to boredom.

Boredom

"I'm so bored, I could die!" "After being married for more than twenty years what can you expect?" "I wait and wait for something to happen but nothing ever does." "If he would only do something to change things but he just sits and sits and suggests nothing at all that would make life more interesting."

These are typical statements.

People dread boredom. Indeed, many people will go to almost any lengths to avoid it. Boredom is felt as emotional doldrums, as emptiness and even deadness. Some people fear boredom as a precursor to serious emotional depression. Boredom is equated with helplessness, hopelessness, and death itself. This is especially true of people who are addicted to stimulation, excitement and tension. Being alone, feeling confortably tension free, stillness, "having nothing to do," inactivity—these are felt as the beginning stages of boredom and are viewed with dread. Some people without conscious awareness generate all kinds of personal difficulties, including hazardous and even self-destructive situations, in preference to potential boredom. I have known men who have undertaken disastrous business ventures because they were bored. Others have taken up sports completely out of keeping with their age and physical condition. I have known women who insist on unnecessary surgical procedures in order to generate excitement and to avoid boredom. Some women become pregnant and have babies because they are bored. Boredom often leads to destructive divorces, destructive relationships, and destructive marriages.

But on an unconscious level, beyond conscious awareness, many of us who dread boredom the most, often initiate and sustain it. Most often we don't know we are doing it to ourselves. Indeed we usually blame others for boring us and for being bores. We make claims on others and especially on our mates and close friends to produce enough excitement and interest to prevent and relieve boredom. To most of us boredom is felt as coming from outside ourselves and as something over which we have no control. We blame people, situations, and fate, but we seldom look to ourselves for either the source of boredom or its cure. Then why, if we dread boredom so, do we initiate it and even feed and sustain it? Why do we seek out people, situations, and activities that are certain guarantees of boredom?

1. Boredom for many of us represents a guaranteed form of emotional anesthesia. There are feelings some of us sometimes prefer to have as little to do with as possible. Some of us don't want to feel at all. Some people have a history of severe pain associated with almost any kind of strong feelings and especially those coming from deeper emotional involvements. Some of us dread angry feelings. Others of us love but dread excitement or what we've come to view as too much aliveness. We don't care to feel envy, jealousy, vindictiveness, possessiveness, etc., which are quite human but other than purely saintly feelings. Some of us no longer trust feelings of warmth, a desire for closeness and love. Some of us fear sexual yearnings of any kind, and so it goes. Entering a state of boredom, while it brings its own drawbacks, is almost a certain guarantee of anesthetizing or deadening other feelings. Of course, the price is high. Boredom is no fun. But the chronically bored person doesn't know this. He or she simply knows they are bored, that life is dull and they can't understand why. Often they blame it on bad luck and wait and wait and wait for a change to occur. It doesn't because only they can make it happen and they don't.

2. Boredom is often used to avoid change and indeed to avoid even the idea that change is possible. Most of us dread the unfamiliar and will go to great lengths to sustain the familiar situation in which we find ourselves. Without awareness we often do just about anything to feed inertia and to prevent movement. Most people prefer to stay with what they know rather than to confront the unknown, however painful the particular *known* may be. Boredom helps to prevent real change and movement. While people dread boredom and think that some superficial antiboring moves will produce real change, this is seldom so. Quick stimulation through meaningless sexual escapades, dangerous adventures, overeating, overdrinking, heady gossip, and drugs will lead to certain disappointment, depletion of energy, more hopelessness, and greater inertia, if not downright paralysis and still more boredom. Unless boredom is understood and coped with on a somewhat insightful level it invariably leads to still more boredom. Boredom breeds boredom and produces an emotional mire that is used to sustain the very condition from which bored individuals claim they wish to extricate themselves.

Life is certainly not a continuous series of fascinating experiences. We must all encounter times that are relatively staid and lacking in excitement. We must learn to differentiate quiet comfortable times from chronic boredom consisting of self-stultification, stupefaction, and paralysis. But even at so-called best some periods of relative boredom must occur in all of our lives. Tolerance and compassion for ourselves during periods of boredom, frustration, anxiety, and depression are enormously helpful in providing an atmosphere conducive to change and relief.

But what of chronic boredom? What can be done?

It is of prime importance to understand that we are the centers of our own lives. Looking to other people, luck, chance environmental situations and changes for solutions to inner emotional problems strips us of the opportunity for adult responsibility and autonomy. More than that, it often confuses and obfuscates problems so that solutions become more distant than ever. The first step then, in ridding ourselves of chronic boredom, is to accept responsibility for its existence. The next crucial step is to understand the psychological purpose it serves and to undermine this purpose. Along these lines we must ask ourselves, are there feelings we fear and are attempting to deaden? Which feelings seem to frighten us the most? As human beings we must tell ourselves that all feelings are entirely human and never cause for self-hate. We must be open to the possibility of accepting ourselves and whatever we feel without self-contempt and rejection. We must also ask ourselves if there are issues in our lives that we try to avoid by using boredom as well as other self-deceptions. These may involve close relationships, types of activities, styles of life, and numerous other situations. Are there changes we desperately want but are afraid to undertake or to even admit desire for? Are we desperately and fearfully clinging to a despised but "safe" status quo situation? Sometimes chronic boredom has gone on for so long and so effectively that these answers are not forthcoming, however much we struggle for answers. In this situation, psychoanalytic treatment may be necessary in order to restore a sense of self, self-responsibility, awareness of feelings and aliveness, spontaneity, and the ability to make decisions regarding one's own life.

Superficial maneuvers and attempts at quick stimulation may bring brief periods of respite. But these periods become shorter and shorter and increasingly difficult to attain, leaving the person more bored than ever. Addiction to excitement as a way of coping with boredom, like all addictions, leads to greater and greater needs, which become increasingly difficult to satisfy. Expectations for stimulation, excitation, and acute pleasure, become exorbitantly high, leaving the victim feeling impoverished and depressed as well as bored. Life's subtler orchestrations are ignored in favor of louder and louder noises in which rate of change is more important than depth or quality. One's sensibilities become dulled so that eventually the individual feels that only events of cataclysmic and explosive magnitude can possibly awaken them. This produces a state of emotional torpor and apathy that closes one off to everyday pleasures, satisfactions, and rewards. In this condition, people are not only bored. They also feel abused, irritated, and downright hostile. They are convinced that everyone else is surely getting a better deal out of life. This leads to further claims on other people for special consideration and satisfaction, making for disturbed relationships and further discouragement, thus completing a series of emotional vicious circles.

In order to help ourselves, boredom must be viewed as a cry of yearning from unrealized aspects of ourselves. These include the use of self in all regards: talents, work, pleasure, and relationships. Real involvement with people, activities, or any aspect linked to the development and evolvement of ourselves is the enemy of boredom. This almost invariably includes considerable struggle and some of us have forgotten how to struggle, and fear struggle. Some people will rationalize, "How can I get involved to the point of struggling with anything when nothing interests me?" It must be realized that:

1. Boredom represents an unhealthy struggle in which one actually expends enormous energy to keep one's self paralyzed. The bored person may not look as if she has energy at all, but maintaining a state of boredom takes great energy. She is actually using all of herself to keep herself *down and out*.

2. Growth in any area—art, music, work, study, care of children, involvement with friends and family, and pleasure—*always* involves struggle—constructive struggle. *In a state of constructive struggle in which a person stretches and uses more of herself than she has previously, she cannot be bored and she will grow.*

3. Involvement nearly always preceeds interest. If we wait for a bolt to shoot out of the sky to illuminate an *interest,* chances are we will wait and remain in a state of apathetic boredom all of our lives. We must struggle (if necessary with the help of a therapist)

to overcome initial inertia in order to become involved. We cannot begin to know whether or not we are interested in anybody or anything at all until we have become at *least* minimally involved. Some small familiarization is necessary before we can tell if we have interest, let alone the possibility of sustained satisfaction. Interest—real interest—comes from real involvement and seldom develops at a distance except in boring daydreams.

4. Bored people are usually more concerned with goals than activities. In fact, they are so concerned with rewards and so little involved with the process leading to goals of any kind, that they neglect the process and miss both process and goals. One of the great enemies of boredom is the deep-felt knowledge that *the process is the product*. Practicing medicine and curing is more important than the glory that comes of effecting a cure. Raising a child is more important than dreams of having a wonderful adult son or daughter. Painting a picture is more important than having produced a prized masterpiece. *The process is the now of it and the measure of use of self.* When we use ourselves compassionately and adequately, we seldom suffer the pain and hunger of unrequited inner yearnings characteristic of boredom. Boredom is a sure indication of lack of self-nourishment, lack of self-use, and lack of self-care. Developing and tapping our inner resources through constructive struggle and real involvement is the only antidote to boredom and self-hate.

Why Are Men Interested in Pornography?

People often ask me questions concerning the prevalence of pornography. The two most common questions asked are: "Why is my husband interested in pornography?" "Is pornography bad?"

I cannot, of course, give specific reasons why a certain man turns to pornography without discussing the situation with the man himself. But as a psychiatrist, I can analyze in general terms men who like pornography and what I feel are the effects of the current wave of pornographic films, newspapers, and books.

Since his very beginning, man has used every means possible to produce sexual excitement and to find substitutes for actual physical sexual contact. In short, pornography is not a new phenomenon; it is as old as man himself. In societies that encouraged it, pornography flourished. But more important, it outlived cultures that tried to repress it. So it would seem that, regardless of laws, opinions and moral judgments, pornography—like crime, taxes, and the common cold—is here to stay.

In preparing this article, I investigated current, readily available pornography in New York City. (I've been told by out-of-town friends and colleagues that New York is no different from most other American cities in this regard.) I read two X-rated underground newspapers, which I purchased at the local newsstand and through ads in those papers selected three X-rated films to see. I also saw one burlesque show and one "simulated" sex show. I read three X-rated novels that one of the underground newspapers had rated as "particularly stimulating."

Very little of what I saw or read was stimulating. In fact, most of it was downright boring. It took considerable will to watch or read the stuff. The novels were poorly written and the films badly acted. Some of the women were beautiful, but their acting was, to put it mildly, mechanical and inarticulate. The male actors (most of whom, oddly, had tattoos and minor skin eruptions) were just as bad. The women invariably had black and blue marks (needle marks?) on their bodies.

The dialogue in the movies I saw bordered on the idiotic, and the sex scenes were so blatant that nothing was left to the imagination. The scenes were almost totally devoid of anything resembling human relations. But worst of all, the films and books lacked humor.

While watching these films, I couldn't help but think back to the "stag" films I had seen during my college days. From a technical standpoint, those old "blue" movies were vastly inferior to today's works. They were not so well lit, directed, or photographed. But they *did* have the saving grace of humor—and, as a result, reflected some flashes of realism and human emotion. These qualities made possible some identification and excitement on the part of the viewer —and, of course, the curiosity of my youth helped, too!

There were only a few women in the audiences at the films I saw recently, and, happily, there were no children. The theaters were nearly full, even though I attended on weekday afternoons. The audiences consisted mostly of middle-aged, well-dressed men, although there were some young and old men present, too. Some carried attaché cases. They all sat quietly throughout the movie and seemed emotionally isolated from each other. When the theater lights came on, many of the men tried to hide their faces from their fellow viewers.

If these films are so bad, if men are embarrassed to be caught watching them, why do so many go to see them?

I feel that men of all ages are curious enough about sex so that they are curious about pornography, too. I also feel that despite the current "liberal" trends, most of us still feel embarrassed, guilty and ashamed of our interest in pornography. Culturally taboo information and material that is not learned through regular educational channels often reaches us through other means. In our youth nearly every one of us learned something about sex (and this includes misinformation) from other children and especially from our peers' efforts to shock or titillate. However mature we become as adults, much of our personalities remains childish. And it is the childish part of man that is interested in pornography.

The chief reason for the interest is enormous curiosity about what other people are doing. This is especially true in the sexual area, and it is especially noticeable in men who grew up in households in which there was sexual repression. Children are invariably interested in where they came from and in all the mysterious activities by which their parents produced them. Psychoanalysts feel that interest in pornography is just a continuation of the child's interest in parental sexuality.

Many adults who feel sexually inadequate are curious about other people's sex activities as a yardstick to measure their own performance. Some men use pornography as a means of assuring themselves that what they do sexually is done by other people—and is, therefore, "normal."

Men who feel this way are often attempting to allay guilt feelings produced by sexual pleasures, because they confusedly believe that sexual pleasure is sinful or less than pure. Men who feel that their sex lives are waning use pornography as a substitute for actual sexual participation. Still others use it as an attempt at self-stimulation, because they vaguely remember that it was quite effective during adolescence, with its enormous curiosity and receptivity to titillation. Unfortunately, you can't be young again, and men who seek to recapture the "thrills" of adolescence are usually disappointed.

Men are generally more interested in pornography than women. I suspect this has much more to do with upbringing than with any anatomical, psychological, or physiological differences. In my analytical and clinical experience—as well as from my general observations—I find that our culture somehow gives women greater maturity. Women generally (although there certainly are individual differences and variations) grow up, leaving most of the "little girl" in the past. Men grow up and bring most of the "little boy" with them into adulthood.

Men are also much more concerned with sexual adequacy and sexual competition. Therefore, they want to know how they compare with other men. Men—secretly and not so secretly—see themselves as great sexual athletes, which makes identification with other sexual performers relatively easy. Through pornography, they can vicariously satisfy their childish fantasies.

In our culture, it is usually simpler for men to be stimulated than it is for women. Viewing nudity and the sexual activity of others seems to have little "stimulation effect" for women, because their sexual needs tend to be more complicated than those of men. This is why most women prefer romantic, subtly stimulating books and films rather than ones with blatant sex.

There are, of course, pornography addicts—men who derive their only sexual satisfaction from pornography. But pornography itself does not produce addicts. Addiction is the result of faulty early upbringing often related to severe sexual repression. Neither does pornography produce perverts or sex criminals. Sex crimes are committed by emotionally disturbed men whose problems have early-life roots in disturbed parent-child relationships. Indeed, people suffering from severe sexual disorders seldom have any interest in pornographic material.

The truth is that the vast majority of men who are interested in pornography—even though they may be embarrassed by this interest —are generally "normal."

Does pornography pose any real dangers?

Not terrible dangers—but there are a few minor ones. Pornography is often the source of considerable misinformation about sex, because many men interested in pornography already suffer from a feeling of sexual inadequacy. Contrary to the ideas commonly promoted by pornographic books and movies, men do not have huge genitalia (nor is size essential for mutual sexual satisfaction); men are not always immediately and repeatedly potent; men cannot sustain erection endlessly or achieve climax after climax; women are not always ready, willing, and, indeed, in constant, desperate sexual need.

Though most people do have sex on their minds a good deal, it is not the be-all and end-all.

Another danger posed by pornography is boredom and the assault on our sensibilities. Too much pornography is purely exploitative, blatant, and downright ugly. I would not care to have children view this stuff until they understand the possibilities of beauty in sex.

I do not think there is any point in repressing pornography. Historic evidence proves that repression does not eliminate pornography. If anything, it seems to ensure an increased interest. I think that whatever small dangers pornography does present are usually counteracted adequately by a healthy emotional background and upbringing.

Why Nice Women Read Shocking Books

What makes some women call a book "shocking" or "dirty," while other women voice no objection to the same book? The answer can be found in the mind of the reader. An attitude toward a book depends on the particular culture and the times in which the reader was brought up, her family background and personal development.

Whenever I hear a woman say a book is "dirty," I question her carefully and listen intently to what she says and does *not* say. Both will reveal to a psychiatrist the origin of the woman's feelings, even though she may remain unaware of the basis of them.

Let me share a few "dirty book" interpretations with you. Here are some of the types of books so classified by women:

1. Books women do not understand. Some women are so constricted and insecure that they will label a book "dirty" rather than admit that they experienced personal intellectual difficulty reading it.

2. Books that advocate new, unfamiliar ideas. Some women have difficulty adapting to new concepts and situations. Tenaciously, they cling to old ideas, maintaining the status quo with righteous indignation. Anything else is "shocking."

3. Books that are particularly sensitive works, especially those that explore and stimulate strong feelings of any kind. Women who term these books "dirty" are usually women afraid to feel or show feelings. They mistakenly equate "feelings" with "weakness" and "lack of feelings" with "strength."

4. Books that describe personal details, activities, and relation-

ships. Women who are detached, sometimes to the point of seclusiveness, often interpret any personal inquiry as an invasion of privacy. These women label "dirty" any book that goes deeply into personal detail.

5. Books that describe sexual activity of any kind: books that are sexually provocative. (This is the category into which the largest number of so-called "dirty books" fall.) The degree of titillation will determine the degree of "dirtiness." Many women attempt to rationalize away these exciting feelings. Therefore, they prefer books that ostensibly have a purpose other than excitation—but that, in fact, were written, sold, and bought almost exclusively for sexual stimulation. The veneer of a thin plot and shallow characterizations make this rationalization easier. Many of these women have difficulty accepting their own sexual feelings and aspirations. Few of them would dare to admit even to themselves any desire to read out-and-out "dirty books."

Now let's talk about women, nice, respectable women, who read books from the largest category of "shocking" books (No. 5)— books that attempt to be sexually stimulating. Why *do* "nice" women read them?

Some women will tell you they read them for every reason other than the true one. Some will say these books aren't dirty at all— even though they do feel, in fact, that they *are* dirty and that this is the sole reason for reading them. These women are not lying; they have simply relegated their motivations to an unconscious level in order to be more comfortable and safe with what they think are acceptable mores. Only a few women will openly state that they read these books for sexual stimulation.

Obviously, women who read such books read them to satisfy some need, appetite, urge or motive. Here are the principal ones I've found in careful psychiatric questioning and clinical resarch:

1. Some women read sexually stimulating books because they have a compulsion to be "nice" and "clean" in all ways. Doing the forbidden is the only way they have of rebelling and feeling free. Reading such books represents doing something "bad," thus rebelling against old patterns and rules.

2. Some women read "dirty" books because they don't find their real sex-life situation stimulating enough. Through these books they receive fairly acceptable, noninvolving, extramarital stimulation.

3. Some women use books as fantasy substitutes for real-life

situations. Whether through fear, choice or chance, living sexual contact and involvements have eluded them, so they identify with book characters in self-involving sexual fantasies.

4. Many women read "shocking" books because these are the most superficial books they can find. This kind of reading demands minimal concentration, introspection, or possibility of change or growth.

5. "Dirty" books are read by some women chiefly as a voyeuristic activity. These women have an infantile need to see other people perform sexually. This need, and the sexual stimulation that ensues, is partially satisfied by the peephole effect of reading the descriptions of others' sexual exploits.

6. Some women read these books in an attempt to broaden their sexual education. Actually, they are seeking new methods of stimulation and satisfaction.

7. Those women who feel guilty about sexual feelings and activities will seek their counterparts in literature. They read dirty books for reassurance: "If the girl in the book is doing it, then I can do it."

8. To some, a sexually stimulating book is a stop-gap alternative to a potential extramarital affair. They choose to read about it rather than do it.

9. Reading a "dirty" book may be a hostile act toward a husband or lover. The wife can compare her husband's ability to those of the men in the book and find her husband inadequate and wanting. This gives the woman secret satisfaction and sometimes ammunition for vindictive triumph. Such women also use books as a substitute and a dilution of desire for their husbands.

10. A "shocking" book is used by some women to get into the mood for actual lovemaking. These women fancy themselves as the woman in the book and will fantasize their lovers out of the same novel.

11. Some women read these books to identify with the characters who have sexual problems. These women are not consciously aware of their personal sexual problems, and many are equally unaware that they seek, through reading, to satisfy complicated, unconscious yearnings.

12. Some women read "dirty" books so that they can secretly feel virtuous and superior—in their supposed purity—to the less virtuous characters in the books.

There are, of course, the prudish or Victorian women who flat-out refuse to read dirty books, however tempted they may be. Then there are women who *choose* not to read such books because they find them boring, poorly written, conveying little information, and giving insufficient human stuff and substance for involvement. Also, to some women, the mechanical descriptions of mechanical sex are stultifying and even depressing. Instead of acting as a stimulant, the book acts as an anesthetic.

Let me close by saying that there is only one *real* danger in reading "dirty" books: the naïve reader may believe their glowing descriptions of sexual prowess and overwhelming sexual responses. These descriptions, of course, are highly exaggerated and are often completely untrue. But because the naïve reader does not know this, she may feel inadequate and dissatisfied with herself and her husband. She may then spend her life in frustration, trying to satisfy sexual expectations that cannot possibly be fulfilled by mere mortals.

Watching Television

Every television program, like any human endeavor, combines constructive and destructive elements. Many programs have enormous therapeutic value because they provide the viewer with entertainment, information, and education. But some shows are insidious, destructive, and detrimental to emotional growth and mental health. And because television is such a popular American pastime, such shows have an unfortunate effect on millions of viewers—young and old.

Programs are harmful in varying degrees. Some are only a ridiculous waste of time; others combine all the unfortunate aspects I've mentioned. What matters in the long run, however, is not any one specific program, but the continuing onslaught of program after program. The cumulative effect is too much for the sensitive human being to absorb without some bad effects. This is especially true of children, who lack adult sophistication and defenses against repeated doses of anything—including bad TV.

What, then, are the major destructive elements and effects of TV? Speaking as a psychiatrist, here is what I think:

1. Television promotes an addiction to mediocrity. Most television executives assume that only an infantile level of programming will be acceptable and profitable. I've heard TV executives say, "We only give the public what they want—and the public only wants mediocrity." Such a patronizing view of their audience is erroneous; it falsely assumes that people cannot change or grow.

2. Television is a mind-blunting activity that has a hypnotic, anesthetic effect. In certain instances, this could be helpful—when a person can't fall asleep, for example. In most cases, however, watching television dulls our ability to fantasize and be creative. This is especially true of children. TV feeds children mechanical, ready-made fantasies, thereby contributing to their intellectual and emotional stagnation. Too much TV watching also causes alienation —from ourselves and others. We cease to know or care what we feel or what others feel; instead we become immersed in what the screen tells us we are supposed to feel. Many nights families will watch TV for hours, saying nothing to each other.

3. TV creates an unrealistic world in which soap opera characters, popular comedians, and other personalities are cared about, gossiped about, and given disproportionate importance. Pleasurable relief from cares is fine, but undue concern about the happenings on "As the World Turns" merely contributes to a loss of contact with reality.

4. Television consumes time, energy, and involvement that could more beneficially be devoted to museums, concerts, plays, and books —all of which contribute to a sense of identity as a full and alive person.

5. Television promotes antihuman characteristics, values, and ideas. People (particularly the young) often begin to hate themselves when, in real life, they find themselves falling short of these "ideals." Among the ideals that some programs promote are arrogance, violence, and revenge.

6. Television encourages pseudointellectual expertise by people who are not experts. Glamour and fame do not make a person an expert in a field he or she knows nothing about. Yet on TV, pomposity and glib talk are too often equated with knowledge. "Celebrity" experts often dispense information that is wrong.

7. Sometimes television commentators will take bad news out of context and present it in concentrated form. This can promote

bitterness, helplessness, cyncism, and depression. It also gives the impression that murder, suicide, muggings, and arson are the only things happening in the country today. Good news, such as the fact that people have friends, families, health, love, and the desire to contribute to the welfare of others, is not considered "news." I would like a program called "Good News" that people could watch before bedtime.

8. TV puts too much emphasis on looks, charm, and showmanship, making them seem great humanitarian gifts and virtues. Viewers are made to believe that good looks are more important than deeper human values.

9. Television promotes the belief that a person will be socially rejected unless he or she owns certain material things. This is particularly worrisome when children are made to believe they must have a special toy to achieve happiness. Aside from the way this materialism distorts values, it also makes parents who can't afford those toys feel guilty.

10. Television generally creates an artificial world. Some programs make viewers feel that there is another planet, one of everlasting beauty and glitter, and if they could find the key and open the door to that planet, then all suffering, boredom and even death could be avoided. False TV worlds are also created for children— for example, a world in which teachers are infinitely patient and understanding. By comparison, real life becomes unhappy and dull. Self-hate and a tendency to minimize one's own efforts is a common result.

11. On sports shows, athletic and physical prowess are stressed beyond their realistic importance, making viewers feel inferior. Such programs also serve to further blur already confused notions about masculinity.

12. Programs that "entertain" through sadistic manipulations and exploitation of people with problems are dehumanizing. These programs destroy human dignity and privacy.

13. Television has a way of encouraging fads that destroy individual differences. It also tends to produce one flat culture devoid of depth or spontaneity.

14. Television promotes hero worship through repeated performances of the same people over and over again.

Those are what I consider the major destructive television elements and effects. Programs that most exemplify some or all of these harmful effects are:

1. Beauty-contest programs on which unctuous, patronizing masters of ceremonies dehumanize young women and promote the importance of superficiality and physical beauty.

2. "The David Susskind Show," on which the moderator patently patronizes both audiences and guests with pseudointellectual nonsense that kills interest in real intellect. Under the guise of discussion, serious subjects are sensationalized and distorted.

3. "Truth or Consequences"—a program in which adults are ridiculed and humiliated on the pretext of "entertainment."

4. "Hogan's Heroes." This program is nothing short of a travesty. It derives "fun" from one of history's greatest tragedies, World War II. Portraying Nazi characters as ridiculous but kindly makes this show unique in its bad taste and unreality.

5. Cartoon features that are violent, distorted, and superhuman are foolishly programmed for children. Such cartoons extol the virtues of unrealistic strength and superheroism; they ignore realities of the human condition.

6. "The David Frost Show." Talk shows in general tend to put show business celebrities in the spotlight as experts, when they are not experts in any field other than show business. Mr. Frost is singled out here because, more than other hosts, he seemed to accept what his guests said with repeated paroxysms of "terrific" or "marvelous." Mr. Frost is an unusually intelligent human being, and if he felt that what his guests were saying was "terrific," then viewers would accept it as such. Unfortunately, what his guests said seldom was "terrific."

7. The Academy Award presentations. More than any award program, the Oscar ceremonies convey the impression that Shangri-la exists—and that only the privileged nobility are permitted to enter. No such paradise exists, and it is ultimately destructive to foster the belief that it does.

8. "Marcus Welby, M.D." This popular show gives the impression that doctors are superhuman, Christ-like people who have no private lives at all but care for their patients twenty-four hours a day. This is totally false. Doctors are human beings with faults as well as virtues. Conveying the idea that they are paragons can cause

adults and children to berate themselves because they fall short of such perfection. Impressionable people also become depressed and resentful when their own doctors do not devote hours and weekends to them, the way the mythical Dr. Welby does with his TV patients.

9. "All in the Family." This program means to poke fun at bigotry and prejudice—an admirable goal. Unfortunately, it has, in my opinion, just the opposite effect. Archie Bunker has become a folk hero instead of the bigoted, narrow-minded boor he was intended to be. Too many people laugh *with* him, not *at* him. Instead of lessening bigotry, I feel that this program heightens it.

TV viewers too often forget that their time, money, energy, and psyches have great value. Be prudent and thoughtful in your choice of programming for yourself—and your family. You'll all be better off for it. And so, in the long run, will TV.

Q: *Four years ago my husband and I bought a country home because he has a very high-pressure job and needs a place to relax. But whenever we go to the country, my husband cleans, mows the lawn, fixes the boat, paints the house, etc. He hardly sits still. Is this relaxing?*

A: All that work may well be relaxing for your husband. Some people relax through activity, especially activity that is different from their normal nine-to-five work. Men who do paper work, or work that involves the intellect, often relax by doing physical things. Actually, very few of us relax by sitting still and doing nothing. Forcing yourself to do so often generates anxiety and tension—both enemies of relaxation.

Q: *My husband is invariably irritated, moody, and just plain hard to get along with on weekends. He is perfectly fine during the week, but is miserable on his days away from the office. He's also nervous and unhappy on vacations. Can you explain this to me?*

A: "Weekend neurosis" is a very common condition. However, the reasons for depression, anxiety, irritability, etc., on weekends and vacations vary from individual to individual. Theories concerning this phenomenon are likewise varied.

In my own clinical experience, I have found that some people suffering from this condition have had virtually no training or experience with leisure time. They come from families to whom vacations and time off were unknown. "Good" people worked all the time. This, coupled with other emotional difficulties, makes vacations seem, to them, demoralizing and destructive. I have known other people who are uneasy on weekends because of the close and prolonged contact with their own families. These people have a compulsive need to maintain distance and can do so only when at work. Still others lack a feeling of self-worth. They see themselves as worthwhile only in terms of being workhorses. Any removal, however temporary, from the position of working and earning dollars is a blow to their already shaky self-esteem, prestige, and identity.

Q: *Do you think that a person's psychological problems show in his political opinions and the way he votes?*

A: I certainly do. Everything a person does is determined by who he is. His every word, decision, and action are symbolic of what goes on in him. The meaning of a particular action is not always obvious or even discernible. Often, it can be understood only in terms of the person's entire life history and knowledge of how he relates to himself and others. This, of course, applies to one's political outlook, just as it does to all other feelings, opinions, attitudes, and actions. The healthier, more emotionally mature individual will be able to bring greater objectivity to his examination and choice of political issues and candidates. But, he, too, will respond to elements of his personal history, however healthy that history may be. Disturbed people tend to be more rigid, prejudiced, and often repetitious in their choices.

Here are some examples of "choices" dictated by psychological determinants. Please remember that, for the most part, people are unaware of what their choice is based on, since the motivating forces are on a relatively unconscious level.

1. The masochistic woman who votes for the candidate who seems to be the most arrogant and vindictive.

2. The compulsively gregarious, overtalkative woman who votes

for the most detached, reserved, silent candidate. She has always confused silence and reserve with profundity, acuity, and strength.

3. The homosexual man who votes for the man who is most attractive to him, but who tells himself that his choice is based on "logical merit."

4. The woman who votes for the candidate who reminds her most of her father.

5. The woman who votes against all candidates who remind her of hated authoritarian parents. She will vote for the candidate who seems most unconventional and rebellious, although she herself is likely to live in a very conservative, conforming, and constrictive way.

6. The man who has never resolved severe problems with his father. He unconsciously sees competent men as competitors, enemies, and potential castrators, and he votes for the man who seems the least determined and easiest to manipulate. He rationalizes his vote on the basis of "humanity, warmth, understanding, and flexibility."

7. The person with a weak sense of identity who sees any change as a threat to his well-being, makes frequent statements like "Don't rock the boat," "Don't change horses in midstream," "We must finish what we started." He tends to vote for people already in office or for the candidate who for him most represents *no change*.

8. The woman who projects her self-hatred onto people who most remind her of herself. She invariably votes for the candidate who seems to be least like her, often someone from an ethnic, religious, social, or economic group that is just the reverse of her own. She will rationalize her choice on the basis of "See how liberal I am."

9. The narcissistic men or women who feel safe only voting for a person who as much as possible reminds them of themselves.

10. The woman who is terrified of anger, who predicates her life on "being nice," on "being universally loved," on never ruffling anybody's feelings. She votes for the candidate who seems most compliant and self-effacing and who is least likely "to make waves." Occasionally she does a complete about-face and votes for the man who seems most arrogant, vindictive, angry, and punitive. This is her equivalent for an unconscious temper tantrum, although she may explain it very sweetly with, "I don't know, I just have the strangest feeling that he is the right man."

11. The woman who feels downtrodden, used, exploited, and persecuted by an uncaring world. She identifies with the "underdog," seeks him out, and votes for him.

Q: *I can almost understand my young son's protest against the so-called "establishment," but not the same rebellious feelings that he has about his family. Are the two connected in any way?*

A: It is only human that we find it easier to accept rebellious attitudes and actions when they are at a distance. But when this rebellion hits home—ah, that is different. Some complaints about both family and society may have a realistic basis. Without knowing the particulars, it is impossible to evaluate to what extent such complaints and rebellious feelings spring from reality, from inner conflicts, or simply from the process of growing up. Many young people feel that their family establishment is an extension of society's establishment, and vice versa. They lump the two together and, in fact, they *are* nearly always intimately connected. As a result, some young people displace problems relating to the family to society so that, for example, a complaint against an authoritative father becomes rebellion against authority whenever it appears in society. In order to grow emotionally, everyone must experience struggle. When deprived of an opportunity to struggle at home, many young people flex their emotional muscles by joining struggles outside the home. This outside struggle can then overflow back to their own families. It is therefore reasonable to expect that youth's rebellious feelings and expressions more often than not will exist simultaneously in both family and society.

Q: *I recently discovered that my teen-age daughter has a drug problem. She is currently hospitalized and receiving treatment. My husband and I blame the town in which we live for our daughter's problem. We moved here two years ago, and I know that up until then she never touched drugs. Her friends here are all on drugs. Perhaps my husband and I are seeking ways not to blame ourselves for what happened, but we want to know if you agree that her new environment could have made her try drugs?*

A: Yes, I do agree. Particularly if your daughter tends to be compliant, suggestible, eager to please, and eager to be liked. Wanting to be one of the crowd can be disastrous, especially if the crowd participates in serious, self-destructive activities. Authorities in some countries consider drug addiction a contagious disease. They believe that each drug addict becomes a carrier who contaminates a considerable number of people, who in turn become addicts. The process grows like a germ-induced, infectious disease. In these countries, drug addicts, like people suffering from other contagious diseases, are kept isolated in order to limit contamination. Authorities claim that they have had considerable success in containing the drug problem with these methods. They point out that this segregation is not meant as a punitive measure, but merely as a therapeutic one in terms of both the patient (addict) and the non-addict population.

Q: *My son, who is eighteen, told me, in an apparent attack of guilt, that he tried marijuana three times. He said the last time was six months ago and swears he will never use it again. My husband and I are frantic. Is marijuana addicting? Can we trust him?*

A: I don't know whether or not you can trust him. That would largely depend on what kind of boy he is generally and what your relationship with him is like. Experimenting with marijuana three times does not make him a confirmed user by any means. "Trying marijuana" has become an increasingly fashionable activity among young people, and I include those of relatively high scholastic achievement. If you feel that your son has emotional problems and if you can communicate with him on a fairly good level, then you might suggest a psychiatric consultation—but not as punishment and not with recriminations.

Marijuana produces no physical withdrawal symptoms and as such is not considered an addicting drug. Prolonged use, however, can be habit-forming, so that a psychological dependence on the drug is established. I feel that chronic users are people suffering from an inability to withstand severe anxiety. They use the drug as a form of narcosis. The great danger is their entering the drug subculture, suffering chronic debilitation as promotion to other drugs takes place, with final graduation to heroin addiction. Of course, users need professional help, but unfortunately few seek it. Fortunately, few marijuana experimenters become chronic users, and even fewer go on to the addicting drugs.

Q: *We keep hearing about the young people who smoke marijuana. How about those who do not? Are they healthier or are they frightened of going against parents and "the establishment"?*

A: We must know a great deal about an individual in order to understand why he does what he does—especially youths.

I know young people who are too constricted to try marijuana or anything else that is not parent-approved. I know many more young people who are self-preservative and who refuse to try anything that may injure their health. I know others who are amply creative and feel no need for stimulation as produced by drugs. I know still others who refuse to conform. They refuse to try marijuana precisely because "everybody else is doing it."

Q: *My son and I fight all the time about indecent books, art, etc. He says I should be more tolerant and enlightened. I ask what about the effect of all this stuff on sex criminals and public safety? We'd like to know how you feel about it.*

A: Sex criminals invariably have a long-standing pathological history rooted in severely disturbed early family relationships. Interestingly, sex offenders are often stimulated by things that in no way would be considered sexually exciting by normal people. If anything, what most of us have come to look upon as pornography seems to be more interesting and exciting to the ordinary "normal," law-abiding population than to the sex offender.

Being subject to constant and chronic overexposure to *any* mediocre, mechanical, ugly material has a poor effect on a growing child's concept of esthetics and values. This is true of mediocre and crass television, films, and books, as well as pornography.

People who are compulsively driven to read or view pornography will do so in any case. I don't believe that censorship can eliminate pornography or keep those so motivated from availing themselves of it.

If future censorship is exercised at all (and why stop at pornography?), I hope that the censors will be concerned with esthetics and good taste rather than with the dangers of stimulating sexual offenders.

Q: *Do you think magazines that specialize in pictures of nude women are responsible for an increase in sex crimes?*

A: I don't think these magazines—or any magazines, films, literature or plays—increase sexual crimes or aberrations. However, I do not think these magazines promote responsible sexual freedom, either. Or that they enhance a woman's dignity or social position. On the contrary, they tend to dehumanize women by making them seem like stimulating "sex objects" rather than "whole persons." No matter how the editors may rationalize the existence of these magazines, their sales are dependent on the temporary satisfaction of the reader's unresolved childhood curiosity or on the superficial, momentary sexual stimulation their photos offer. Under the guise of being "modern" or "anti-Victorian," these magazines inadvertently promote the constrictions of the Victorian Age, including a separation of human relatedness and sex, as well as undermine human dignity and self-esteem.

Q: *I love to read astrology columns for fun, but I have friends who are really addicted to magic, superstitions, astrology, spiritualism, and all that kind of stuff—and they spend a great deal of money for such advice. Why?*

A: The "not-for-fun" people believe in this so-called magic because they don't adequately believe in themselves or the world they live in. Their lack of self-confidence makes it difficult for them to tap their own resources in facing and coping with the real world. They would rather seek direction from outside "magical" sources than from mature inner struggle. These people are attempting to recreate a childhood when life seemed simple and safe and parents knew all the answers. As adults, they substitute magic for parents. Unfortunately, this "magic" is often very expensive, economically and emotionally, especially when doled out by charlatans.

What Spending Money Reveals About You

Some people say—and believe—that "money is the root of all evil." That just isn't so. Money doesn't make people sick or corrupt. Sick people make sick or corrupt use of money, just as they do with other things in life.

Money represents time and energy. It is a medium of exchange and, as such, it offers the possibility of enhancing human relations and communications. Unfortunately, as in other areas of human endeavor, constructive possibilities for using money can be displaced by destructive ones. So money has come to represent more than it should. To too many people, money has become highly symbolic. Everyday we hear expressions like: "I feel like two cents. . . . I feel like a million dollars. . . . Sound as a dollar. . . . Phony as a three-dollar bill."

In these expressions, the symbolic meanings attributed to money are clear. Sometimes, however, the meaning a person actually assigns to money exists on an unconscious level and the person is unaware of it.

How you feel about money, spend it, and use it, tells much about you. This is particularly true in marriage. Often the way a couple acts together in money situations reveals how they feel and relate to each other generally—a good deal of which they may not be aware of at all. Attitudes regarding money are very similar to those about sex, inasmuch as both usually reflect a great deal about how we relate to ourselves and to other people.

Let me describe the most common symbolic meaning of money. Bear in mind that these symbols can overlap: money can symbolize many things to the same person at the same time. Even more peculiarly, money can symbolize opposite values to the same person. Here, then, are some symbolic meanings of money that I have come across in clinical practice.

1. Money is all that is evil, dirty, mysterious—even death itself —while poverty represents all that is good, clean, light, and alive. I knew a man who felt this way but who, at the same time, also felt that money meant respectability and acceptability, while poverty stood for rejection and self-hate. He was in constant conflict about money. Without knowing why, such a person can fluctuate between great efforts to accumulate money and equally great efforts to fail

financially in order to divest himself of every cent he worked hard to make.

2. Money is knowledge, culture, and expertise. People who believe this will repeatedly ask the richest man or woman they know for all kinds of advice on any subject, simply because they believe that to be rich is to be all-knowing. They will also strive for money of their own so that they, too, can acquire the instant wisdom that comes with money.

3. Money is an antidote to self-hate, self-rejection, and depression. Some people believe that money will give them self-esteem as well as an ability to relate successfully to others. Here money symbolizes the end of misery and the beginning of happiness. When it brings neither, the believer sometimes feels that he or she simply must get more money. When more money still doesn't solve the problem, the feeling of emptiness deepens. I have seen great depression ensue when people realize that money does not "bring" or "buy" what it is supposed to.

4. Money means friendships with important people. Those who feel this way will display their money in expensive dress and possessions (such as jewelry, high-priced cars, furniture, etc.) in an attempt to impress and to attract the "right kind" of "important" people.

5. Money is power, prestige and status. Here, too, ostentation with the aim of impressing others is often an attempt to hide underlying feelings of worthlessness. Some people will throw money around by overtipping or overspending just to show themselves and others that they "have arrived." But it doesn't work! These people are often shocked when they realize that money, however much they acquire, does not really change basic feelings of unworthiness, nor does it confer real self-confidence.

6. Money is blood. As a result, spending money is like hemorrhaging or giving away vital pieces of one's self. People who feel this way are stingy people. They can't spend money unless they are convinced they are getting the best deal possible. "Being taken," or getting the worst end of a bargain, can bring on terrible feelings of despair, even an urge to commit suicide. Usually people who can't spend money (assuming they have it to spend) can't spend emotions, either. They are very detached and constipated emotionally— as well as financially.

7. Money is mastery, a manipulative tool that procures love or

control over people. I have known parents who can't understand why their children do not love them even though they have given their children so much money. For these parents money equals love; they feel that the money-love they have given is as good as emotional love. Some women, to whom money equals love, will see their husbands' failure to earn a lot of money as his failure to love his family enough. In effect, these women are saying to their husbands, "If you loved me you would go out and earn more money for me."

8. Money is the medium of exchange in a game called "Papa and the Little Girl." The husband gives his wife a weekly allowance. She is Little Girl, he is Papa. This stems from and enhances a dependency relationship in which he needs mastery and she needs to feel weak and protected. The husband may complain that his wife refuses to learn how to care for money, and the wife may complain that her husband won't treat her like an adult, but neither will take responsibility for changing until they examine and change their emotional outlook toward themselves and each other.

9. Money is an emotional compartment. People who believe this never really share money, nor do they share emotions. They get married and maintain separate bank accounts—and usually separate emotional accounts, too.

10. Money represents health and longevity. You hear people who believe this say, "Money buys the best medicine, the best doctors! . . . Imagine, John Smith died and he was actually a millionaire!" The belief behind these words is that money magically buys life and a way to cheat death.

11. Money is nobility and an entree into a special circle of superhumans who live in a heaven on earth. It is often a big shock to people who believe this that human functions, limitations and problems exist and continue to exist no matter how much money they accumulate.

12. Money is things—innumerable things, such as cars, clothes, appliances, houses, lawns—things that, if possessed, will replace a missing self and a missing sense of belonging.

13. Money is a plaything, a child's toy. "I just love to handle money. I like the feel of it in my hand. I just like to jingle coins in my pocket. I just like to count money." Some thieves have this very childish feeling about money. They'll steal it to play with it, without actually valuing its buying power.

14. Money is freedom. It makes work unnecessary and permits its possessor to spend his time as he wishes. This view of money may or may not be coupled with the belief that money equals longevity.

Q: *My husband is always in some kind of financial entanglement. It is not that he is unsuccessful. We live very well, and we seem to have ample money. It's just that he is more often than not in a stew about one or another "deal" and goes about harassed and worried. I am quite willing to live a simpler life, and we've discussed this. But somehow he always manages to get into new and, I feel, unnecessary involvements and headaches. How do you explain this kind of behavior?*

A: There are many explanations, and the correct one would consist of the combination of factors appropriate to the individual. This would entail a detailed study and firsthand knowledge of that person. However, let me list some of the dynamics found in people with this kind of problem. Remember, we often find a combination of several of these "characteristics" operating in highly complicated patterns.

1. The chronic quest for power, prestige and money, in an attempt to mitigate underlying (and unconscious) feelings of inadequacy and personal worthlessness. The individual here feels that he really owns nothing at all and is stuck with his feelings of personal impoverishment, regardless of how much he actually amasses.

2. Self-hate and punishment, in which the individual uses pressures and entanglements to impose a state of unrelenting emotional pain.

3. Poor judgment, in which he sees himself as limitless in effort, energy and time.

4. The need for maintaining emotional distance from himself and from his loved ones. He "dilutes" his relationships with a constant preoccupation with business worries.

5. The irrational but unconscious search for the one magic deal, which will produce unlimited dollars, security, self-esteem, and solutions to all his problems.

6. The search for excitement, to mitigate feelings of emptiness and inner deadness. Here, there is often a need to set up and resolve larger and larger and increasingly precarious problems.

7. The unconscious, unresolved need and search to please and to get approval from a mother (and/or a father) often long since gone. This need is sometimes transferred to a wife.

8. Total unfamiliarity with leisure. To this individual, life is work and work is life. There has been no experience with anything else. Learning about different activities can be most painstaking and difficult.

Q: *My husband is obsessed with making money. He is very good at business, but really has no other interest at all. He is not stingy, but money is his entire life. I've heard that this kind of thing is tied up with childhood constipation. Can this be true?*

A: Some psychoanalysts feel that men who are enormous money gatherers, especially those who are in fact stingy (unlike your husband), have been arrested at what they call the "anal stage" and may have a history of childhood bowel retention and even severe constipation. Money, according to this theory, is seen as symbolic feces and stinginess as a kind of symbolic retention. While elements of this theory may be true, I feel that it is an oversimplified explanation. Money means many things and a combination of things to different people.

Some men see money as power and prestige and as a means of attaining personal safety and security through mastery over other men. Others seek it as an unconscious way of evening scores or buying affection and admiration, as well as a route to feelings of accomplishment and self-acceptance. Some people have the unconscious delusion that money buys longevity—that the very rich don't really die, that the accumulation of a great fortune ensures immortality.

Unfortunately, what is often lost sight of is the fact that money represents a man's labor. *As such,* money becomes a healthy exchange of energy and an important form of communication.

Q: *Whenever my husband and his friends get together, they compare notes as to their personal economic status. I usually laugh at this because they remind me of little boys comparing marbles or toys. But when they talk about other men who are not present and use the expression: "What's he worth?" it grates on me. I find the phrase offensive and dehumanizing. I have told my husband this, but he only laughs, saying it is nothing more than a casual expression and I should accept it as such. What do you think?*

A: I agree with you. Nobody uses words or expressions casually or accidentally. The words we use invariably reveal how we feel deep down inside. It is unfortunate but true that many men measure themselves and others in terms of personal fortunes or money-making ability. This concentration on material existence *is* dehumanizing, and prevents us from relating to a person's more important attributes: sense of humor, intelligence, ability to form relationships, etc. When men don't recognize the importance of things besides money, their lives and their friendships are seriously impoverished and usually emotionally fragile. Feeling emotionally impoverished feeds a man or woman's need for greater "net worth"—thus completing a vicious cycle which makes us increasingly vulnerable to the ups and downs of life.

Q: *I have been married for six months and everything is just fine—except for money matters. My husband insists on giving me a weekly allowance, and then wants a detailed explanation whenever I need any additional thing. I feel he is treating me like a child and/or a spendthrift. I am neither. I want our money handled more equitably, but every time I mention this, he says I am making a big fuss over nothing. What do you think?*

A: I agree with you. The sooner you and your husband settle this matter, the happier you both will be. Money very often becomes the symbol of hidden power and a means for one marriage partner to dominate the other. Tight money control sometimes indicates lack of confidence in one's partner. When this situation occurs, heroic efforts must be made to build self-respect and mutual trust. And it is much easier to do this in the beginning, because the more firmly the bad habit is established, the harder it is to change without causing hostility, resentment or—in extreme cases—a complete communications breakdown.

The ability to manage money properly is neither a masculine nor feminine trait. Men and women are equally good or bad at it, depending on their maturity and ability to cope with reality. It is very important that both husband and wife have a chance to manage the family's money. Sharing family responsibilities and experiences democratically makes for a healthy adult relationship. It also provides a sense of security for children, because it lets them know that both mother and father are full adults and that either parent can handle a financial situation should the other be incapacitated. It is indeed pathetic to see elderly widows whose husbands have treated them like children for so long that they are completely helpless after the death of their husbands.

Q: *My friend's husband is an absolute tightwad. He has a positive seizure if she buys a dress, shoes, anything—even if she really needs it. They are not poor by any means and the wife is not a spendthrift; it is just that he wants to put the money in the bank. What's going on?*

A: Money is probably this husband's security blanket. He may view any expenditure on anything other than what he considers an absolute necessity to be frivolous and dangerous. The danger stems from the feeling that a slight drain on dollars will lead to a massive flood—and to an empty bank account. When a person suspects that his security is threatened, he can experience extreme feelings—and other complications as well. Any expenditure of money by this wife may be erroneously interpreted by her husband as selfish, uncaring, ruthless, and disloyal. Some men with this problem have the notion that only males are capable of financial prudence—and that, therefore, they alone should control the family purse strings. Some of these men view emotional spending (of tears, laughter, etc.) as well as money spending as a female liability that must be avoided or controlled at all costs.

Q: *Our neighbor straps himself financially by buying a very expensive new car every year. We would feel lucky to have him as a friend regardless of what kind of car he drives. Other friends feel the same way, yet our neighbor has this "thing" about having to get that shiny new car regardless. Do you know why?*

A: You may· have a high regard for your friend, but unfortunately, he seems to have little respect or admiration for himself. Many people see possessions—especially cars—as extensions of themselves. Some men are more concerned with the automobile part of themselves than with their own inner beings. To such a man practical considerations have nothing to do with decisions that inflict financial hardships on themselves. Your friend sees driving a lesser car as degrading, a blow to his pride, a lowering of self-esteem and self-acceptance that could bring about self-hate and depression. Unless they resolve this problem, such people need bigger and bigger cars, diamonds, houses, bank accounts, etc., in their futile attempt to counteract growing feelings of self-worthlessness. Getting these things, however, will have no sustained effect—and, as with drugs, the requirement for satisfaction gets larger and larger and finally becomes grotesque and very self-destructive.

Q: *My husband gambles away huge sums of money. Often my children and I must do without because his hunch doesn't pay off. My neighbor's husband is a gambler, too, but he sticks to two-dollar bets. What is wrong with my husband, and how can I set him straight?*

A: All people, men and women, gamble at one time or other in their lives. But the occasional two-dollar bettor must be separated from the destructive chronic gambler. These compulsive gamblers are emotionally sick people, and punishment, harsh treatment, or preaching not only does no good but may even make matters worse.

The overwhelming compulsion to gamble invariably springs from deep-seated emotional problems. It is always connected with other character problems and difficulties in relating to people.

Compulsive gamblers are often emotionally immature people with poor judgment and little ability to accept responsibility. They also have a low frustration threshold and, as with children, find it difficult to wait for anything they want. They want it *now*—and they gamble to get it.

People who suffer from any emotional disturbance do so because of their own unique problems. There are, however, several problems that compulsive gamblers have in common:

1. A more-than-ordinary desire to rid themselves of feelings of

emptiness and poor self-esteem.

2. A fear of sustained adult sexual involvement. Gambling is their substitute for sexual activity.

3. A belief in magic—and the feeling that the "big win" is just around the corner. The win, they think, will make for inner peace, outer paradise, and happiness.

4. A need to be free of sustained involvements with people, activities or routines.

5. Deep-seated self-hatred and the feeling that they are not entitled to anything. This leads to an appetite for more and more gambling, which is coupled with the need to lose more and more. Many gamblers openly admit a feeling of great relief when they have lost everything and there is nothing more to lose.

6. Compulsive gamblers are compulsive liars. They also have the knack of being able to manipulate people, to talk them into investing in their wild schemes.

You ask how you can set your man straight? You must stand fast against his manipulations and resist any urge to give him money. Money is to the gambler what alcohol is to the alcoholic. You should handle and administer all family monies.

Most compulsive gamblers rationalize away their sickness and are poorly motivated for treatment or change. This is tragic because psychoanalytic treatment is badly needed. However, I also recommend an organization called Gamblers Anonymous, P.O. Box 7, New York, N.Y. 10001. This group is often more palatable to the sick gambler than psychoanalytic treatment.

Q: *A friend of mine owed me money for a long time, but I never reminded her of it. Recently, I needed the money she owed me, so I simply asked her for it. She repaid me, but has since been very angry with me. Can you possibly tell me why she reacted the way she did?*

A: Probably because she is embarrassed. You disturbed her idealized, false picture of herself. You confronted her with the fact that she is not a responsible, spontaneous payer-back. You should not feel guilty about your action; you were right to ask her to repay the money.

Q: *Why have I become such a compulsive bargain-hunter? My husband and I must live on a budget, but even I can recognize that I have gone overboard about "buying cheap." Whenever I hear of anyone paying less for something than I paid, I blow my top. At first my husband laughed at my outbursts, but he doesn't anymore. He is beginning to be outraged by my behavior. What can I do to stop?*

A: Because you can admit that you have become fanatical about your bargain-hunting, you are not as bad off as you think. Yes, there is a difference between enjoyable, constructive comparative shopping and your compulsive actions. Compulsive behavior destroys spontaneity and happiness. Very often people are the victims of compulsive behavior for years without being aware of it (although you are aware)—and without having the slightest idea how they got into the predicament in the first place. Unfortunately, human beings always seem to find ways to hurt themselves and to kill personal happiness. Your method—buying everything only at the absolute lowest price and generating self-hate and recriminations if you find that what you have paid is *not* the lowest price—is not uncommon. Such actions—like all compulsive actions—have their roots in anxiety that stems from feelings of inadequacy and worthlessness. People try to dispel these feelings by attaining perfection in certain areas. Your way is to buy things at the lowest price. By attaining this perfection you will become "perfectly good"—and, as a perfect person, you will not be filled with self-contempt.

In my practice I've seen patients with low self-esteem who cannot buy themselves anything unless it is "absolutely necessary" or unless "everyone else has it, too" or unless it is bought at the absolute lowest price. When self-esteem is at its lowest, the desire for perfection becomes so great that often such people cannot even buy something for someone else lovingly or freely.

You can't always get things at the lowest price; everyone makes a bad bargain now and then. Why? Because we are human. And unless bad bargains become a way of life, they should be accepted without recriminations. But this requires increased self-esteem and lowering those unrealistic self-imposed standards of perfection. Some people need professional help (psychoanalytic psychotherapy) in order to do this.

Q: *My wife is bright, extremely devoted to me and our children and gives me no cause for complaint except one: she is obsessed with clothes. She keeps buying them at a fantastic rate, even though she can't possibly wear everything she has now. If she's not out there shopping for clothes, she grows restless and insecure. My wife is not putting us in the poorhouse with her purchases, but her habit is one I'd like to know more about.*

A: Some women (and men) think of clothes as an extension of themselves. By continually buying new clothes they are unconsciously seeking a personal perfection that does not exist. Such people feel that others judge them only on a surface level. How they decorate that surface becomes inordinately important.

People who have feelings of inner worthlessness are particularly concerned with outer trappings and the impressions these trappings (clothes) make on others. Being "stylish" also becomes important. Such women consider anything less than a closet bulging with clothes as a threat to their security and their fabricated feelings of self-esteem. Actually, clothes become more important than the individual herself; she needs the clothes because she feels they are her only way of evoking the admiration of others. She needs clothes to relieve her feelings of anxiety and weakness. Sometimes psychotherapy is necessary to put women (or men) in touch with their real human assets so they can rid themselves of a compulsive activity—such as buying clothes, or whatever other form this problem takes.

Q: *Why can't I give up my obsession with becoming rich? I feel that I'm missing so much by not being wealthy. I've tried to tell my-self that a larger house, world travel, more jewels—and all the other things that money can buy—are just "things" and not all that satisfying. But my craving for big money persists, and it makes me unhappy. I know that I ought to be satisfied because my husband has done well and we have so many things other people don't have —and many things we didn't have when we first married. But I do so want to be really rich! Why?*

A: You are suffering from a common American and European malady that I call "Shifting Unachievable Goals." The principal symptoms of this chronic emotional illness are: (1) general disregard and contempt for one's achievements, however worthy these may be; (2) self-hate; (3) unhappiness and depression; (4) hopelessness; (5) emptiness; (6) a sense of deprivation and ingratitude; (7) cynicism; (8) bitterness and greed. These symptoms may exist singly or in combination; they may be obvious or hidden; they may be moderate or severe.

The malady also consists of setting up obsessive goals that, when achieved, are immediately replaced by new and more exorbitant goals. This keeps the victims in a constant state of instability and discontent; it pushes them on and on in an unhappy, meaningless quest for goals that give them no happiness. This mythical kind of happiness can *never* be achieved.

Shifting Unachievable Goals is known to attack any and all areas of one's life, and may easily shift from one area to another. These may include your sex life or your professional attainments and can even extend to your children and their accomplishments.

In your case, the disease has localized itself largely in the area of money, although I'm certain it reaches other areas, too. But, an obsession with wealth is quite common in our civilization.

"Money Magic" is a very widespread delusion. Of course money is important and helpful. It can buy necessities and niceties. But, as we have heard so often, it *can't* buy happiness. Money does not produce magical results. If you have any doubt about that, just ask anybody you know who has a lot of money. Millionaires are subject to the same human problems—depression, sickness, phobia, compulsion, death, etc.—as poor people.

Your concentration on the money you *don't* have keeps you from enjoying the money you *do* have. Your quest for more money also prevents you from exploring real problem areas in your life. But most of all, your craving for money pushes you further and further away from the possibility of accepting yourself and discovering true happiness.

VIOLENCE IN SOCIETY

The papers tell the story every day: woman raped, man robbed, plane hijacked, war continued. Is man really more civilized today? Our industrial and economic achievements are phenomenal, we have reached heights of scientific discovery, artists are prolific, and we call ourselves humanists, regardless of profession. Yet the 1960s and '70s has seen a proliferation of violent acts and of man's inhumanity toward man. Can this aggression be curbed, or is it a sign of the degeneration of our advanced society? If we can better understand that violence against society is a result of poor interpersonal communication and of repressed anger among individuals as well as nations, perhaps we can generate more public interest in stemming the hostility we are currently witnessing around us.

Q: *In view of the constant anger, war, and violence taking place throughout the world, do you think that aggression and war are inborn human instincts?*

A: Some psychoanalysts believe that aggression is instinctual, but I do not. I do believe that anger is a normal human characteristic. Unfortunately, we often repress anger so excessively that it accumulates and becomes explosive and dangerous. Aggression and war are not natural human phenomena. They are the results of repressed rage (a perversion of healthy feelings and expressions of anger), hurt neurotic pride, power-striving to bolster grossly inadequate self-esteem, projected self-hate, and ruthlessness. All of these feelings are the result of inadequate development of feelings for others. Better communications and relations among people are vitally important if we are to diffuse these negative traits; so is the improvement of socioeconomic conditions for all people. As I have stated before, psychotherapy for *all* world leaders would be immensely helpful.

Q: *I have a friend who insists that our law and order are breaking down. Do you feel we need stronger law enforcement?*

A: Law and order break down because communications and relations between people break down. These breakdowns are often due to loads that are too heavy. Today, our environments have become too complex. Law is only as effective as the people who make it and who live by it. Our current problems indicate that the "ostrich phenomenon" has been in full sway for some time—meaning that too many of us have lived with our heads buried in the sand while people-to-people problems have been simmering for years.

As a psychiatrist I feel that we need better communications, understanding, and insight rather than more law, order, or enforcement. If we are sick, we must try to understand our social ills by honestly bringing them to light where they can be cured. To repress these ills is to compound them and make for destructive psychological and social upheavals and explosions.

Q: *Can you explain why movies and television programs with a high violence content are popular?*

A: Curiosity is one of the prime human characteristics, which means that people are interested in learning about all facets of the human condition. Violence is particularly attractive to people who —for whatever reason—feel "dead," empty, bored, or resigned and in need of stimulation. However, the stimulation derived from violence does not have a sustaining or fulfilling effect; it can never take the place of honest involvement or activity that results in real self-fulfillment.

Q: *People must get something out of reading about and seeing so much violence and horror; otherwise, why would there be so much of it in our current books, films and television?*

A: Many people suffer from a paralysis of their feelings. For many reasons—personal hurts, a world in which it becomes increasingly complicated to live—they have lost their capacity to feel. It is almost akin to a kind of anesthesia, and it makes for feelings of great inner deadness or emptiness. The more deadness there is, the more stimulation is required to feel *anything*. In cases of extreme deadness, the victim will often seek brutality, pain, and suffering (strong stimuli) as a means of feeling something—anything at all.

Q: *My husband and I are constantly dismayed by the filth we see on the city streets. Why are people such slobs? What do you think makes them litter?*

A: There are several rather basic reasons why people litter:

1. People learn by example. Many who litter in their own community are ultra clean when they visit an area that is well kept. Some people feel that so long as the city is dirty, they'll help keep it that way.

2. Lack of self-respect and lack of respect for others often cause people to treat their physical environment with contempt. Repressed anger, especially among people who feel that they are being treated poorly by the community, is another reason for littering.

3. Littering may be evidence of a general lack of caring and responsibility. Litterbugs say, in effect, "I don't give a hoot about you."

4. Some people have no feeling for, or identification with, their community. In short, they feel like displaced persons who do not "belong." When these people litter, they don't feel that they are dirtying their home because they actually feel homeless.

5. Unconsciously, some people actually identify with garbage or litter. Spreading garbage in the street is an unconscious way of decorating the streets with themselves. Like certain dogs who seem to stake out their own private fire hydrant, people use littering as a way of making a particular area seem like home.

6. Lastly, some people have an obsessive need to be clean. To protest against their own tyrannical need for cleanliness, they litter.

Q: *Many people are saying that one reason young people have been causing so much trouble these days (student riots, etc.) is that their parents brought them up on the permissive theories of Dr. Benjamin Spock. Do you think there's any truth in this?*

A: Emphatically no!

The behavior of students (and there is both health and sickness in their behavior, in my opinion) or anybody else individually or en masse is always a highly complicated phenomenon. Human behavior (protest demonstrations included) invariably has profound familial, sociological, economic, political, cultural, and internal psychological roots. To blame the theories of Dr. Spock makes for a vast oversimplification and a mockery of the science of human behavior. It also demonstrates an enormous distortion of Dr. Spock's work, as well as ingratitude for his most significant contribution.

Dr. Spock never advocated excessive or inappropriate permissiveness. He was always aware of the necessity for limitations. But he was against unnecessary and compulsive adult despotism toward the very young. His book goes on as a classic of its kind and has no parallel in the comfort and practical knowledge it brings to young mothers.

Q: *Do you think our country has a suicide complex? I'm referring to the fact that millions of people refuse to pay any attention to ecology.*

A: No, I don't think we have a suicide complex. I think that most of us want to live but just don't want to grow up. There are several reasons why ecology is ignored.

1. We don't like to face problems.
2. We don't like to make sacrifices, however constructive those sacrifices may turn out to be.
3. We don't like to take on responsibilities.
4. We are not adequately tuned in to the fact that all people are interdependent and dependent on the earth and its *limited* resources.
5. Ecological education, which really consists of lessons in anti-ruthlessness, must begin at home—at birth.

Q: *Someone told me recently that most automobile accidents are really due to emotional disturbances. Do you think that this is true?*

A: For many people, the car and the road become extensions of themselves. On an unconscious level, other cars and drivers, as well as traffic authorities (lights, signs, police), represent brothers, sisters, authoritarian parents, competitors, rivals, and potential enemies. You can therefore readily see that many traffic offenses and accidents are not accidents at all. They are often acted-out desires and impulses directed by unconscious forces. For some, a car becomes an avenging weapon with which to give vent to aggressive, hostile, and sadistic impulses. For others, the car becomes a sexual symbol used to compensate for feelings of sexual inadequacy. Still others act out fantasies of grandiosity and limitless power. A large group of accident-prone drivers are self-hating and self-destructive.

They have an unconscious need to get hurt. Others want to get hurt in order to satisfy a need for sympathy, dependence, and attention.

I feel that, in this, as in most other neurotic manifestations, the most prevalent problem is that of neurotic pride. People will kill and be killed in the service of hurt pride. I feel very strongly that chronic traffic offenders—nonaccidental accident producers—are in need of psychiatric treatment rather than of fines and punishment.

Q: *As a psychiatrist, do you have any plan to stop skyjackings? I'm assuming that people who hijack planes are crazy and that perhaps there is a psychological solution to this problem.*

A: Studies on skyjackers reveal that these men and women are disturbed. Most of them feel that if they can start life anew in another place, with lots of money, all their problems will be over. They do not realize that they are taking the same person with the same problems and just putting him down someplace else. Money does not solve problems, but disturbed people think it does. To them, money means instant glory, peace, and happiness. That is why, to date, the skyjackers have demanded huge sums of money.

Skyjacking is like a contagious illness, and people who lean toward this "acting out" behavior become more disposed to it when they read about skyjackings or talk about them. Even worse is the threat posed by people who are sicker—people who are enormously self-destructive and potentially dangerous to others, people who are radically psychotic. So far such people have not tried to hijack planes. If they did, they would have no goal in mind—such as Cuba, money, etc.: all they would want to do is go down in a blaze of glory. They wouldn't care about anyone else on the plane; they would not listen to reason; they would not let passengers go; they would not be scared; they would be concerned only about fulfilling their own desires to make "headlines" in their last moments.

The solution to skyjackings is not psychological; it is practical. And it must be carried out by both passengers and the airlines. For example, I believe that all baggage—not just hand luggage—must be examined before passengers board a plane (much as baggage is examined in Customs). And metal detectors must be set up in all airports to reduce the possibility of firearms being smuggled aboard aircraft.

The solution cannot be left to one country or one airline—because such a solution will not work. The U.N. should take an active part in solving the problem; no country should accept these sick people as refugees. The U.S. government should give all possible help to airlines as they seek to develop and install the most effective detection procedures, because air travel is an important part of American living and should be made safe.

I do have a plan to stop hijackings in the event that the above procedures do not work and there is a distinct possibility that they will not. In that event, I would suggest that the following steps be taken:

1. No baggage is to be carried on passenger planes. (Baggage space and weight could conceivably be converted to more passenger room.) A second plane will carry only baggage, and it will be at your destination when you arrive. No hand baggage can be carried on board the passenger plane. It must be handed over to the airline, which will search it thoroughly, then deliver it to the passenger who is already on board the plane. (This way, businessmen will be able to do their work, medicines can be delivered, etc.)

2. All passengers will have to change into uniforms or smocks, which they will wear during the flight. While the plane is aloft, passengers' clothes will be stored in individual fireproof, bombproof capsules. The capsule will be handed to the passenger when the plane lands.

Yes, I know these seem like drastic measures. But if skyjacking continues, drastic measures may well be necessary. There will be some inconvenience for both passengers and airlines, but it will be worth it. Even with delays, air travel is still the quickest way of getting from here to there. And air safety is still first.

Q: *I am horrified by capital punishment. My feeling is that this is a most primitive condition. Could you tell me the psychiatric point of view?*

A: I think it would depend on the individual psychiatrist.

I feel that antisocial acts are evidence of sickness (emotional disturbance). I believe that there should be more research on this kind of sickness and that sick people should receive psychiatric treatment. I do not believe in punishment—capital or otherwise—since it is neither research nor treatment.

Q: *We have a young daughter, and as it happens, she is a nursing student. This I suppose sensitizes us even more (if that's possible) to the horrible murders that took place some years back in Chicago. Isn't there some way psychiatrists can predict and help prevent such mass murders, since the murderer is clearly insane?*

A: Human behavior can at best never be predicted with accuracy. That we can predict it so well is a credit to our advanced state of learning and skill. Countless sick people are so well evaluated and treated by experts that they are saved from becoming suicides and murderers. These expert examinations, studies, decisions, and preventive actions take place every day in hospitals and private offices. Since the results are excellent, they are not sensational and we do not read about them. Of course, psychiatrists, like surgeons, "lose" patients. However, with proper evaluation and treatment, this seldom happens.

The fact is that we do have much information concerning the anatomy and physiology of murder and considerable skill in the application of this information. But (and this is a big one) there is little we can do if we are not given the opportunity to apply this information through our skills. In short, we cannot be effective unless we have the opportunity to see and, if necessary, to treat the patient. Also, there are still gaps in our knowledge of human behavior. This includes our knowledge of violence. Vindication and punishment do not advance our knowledge or close these gaps one iota. It is a pity that much that can be learned from the very sick "criminal" is often lost to the electric chair.

Much of the problem is a socioeconomic one. We need more money so that we can have more diagnostic centers, more psychiatric evaluation and treatment in child community centers, more orientation toward diagnosis, research and treatment centers in prisons, and the means for following up this treatment after release from prison. All this requires public interest and pressure. Unfortunately, public interest is piqued by sensational crime but seldom sustained long enough for real, constructive change to take place.

Q: *Violence seems to be on the increase everywhere, and we keep hearing sociological, political, economic, and legal explanations of it. But how about psychiatric understanding in this problem? I*

*realize that this would fill a book, but at least give us a clue. The
subject is surely of monumental importance.*

A: I'm not sure there is actually more violence now than there
was in the past. I *am* sure that we hear more about it, since our
means of communication are so improved and our population continues to grow.

While there are many factors, I think violent acts on every level
are intimately connected to an inability to handle feelings of anger.
Many people see anger as a shameful, sinful emotion, which they
must repress at any cost. The cost is invariably high. It may take
the form of psychosomatic illnesses, severe anxiety, or depression.
It also converts people into emotional time bombs, who need only
the slightest stimulus to join a fight, a brawl, a crusade, a mob. A
word, a rumor, an imagined insult can trigger the explosion and
release pent-up rage.

Human beings get angry, and this is normal and natural. Too
often, however, this natural process is perverted and converted into
dangerous channels—dangerous for ourselves and others. Indeed,
I feel that we twist and pervert angry feelings more than any other
emotion—and for this we pay a terrible price. We hurt others, and
we distort ourselves. Of course, cultural or environmental glorifica-
tion of violence reinforces the psychologic factor. Sports, recreation,
and spectacles—like football, wrestling, fighting, hockey, war news,
war movies, violent Westerns, small children playing with guns,
military parades—all help fuel the time bomb.

You are right—the whys, whats, and hows of anger and violence
could fill a book. I wrote *The Angry Book* because I, too, feel that
the subject is of monumental importance.

CHAPTER 11
Growing, Living, and Aging Toward Health

Growing up is a process that should take each of us our entire life-time. One sign of good mental health is a desire to keep learning, to keep increasing involvement in life's processes, including awareness of self and others. This goal can be expressed by what Karen Horney has called "self-realization." Happiness itself is an elusive entity; those who strive toward self-realization, however, may find that they are content without being resigned, busy without being pressured, confident without being narcissistic. But this is an involved process and one that best goes on all of our lives.

Older people are sometimes better able to experience themselves for themselves alone, and aging can be a rewarding, exciting part of life. Some of us may go through identity crises in our thirties or forties; some may wish to start psychotherapy in their seventies or eighties. Such important life decisions need not be limited by time or age.

The Keys to Happiness

Whenever I have been asked to name the most sought-after condition of human existence, I have always answered (and probably always will) that the condition is happiness. We all know the story of Diogenes, who long ago took a lamp and set out to find the truth. Today the world—and psychiatrists' offices—are filled with men and women who are trying to find a road to happiness.

While happiness is certainly not everything in life, it is an enormously important facet of human existence. Happiness is, to many, the feeling that makes life truly worthwhile.

What exactly is happiness? Well, to me happiness is feeling good. Other simple ways of describing happiness include: being at peace with oneself; feeling comfortable; enjoying self-acceptance; being basically pain- and tension-free.

As simple as it is to define, happiness is not simple to find and is even less simple to sustain. Fantastic experiences, magnificent accomplishments, tremendous good fortune, and enormous assets sometimes make for moments of brilliant glory, exhilaration, and triumph, but these moments of great stimulation and heightened sensations, or "highs," usually have little or nothing to do with happiness.

Happiness is seldom composed of what I call mountain-peak experiences—highs or lows. Happiness takes hold in more down-to-earth, less rarefied air; it breeds in the atmosphere of just plain everyday life, and is nurtured by the ordinary rather than the glorious.

Happiness is found more frequently in times of struggle than in times of triumph. Again and again I have heard wealthy and famous people tell me that their days of happiness were over—that they had been happy long ago, when they were "struggling" to make a living, to attain a career, or to raise children. Once they had successfully achieved these goals, once they had "arrived," everything seemed empty—and happiness disappeared completely from their lives.

If happiness is composed of prosaic, common, everyday stuff, why is it so difficult to attain?

To answer this question, it is necessary to realize that we live in a society that deprecates simple happiness. Our society puts down the "feeling good" quality that I consider so important. Instead, society extols the value of supreme moments, heightened sensations, and great accomplishments. As a result, most Americans have come to regard that simple, "feeling good" quality as not good enough—and possibly even something to be ashamed of—because it doesn't measure up to all kinds of glorious standards that society sets. These standards include a great variety of impossible goals, many of which exist purely on an unconscious level and are, therefore, impossible to reach. When these false goals are not attained, people feel disappointed, depleted, and empty.

One of these false goals includes expectations about happiness itself. Not only have human beings been falsely led to believe that happiness is supreme, ecstatic bliss, but they have also been led to believe that once achieved, this divine state of total euphoria should continue endlessly.

Society believes that in order to achieve happiness you must enter a land that is not open to everyone—and that, once entered, the land is never left. This is the "Shangri-la Fantasy" that I have spoken about before. The key to this Eden-on-earth is thought to be money, marital status, looks, power, fame, admiration, owning the right things (car, clothes, jewels, etc.). How many times have you heard (or thought): "If only I had this I would be happy." Sometimes these possessions do help give to you a momentary "high," but the sudden realization that they did not, after all, bring lasting *happiness* often results in disappointment and depression.

Unhappiness is as much a part of the human condition as happiness. Acceptance of all facets of the human condition contributes to realistic happy possibilities. But our culture and society in general fails to prepare people for life's more difficult times. Too many of us unconsciously feel that these negative things should not happen to us. We feel especially resentful and unnecessarily miserable when unhappiness occurs despite the fact that we have done all the "right" things. I've heard many people say "How can this happen to *me* when I've worked so hard?" Being unhappy in unhappy situations is entirely appropriate, but so many of us suffer more than we have to by unnecessarily prolonging unhappiness.

There are two main destroyers of happiness. The first is impossible expectations. These include fantasies and unrealistic, idealized expectations that we have of ourselves, parents, children, mates, friends, Congress, the President, the country, the world, and the human condition generally. They also include our unrealistic hopes that the joy of attainment of things, prestige, status, etc., will be enormous and will last forever. In my psychiatric practice, I see many people who suffer from severe depression. Most of these individuals achieved the particular goals to which they always aspired, yet their impossible expectations remained unfulfilled. Loved ones still got sick and even died; aging took place; children went off to lead their own lives (and became relatively disinterested in their parents); friends turned out to be less than perfectly devoted; and all kinds of familial problems stubbornly remained a part of life—despite success.

The fact remains that no matter what a person achieves, he or she is not exempt from the simple truth that life is indeed tough. We not only make it tougher, we also destroy our potential for happiness by refusing to recognize this fact, and by insisting on building and clinging to expectations that must eventually lead to disappointment, frustration, and unhappiness.

The second destroyer of happiness is self-hate. As human beings, we have a capacity for happiness beyond the realm of any other creature on this planet. We have greater intelligence, feelings, sensitivity, humor, the ability to relate, to cry, to laugh, to make choices and decisions, to love, to think, to reproduce. But we also have many limitations and human characteristics that are less than ideal. Not one of us is exempt from being suspicious, distrusting, untrustworthy, hypocritical, prejudiced, self-serving, possessive, jealous, envious, and capable of bad judgment.

We must accept these human frailties. If we don't, we close ourselves off from the human satisfactions that are possible and available. Self-idealization and self-glorification lead to self-hate, and cut us off from the very real assets we have and need to use in order to be happy. Hating any aspect of ourselves is hating the human condition. Despite our noblest attempts, we will all remain limited and imperfect, as will the world at large. Cries for personal perfection and justice will invariably lead to frustration. You must learn to accept human shortcomings.

Times of personal liabilities are times when we most need self-acceptance, self-love, and compassion. It is at such times we must protect and cherish ourselves. But to do so we must recognize self-hate. The most common forms include second-guessing, self-recrimination, depression, worry, excessive moodiness, accident-proneness, psychosomatic illness. Outside pressures are also functions of self-hate; such pressures consist of relationships with people who treat us badly; working in jobs we hate; seeking or remaining in situations that are degrading, dehumanizing, and even dangerous. True compassion for ourselves entails taking a firm stand against self-hate, whatever form it takes—as soon as it is recognized. Self-compassion leads to self-esteem, and puts us in touch with constructive aspects of ourselves, aspects that are necessary for the effective pursuit of a human, realistic happiness.

The fact is we *can* be the captains of our own lives and we *can* do a considerable number of things to help ourselves to happiness, if we are so motivated. Here are six things you can do to help yourself "feel good" or find happiness—within the human possibility:

1. Remember these truths: Life is tough. Justice is good, but rare. Exorbitant expectations of any kind must lead to disappointment and unhappiness.

2. Learn to accept your human assets as well as your human limitations. You can be right or you can be wrong. You can be sick or you can be healthy.

3. Learn to recognize self-hate both inside and outside yourself, and immediately take a firm stand against it.

4. Make maximum use of compassion in accepting all aspects of yourself, so that you can grow and attain happiness.

5. Remember that happiness is everyday living. Eating, breathing, seeing, relating, loving, talking, listening, walking, etc., are the things that make life beautiful. Using your whole being as much as possible to experience these wonderful aspects of life is what makes you feel good—and "feeling good," after all, is what happiness is all about.

6. If you have made a genuine, wholehearted attempt to achieve the "feeling good" kind of happiness, but it still is unobtainable, professional help may be necessary in order to help you extract yourself from an unhappy emotional morass.

There are times when all of us need compassion, tenderness, and love from another human being to stir up our own dormant self-compassion and love of self—both of which are necessary in order to be happy.

If You Lie About Your Age . . .

Everyone lucky enough to survive birth *must* get older. Clothes, cosmetics, hairdos, etc., can make women look better, but they cannot stop the aging process—only death can do that. So it is that getting older, chronologically, is the very stuff that life is made of.

Unfortunately, however, a great many women have been caught in an extremely destructive trap; they have become ensnared by what I call "the youth cult sickness." These women have been subtly and blatantly taught by books, television, movies, advertisements—even by their own mothers—that "young" is the only way to be, that young is "good" and old is "bad." Consequently these women invest too much pride and have too high an emotional interest in staying young. Each passing day is an assault on their self-esteem. To them, getting older—which is actually living—brings on enormous, often unconscious self-hate and self-rejection.

If you are to live and live happily, self-acceptance is of prime importance. This means accepting yourself as you are at any given moment, at any given age. Self-acceptance does not preclude improvement and growth. On the contrary, it is self-rejection, self-hate, and the denial of reality that make healthy growth impossible. To cling compulsively to youth is such a fruitless and frustrating endeavor that it invariably leads to malignant hopelessness and resignation. It robs women of energy that can be used for more appropriate interests. To cling compulsively to youth is a vicious cycle: the more time and energy a woman spends trying to stay young, the more helpless she feels, and the more hopeless she feels, the older she becomes.

I find it very sad when a woman refuses to admit her age or even lies about it. This is ample proof to me of that woman's self-rejection and self-hate. Evidently she has been caught in the need to satisfy a superficial vanity. Such vanity will make her older than she is, older than the woman who freely admits her real age.

Whatever a woman's age, if she has relatively good health, she will have sufficient energy, reflexes, and physiological ability to pursue nearly all the activities she wants to pursue.

Our culture, unfortunately, puts too much stress on being in *top* athletic, youthful, physical shape. There is no need for anyone except professional athletes to spend time and energy cultivating professional athletic condition. Many people kill themselves trying to become what they physically are not. Chances are that most of us have a storehouse of energy and reserve assets that we can use in emergency. Mature people don't need the unlimited bounce of the exuberant teen-ager because only a small percentage of our total energy is necessary at any one time for enjoyable living. But all of this depends on whether a woman is vegetating or living, living in a state of emotional resignation or in a state of emotional youth.

What is "emotional youth"? To me, it is the stuff that makes for self-acceptance, interest, and motivation toward growth, self-extension, and change. It is the open willingness to explore new and unfamiliar territory. Youth to me means *change* and *growth*. Emotional old age means *resignation* and *stagnation*. A woman caught up in "looking young" to the exclusion of real interest in honest growth is old indeed. For me, a pretty, unlined, inexperienced face is fine for a very young girl. On a mature woman, such a face denotes old age and death. On the other hand, a face that shows struggle, experience, growth and change, plus the potential for still more change and development, is a beautiful face, a truly youthful face. It is the face of a woman who accepts and welcomes chronological aging, because to her aging means living and the opportunity for still more living, more experience, and more growth. One must age to live, and to any self-accepting woman living in the present is far more fulfilling than the superficial vanity feedback a mirror or a prized possession can bring. Certainly a youthful woman should enjoy good looks and accept every opportunity and means to enhance them, but she should not confuse good looks with self-growth.

For youthful self-growth to take place at any age, there must be an emotional investment in other people, in causes, in events, in the real world in which one lives—as opposed to the superficial, tinsel, teeny-bopping world created by people who are selling something. The youthful woman must care about herself and about other people. To the extent that she develops new insights and new maturation with regard to herself and the people of the world she lives in, she will be young. With new interests and new and real involvements will come still more interests and involvements, and her emotional vitality will increase, whatever her chronological age. Growing young in this way leaves little time to worry about getting old. Any vitally involved woman looks infinitely younger than women who spend their time fruitlessly trying to plaster down and trap youth.

It is also important to realize that many women cannot grow emotionally younger until they have grown chronologically older, It is almost as though these women had been born old—they are rigid and vain, and they spend all their energy trying to satisfy their immediate appetites. Sometimes, as they get chronologically older, they become wiser; they learn to separate the important from the unimportant. They can finally separate themselves from the objects they've acquired, and they understand the difference between things and people. These women then become more than just sexualized objects; they become *whole* women. They develop new and richer philosophical insights and even become emotionally freer and more flexible. They become less threatened, feel less vulnerable, and develop more self-esteem. They become more self-accepting and more accepting of others—they live, let live, and even care. They are growing older happily and without fear because they are truly becoming younger.

Q: *Do men have the same problems with their vanity and the whole "youth cult" thing as women do? Are they equally disturbed by aging?*

A: Definitely!

Q: *Do you feel that emotional factors play a part in determining a person's life span? If so, which factors do you think lengthen a person's life?*

A: We all know that physiological factors such as diet, physical activities, inheritance, etc., can help to determine a life span, but I feel that emotional factors play a large role, too. I consider the following extremely important life-lengthening emotional factors:

1. A relatively stress-free life.
2. Compassion for oneself and one's human limitations.
3. A good relationship with oneself and with at least one other human being. (Love of oneself and another person is very important.)
4. Being cherished by the immediate community in which one lives.
5. Curiosity, interest, and involvement in any activity.
6. A sense of satisfaction from helping a person, people, or society as a whole.

Q: *I have heard that the human brain is the same as a giant electronic computer. If this is true, does it mean that human thought, behavior, and breakdown will someday be understood exactly the same way today's computer experts understand electronics?*

A: I sincerely doubt that day will come. First of all, the brain is *not* the same as a computer. Computers and other electronic devices try to imitate brain functions. At best they suffer by comparison because these imitations are primitive, rudimentary, and gross when compared to the human brain.

The human brain and spinal cord (comprising the central nervous system)—and the body to which this system sends messages and from which it receives messages—is still the finest, most intricate, most complex, most capable, and most undefinable entity on earth. One average human brain contains a biochemistry capable of more permutations and combinations than all the electronic devices manufactured to date put together. The brain—as part of the organism comprising a whole person—is alone capable of feelings, moods, self-contemplation, change, growth, and the very cornerstone of life—reproduction.

Q: *I hear girls at my college talking about who they are, seeking their identities, questioning about "doing their thing." I am a junior; I work, I go out, I enjoy myself, and I hardly ever wonder about* who *or* what *I am. Am I stupid, dull, bland, or just out of it?*

A: A few of the girls you speak of may be really struggling, searching, and growing. I suspect many are intellectualizing, theorizing, and posturing. The search for identity can become a wasteful affectation. Unfortunately, this kind of outside looking and theorizing sometimes goes on into later life and becomes a substitute for real involvement, relating, and living.

You do not seem "out of it" at all. You sound as though you are quite involved with your work and social life. People who are "involved," who are themselves, and who enjoy living spend little time theorizing—they are too busy being and doing.

Q: *Sometimes, even when I am feeling very good about myself and my relationships with others, I just want to be alone. Is this normal?*

A: Nowadays, people are often made to feel that they must never want to be alone. Unfortunately, chronic outgoingness is extolled as healthy, while an occasional desire for solitude is condemned as mental sickness. To me, wanting to be alone is evidence of mental *health*. There are many people who would like to be alone, but who are afraid; they need the constant presence of other people. When they are alone, the desire for tranquility and self-reflection turns to agitation and self-hate. To be alone and relaxed in one's own exclusive company, without feeling lonely, is an indication of good self-esteem. These people have the healthy feeling that they are *not* alone at all—they are with a *real* person and a friend: they are with *themselves.*

Q: *I am thirty years old and still don't know what I want to be when I "grow up." I panic whenever I think about a direction for my life. Why can't I make this kind of decision? What should I do?*

A: Any decision involves choice and no choice is all-inclusive or perfect. Choice means we cannot be all things or have all things. While we have appetites for many things, choice means we must construct a hierarchy of values—that is, we must determine the relative importance of people, activities, or things that we are interested in. Therefore, when we make a choice—and the decision to act accordingly—we gain some things but we must give up others. As to what career to choose, this also means surrendering the fantasy that it is possible to be all things—to be free of commitments and responsibilities, to sustain freedom from routine and from involvements. Surrendering this complex fantasy enables an individual to make a choice relating to persons and to work; it means giving up the fantasy of perfection. Yet it also means enjoying the satisfaction that comes from solid involvement and commitments to one's choice.

Some people develop an inhibition to commitments and involvement. They feel that making this choice—to dedicate themselves to someone or something—will deprive them of freedom they never really use and will deplete their feelings of self or identity. They also feel that once a choice is made, they make a real emotional investment and can never again change their minds. Therefore, they make no choice at all and remain deprived of the potential rewards choice would bring. Psychoanalytic help is sometimes necessary to help them overcome this difficulty.

Let me point out that you are probably more "grown up" than you realize. No special light comes on to announce the arrival of maturity. You ask what you will *be,* when in fact, as with all of us, you have been and are in the process of *being.* You have been a person all of your thirty years, relating in many ways to yourself and to other people—and this constitutes the main body of *being* and living.

Q: *I wonder if you can tell me if there is some way to keep one-self from playing the role of* witch—*a most undesirable role.*

One of my goals in life—if not perhaps the only goal at the present time—is to be the charming, gracious, loving person that some people think I am. It seems, however, that these fine qualities are too often stifled by quick slips of a vicious tongue that seems almost impossible to control.

I have three fine children who hate me. I have lost two husbands and am about to lose a fiancé because of my witchiness.

Should I seek counseling?

A: Nobody is exempt from what you call "witchiness." Being human, we have all kinds of human feelings and characteristics. These include arrogance, hostility, visciousness, jealousy, and envy, as well as charm, grace, and lovability. Excessive "witchiness" is often due to excessive attempts to repress those characteristics we have come to view as less than saintlike. Acceptance of ourselves and all of our feelings and moods, including those we have come to look upon as "witchy," helps to prevent explosive and uncontrollable outbursts. Attempts to be exclusively charming, gracious, and loving usually leads to repression of anger. This makes for an unconscious accumulation of rage until it uncontrollably and unaccountably bursts forth in seemingly inappropriate situations. Excessive arrogance and vicious behavior is often an indication of fear of one's own hidden and strong feelings as well as fear of what other people think of us. Psychotherapy can help us to reveal and accept all aspects of ourselves so that excessive repression, excessive preoccupation with other people's opinions, and excessive, uncontrollable outbursts become minimal. This makes for a better relationship with ourselves as well as with other people.

Q: *I would like to be more of a friend to myself. I envy people who are interested in golf, books, museums, Bridge, symphony music, etc. These pastimes don't seem to interest me. Other people enjoy these things so much, I would like to share that enjoyment and broaden my horizons. What can I do?*

A: You may be putting the cart before the horse. Contrary to popular opinion, interest in the more sophisticated and complicated activities does not suddenly spring up. Involvement is the mother of interest. First you must commit and involve yourself sufficiently so as to familiarize yourself; so as to learn; so as to expose yourself sufficiently to the possibility of interest.

Initial involvement may be difficult, but could be very rewarding. For example, you may have to discipline yourself to involve yourself with listening to a number of seemingly "boring" symphonies before your ear and heart become attuned to the pleasures this music can give you.

How can you be interested enough to enjoy Bridge before you become involved enough to learn how to play? As it becomes pleasurable, involvement will become easier and interest and motivation will grow. Thus a pleasure cycle will have been started.

Q: *Is it all right to ask for help when a person really feels she needs it?*

A: Everyone needs help, but many men and women feel that there is something wrong with needing it. Independence simply doesn't exist. However mature, well-developed, and self-reliant we are, we still need people and help. This is a human condition, and there is no avoiding it—no matter how much we exaggerate the virtue of self-reliance. It is important to understand this and to teach your children that needing help should not fill them with shame and self-contempt. While it is important that children rely on themselves, it is also important to teach them to ask for help when they need it.

Q: *I know that your book* Lisa and David *was fiction although based on fact, but I can't help wondering what the future of this boy and girl would be. If you were to write a sequel, what would happen to them?*

A: I'm very happy that you recognize Lisa and David as fictional characters. I receive many letters from people who insist that Lisa and David actually do exist and want to know what happened to them. Several professional people were quite angry with me when I "refused" to send them "case material."

Let me say that since I feel that my several aims were fairly well satisfied (by the film as well as the book), I don't think I would ever write a sequel. I wanted to demonstrate that people, however sick, retained some need and ability to communicate; that real communication—the exchange of emotionale, the wonderful chemistry that sometimes occurs between people—always has a therapeutic effect; and that psychiatrists are human and can be helpful.

While there has never been a Lisa or a David, I have known people who suffered in much the same way and a few who were fortunate enough to relate in much the same way. However much sicknesses are the same, people who have them remain highly individual. This makes it impossible to predict the outcome without intimate knowledge of the person, and even then we can be wrong.

Nevertheless, in order to answer your question, let us pretend that Lisa and David *are* real (and I must say that, in my own feelings, they have almost become real). I see David as evolving into an adult capable of a considerable potential for health. I see Lisa as having a much more difficult and tenuous time of it. While she is well on her way and has given up some very severe defenses or symptoms, she still has a long way to go in the development of a "self." I see them both as needing and profiting from treatment for years. I don't see them as relating to each other in a sustained healthy, adult way for many, many years, if at all. For me, they enjoyed a brief but wonderful moment when "something" happened between them, which sparked them back to themselves, to people and to life.

Q: *Do you believe that a person should be told if he has an incurable disease?*

A: Above all, this is a highly individual matter and must be evaluated with the greatest care by both doctors and relatives— people who know the patient as well as his circumstances. If necessary, the family might also consult a psychiatrist. Many people who receive this information simply stop living long before death actually takes place. Others commit suicide, even though no untoward physical pain is present. Months of relatively happy living may be destroyed.

I feel that, for the most part, giving this information to a patient is gratuitous and destructive. Most patients deep down somehow know the truth. Some can face and accept it, and they do just that. Others cannot tolerate this confrontation, and they manage to rationalize away the obvious truth of their impending doom. I have known more than one brilliant doctor who must have realized that his prognosis was hopeless but who chose to deny the truth, camouflaging and rationalizing symptoms and ascribing them to benign conditions that any young intern knew couldn't possibly exist. These men needed hope, however irrational, to go on with dignity and make the most of their remaining days.

It would be cruel and to no constructive purpose to deprive them of whatever emotional comfort they were able to create for themselves, by a confrontation with "truth."

Q: *Can you tell me if it is good or bad for a thirteen-year-old girl to attend the funeral of a loved uncle? I think it is realistic and part of growing up. My husband feels that it is exposing a young person to unnecessary trauma and that there will be plenty of unavoidable such situations later on in life anyway.*

A: I agree with you that it is necessary to experience, to adjust, and thus to come to accept life's realities, including the fact of death. Inappropriate overprotection may prove to be more destructive than traumatic situations. But timing is all important in these situations. Some people can handle tragedy and its concomitant ceremonies early in life while others require a longer growing up and adjustment period. It is important to respect people's sensibilities. Some people simply cannot face certain painful confrontations, and forcing them to do so may have destructive emotional consequences. In this, as in other issues, it is important to know the individual in question. People, and especially children, will often indicate a desire either to confront or to postpone confrontation with highly emotionally charged situations. Compassionate judgment based on respect for individual needs and desires usually produces the right answer.

Q: *I make and break New Year's resolutions every year, as I'm sure many other people do. I wonder if you care to comment on what this is all about.*

A: I feel that New Year's resolutions are really magical, ritualistic attempts to become "a better person." Examined closely, some aspects of the resolutions, you will find, are realistic and in keeping with human limitations and a desire for growth. Many of them, however, are more related to unrealistic strivings in the service of becoming a more ideal and glorious person. The "better person" here is really a superhuman person, who is expected to be too good, or too great, or too hardworking, etc., and just too much for one human being to become. The failure here is due not to lack of willpower but to exorbitant goals.

In general, willpower does not play nearly as important a role as most people think. One cannot spend the many hours of one's life being one kind of person and then change by an act of willpower because it is the beginning of a new year. Real change and growth happen slowly and with hard work and are more intimately linked to insight (real knowledge of oneself) than to willpower. Real change is most effective when it is in keeping with the real assets and limitations inherent in being human, and it can commence at any time—New Year's Day or any other day.

Q: *Every once in a while I decide I'm going to give myself a good time and make plans for things I really want to do. Is this just indulging myself—and is it all right to do so?*

A: I hope you indulge yourself often. By "indulging yourself" I mean spending several hours or even days on your own exclusive enjoyment. This time should not be taken at the expense of others, yet it should be given to the pursuit of pleasure for oneself. Many of us feel guilty when we indulge ourselves, because we think we don't deserve the time and effort we expend in the pursuit of our own pleasure. We feel we must share pleasure with someone else. Some people feel that self-indulgence is justified only when everyone else has been taken care of first. This is a great pity! A day devoted to ourselves—no strings attached—can be a wonderful morale booster. This is not selfishness; it is just good mental health.

Q: *Is it okay to participate regularly in some "mindless" activity or hobby? (By "mindless" activity, I mean one that is mostly physical and keeps your mind off your work and everyday problems.)*

A: Of course it's okay, and frankly, I don't care if it is golf, knitting, vigorous walking, fishing, gardening, etc. The main thing is that you get involved as completely as possible.

It doesn't matter whether the activity involves a great deal of movement or energy, but it must not involve planning, strategy, or "brain work." Strong feelings of competition and concern about perfection or winning spoil the therapeutic effect of this activity. Resting your mind is good for you psychologically and physically, and mindless activity helps do it. Very few people can relax merely by doing nothing.

Q: *I really believe there is some secret formula that will bring absolute and constant happiness. But how do I find that formula?*

A: A vast number of people believe in a Shangri-la, a secret, perfect place that only the worthy or lucky may enter. Residence in this mythical paradise, the believers feel, can be obtained and sustained through a number of sources: religion, money, fame, love, work, art, social attainment, creative enterprise, marriage, psychoanalysis, children, or glory. Unfortunately, when and if any of these magical goals are attained, bitter disappointment ensues—because Shangri-la does not exist. People are complex and can experience many moods and feelings. Happiness is merely one of them. Expecting to be happy all the time puts unreasonable demands on yourself and makes for more unhappiness when you are unable to achieve the impossible.

Q: *In high school I dated a boy for about a year. We liked each other a lot but broke up. Eventually, we both married other people. After all these years, even though I am happily married, I now find myself thinking about him. Why?*

A: Childhood romances and fantasies often remain with us till the end of our days. This happens because people tend to idealize these young romances and to embellish them with a purity, passion, and perfection that simply doesn't exist in real life. We use these fantasies to escape from the present in much the same way that we use romantic films or novels.

People who have the opportunity to reestablish childhood romances are bound to be severely disappointed and hurt. They find that the years have changed a great many things, including their immature outlook. In the main, therefore, the individual we were once in love with now falls sadly short of the fantasy perfection the years have caused us to endow him or her with.

Frankly, I prefer real bread to fantasy cake. There is no substitute for the joys and rewards of real living. The past is gone; the future isn't here yet. There is only the present. The people to whom we relate in the here and now are the people who are important in our lives. Making your present life meaningful will give you greater pleasure than any fairy-tale romances in your past—however beautifully wrapped in fantasy they are.

Q: *Is it true that it is impossible to change one's way of looking at life after middle age? For example, can a relatively rigid and closed kind of person change and become more open even if she is past fifty?*

A: With motivation and willingness to struggle, a person can grow and change regardless of age.

Q: *I know I have neurotic problems, but I'm sixty-eight years old and I'm wondering whether it's worth starting psychoanalysis and if there's any real hope of resolving my problems at this late date. Also, I hear that psychoanalysts are not too interested in older people.*

A: The fact that you are sixty-eight and have written this letter is an indication that you must have been resolving problems all your life. As to professional help, there are psychoanalysts who are particularly interested in older people. Goals in treatment may be different for people in different age groups. I think that everyone is entitled to whatever self-fulfillment and self-realization are possible in whatever time he has. The ability to change is relative to the individual. Motivation is more important than age. Old people who want to change and grow can do so regardless of chronological age. I have met "old-young" people and "young-old" people, but I've never met "really alive" people who were not constantly growing and changing.

Q: *My seventy-five-year-old mother is quite depressed and says she would like to talk things over with a psychiatrist. Our family doctor feels she is rather old for psychotherapy and has put her on medication. Can older people be treated effectively with psychotherapy?*

A: People can be helped and can grow no matter how old they are. While therapeutic goals may be different for people of different ages, older people do comparatively well in psychotherapy in the hands of an expert. In the case of depression, as with other emotional disorders, the expert is a psychiatrist, preferably one with psychoanalytic training.

The fact that your mother would "like to talk things over with a psychiatrist" indicates considerable motivation to get well. Her chronological age must not be held against her. It would be best to heed her wish.

Q: *My father died two years ago. Since then, my mother (who is now seventy-two) has made a fair adjustment to widowhood, but still has periods of depression. I think she is making herself more miserable by refusing to move from the apartment where she and Dad lived for so long. Wouldn't she be better off moving to a place that has no memories?*

A: Your mother's reaction is not at all unusual. As for her moving, there is no one rule that works for everyone. Some people are better off moving from a home they shared with a lost loved one; others find that staying put has a better effect. While reminders of your father might bring your mother pain, they can also bring her joy and fond memories. Your mother's apartment is familiar to her, and she probably feels warm and secure there—especially because of its memories. The place she shared with her husband is *home,* and staying there could be therapeutic. In any case, the decision to move or not to move *must* be your mother's.

Q: *My husband will be sixty-five in five months, and he is retiring one month after his birthday. He has no hobbies, reads very little beyond the newspapers, and through the years has been completely devoted to his work and the children, who are now all married and away. Although we will have no financial problem and although my husband is a perfectly healthy, vigorous man who looks much younger than his age, I am quite concerned about how he will occupy his time. Do you have any advice?*

A: More and more people are living healthier and longer lives, and more and more of them are poorly prepared to use their non-working time effectively, healthily or enjoyably.

Too many people look forward to retirement with vast and impossible expectations. They have deluded themselves into believing that retirement is synonymous with utopia. Similarly, many people believe that financial success and happiness are one and the same. Of course, neither is true. The anatomy of happiness and personal equanimity is very complicated, and most people who are "living for the day when they can retire" are missing the fulfillment that comes of living full lives in the present—the here and now. I feel that the working years almost invariably turn out to be the best years of our lives and that they should be extended as long as possible.

I further feel that men do best psychologically and physically if they are engaged in gainful work commensurate with their age and physical limitations *all* their lives. Forced retirement of vigorous men, due to chronological age, can have disastrous results. Most men invest a great deal of pride in their work (gainful employment) and derive considerable self-esteem from this all-important area. Retirement often brings on feelings of worthlessness, emptiness, loneliness, disconnectedness, and bitter disappointment.

Unfortunately, few people are geared to retirement. Those who are have been making the adjustment for years. This adjustment does not consist of utopian daydreaming. It consists of sustained familial and social involvement, as well as a diversification of interest (reading, politics, hobbies, etc.), which started early in life and which will continue all their lives. Unfortunately, it is impossible to develop interests and involvements suddenly—on order. A warm climate, an income, a new hobby are no substitute for life-fulfilling work.

Q: *When I was a youngster, I used to write verses and stories. When I married, I wrote occasional short pieces for the local newspapers. After my two daughters grew up and married, I took some courses and began to write children's stories. I have had many juvenile stories, poems, and books published. Now, at aged sixty-three, my creative drive has come to an end. I wouldn't mind if I could live happily with this situation, but it makes me miserable. A doctor told me that creativity usually ceases when a person reaches his sixties. Do you feel this is true? If not, can you suggest something I might do to revive my desire to write?*

A: I think that what the doctor told you is nonsense. People have the capacity to grow, to change, and to be creative whatever their age. However, many people select an age at which they consider themselves "old." Interestingly, you wrote, "now, at *aged* sixty-three," instead of, "at *age* sixty-three," indicating that you feel "aged" at sixty-three. But your displeasure with your current non-productivity indicates that you feel quite alive and creative, and that these feelings will not permit you to resign from life. Therefore, you must ignore your doctor's observations on creativity and take a chance on your own proven ability.

I suggest that you begin by writing simply for the pleasure of it, rather than to meet some editorial standard. Many people stop writing (or painting) because they become fearful of a failure to meet impossible demands they set up for themselves.

P.S. Many, many beautiful and wise works have been turned out by people who could only have done them after experiencing a long, full life.

P.P.S. I firmly believe that creativity makes for longevity, and that longevity makes for creativity.

Q: *Is it a good idea to prepare for retirement during your active working life?*

A: If you are doing so, then you are one of the rare ones among us. Most of us do not realize that to retire successfully takes a great deal of preparation. Much more is required than just financial planning. People cannot suddenly become involved in hobbies, various forms of entertainment, and leisure interests and activities. They must develop these interests over a lifetime if they hope to be emotionally prepared for retirement. Without adequate emotional preparation, retirement often leads to destroyed morale, boredom, depression, and physical deterioration; it may even precipitate an early death.

Those whose work has been their major interest are better off not retiring. It is better for them to keep working, even in a limited way.

CHAPTER 12

An In-Depth Interview with Pat Loud

What constitutes a "typical" American family? Is there really any such thing? A family and its members, living together day after day, create a unique entity with its own very special joys and difficulties. When National Educational Television chose William and Patricia Loud and their five children as the prototypical American family, all seven initiated a period of examination relative to personal life, to dealing with others, and to dealing with society. Though the Louds subsequently divorced and the family unit changed radically, a kind of necessary individual analysis on the part of each member made for greater maturity and re-thought-out relationships.

Pat Loud discovered what she wanted out of life during the months that the camera examined her and her family. A woman with a keen interest in life and what she could actually make of it, she abandoned her unrealistic fantasies about love, dependency, and maternal nurturing to look at her own needs and wants and see how she could fulfill them. Today, she is involved, fascinated and open to her own growth and development. She is a healthier mother and woman now because she cares about herself and her own potential. As more individuals, couples, and families learn the important lesson Pat Loud has learned, we can hope for a more alive, more fulfilled, and perhaps more constructive society.

Pat Loud Talks About Love, Marriage, Divorce—and Herself

More than two years ago, National Educational Television decided to spend a great deal of time, money, and effort to produce a new concept in TV programming. Television cameras were placed in the home of an upper-middle-class Santa Barbara, California, family: William and Patricia Loud and their five children: Lance, twenty; Kevin, eighteen; Grant, seventeen; Delilah, fifteen; and Michele, thirteen.

From May until December 1971, cameras recorded the everyday comings and goings of the family. The resulting miles of film were edited into twelve one-hour segments to be shown on TV. The title of the program was "An American Family."

Even before the program appeared on television, social scientists were predicting that the series would be an important human document, a great contribution to better understanding of the American family. The Louds, regardless of their socioeconomic standards, were being touted as the *typical* American family from whom other typical American families could obtain support—because the *typical* Louds's typical problems were every family's problems. The program was lauded in previewing raves and hailed as a forthcoming cultural event—an eye-opener on all levels.

When the program was shown on TV in January through April, 1973, the raves gave way to criticism from critics and viewers who felt: 1. The Louds were not, after all, a typical American family; 2. The program had an exhibitionist, soap-opera quality; 3. The Louds seemed shallow, cardboard figures; 4. The program was just plain boring; 5. How dare TV film the deterioration of a family?; 6. How dare a program discuss a son's homosexuality?; 7. The very presence of the TV camera in the Louds's home killed the "true-to-life" family feeling; 8. The TV program was responsible for the Louds's subsequent divorce.

How strongly some people disliked the program—and the Louds—was evidenced by the impolite reception three Louds (Bill, daughter Delilah, and son Lance) received from a TV audience in Atlanta, Georgia, last April, when they appeared on a talk show.

Although I felt that the program had been over-touted and that it missed its mark, I could not feel pessimistic about the Louds as human beings. I could not, however, get to know the Louds from the show—and I was very anxious to get to know them—especially the wife, Pat. On the program she seemed elusive and remote, but she also seemed to me to be the most interesting member of the family. A sense of her resolute strength came through to me on the TV screen. I was anxious to have a chat with Mrs. Loud to find out what she was really like.

In New York to discuss a business project, Pat Loud agreed to come to my office, where we chatted for hours before having lunch, and then continued again for another session. Let me say here that at no time did I analyze Pat Loud as a psychiatrist would analyze a patient. She was *not* a patient but a subject I was meeting as a psychiatrist-writer.

Pat Loud is tall, thin, large-boned, and graceful. She was simply dressed and wore little make-up. I found this in keeping with her direct, open, natural approach to our interview—and to life in general. There is nothing cute, affected, or pretentious about her. She is a beautiful woman. Her face and hands are mobile and expressive, and her eyes and mouth project much inner warmth, vitality, and strength of feelings. When she laughs—which was often—her cheeks dimple. In person, she looks much younger than her forty-six years. It didn't take me long to discover that the Pat Loud I saw on the TV screen was not the Pat Loud sitting across from me in my office.

She told me that her maiden name is Russell, and that she is of Irish-Scotch origin. I had guessed as much because she reminded me of John Steinbeck's women in *Grapes of Wrath*. As with those women, Mrs. Loud's face radiates strength and substantiality; it tells me that she is a person of determination and reliability. She is articulate and knowledgeable. She has never been a big-city person, so she lacks some cosmopolitan sophistication, but she expresses herself feelingly and without evasive intellectualizations.

"I was raised in Eugene, Oregon, in a middle-class Catholic family," she told me. "My parents were extremely devoted and loving to each other, as well as to me and my brother." Being a cherished and loved child in a warm, stable household was no small force in producing Pat's present strength and solidity. Her ability and intelligence were held in high esteem so that she went on to Stanford University, where she majored in history and minored in English literature. She says that her own family was conventionally "Victorian."

"My father seemed to head the family," she admitted, "but when I think about it, it was my mother who provided me with the necessary strength and resilience. Mother was diplomatic enough to apply wisdom and support without usurping my father's personal or family prestige." In looking back, Pat remembers, "My parents lived a beautifully romantic idyll; they were madly in love with each other. Dad used to recite poetry to Mother."

Not surprisingly, young Pat fantasized a similar marriage for herself. She dreamed that she and her husband would be madly in love. This marriage fantasy, coupled with her early Catholic orientation and cultural influences that existed twenty-five years ago, accounted for her willingness to forego a career for marriage. Girls of that generation (and even today's generation) were ready and eager to surrender professional pursuits and intellectual endeavors in favor of becoming wives and mothers.

William Loud was six years older than Pat. She had known him since childhood; he was her brother's friend. She was in love with Bill throughout college. To Pat at twenty-three, her marriage to Bill Loud, and their subsequent family, was the culmination of her familial, personal, and cultural dreams.

"Life with Bill was fairly happy," she says, but she also indicates that something was wrong. That something, I suspect, was that Pat Loud was beginning to feel important stirrings within herself. These stirrings were her need for personal growth—a need that, like other women of her generation, she repressed in order to avoid inner conflict and anxiety, until her intelligence and sensitivity could no longer allow her to cover up what had become so obvious; that her marriage to Bill was not what she had expected; it was not a duplication of her parents' marriage.

While Bill was compassionate and caring, he never offered their marriage the involvement and sharing that Pat's father had given his. Pat sensed that her husband led a life apart and that his surface charm, humor, and striving for material success masked deeper feelings. Looking back, Pat told me that Bill's detachment prevented her ever getting to know him. Despite years of marriage and five children ("I was very fertile," she laughs), despite having gone through much together, Pat admitted: "I feel that the real Bill Loud has eluded me."

Pat's statement is not an unusual one for wives—or ex-wives—to make. Many relationships fail to produce deep understanding and exchange of feelings. The result of such relationships is frustration and anger. However much one tries to bury these feelings, however one tries to avoid facing up to them—they are there, growing and festering.

Pat Loud knows all about such feelings, but like so many women, especially women with children, she kept them from showing. Keeping a family together is no minor motive or effort for an earthy, serious woman. Besides, to let these feelings take over would be to shatter Pat's childhood illusions, that marriage to Bill Loud was the be-all and end-all of life, and that her marriage would be like her parents' marriage.

So Pat hung on to her illusions—even though she realized she was being treated like a child instead of a wife. Bill was in charge of the money; he doled out allowances to the kids—and to her. He seemed to be the boss in charge of all important decisions. She realized that she sustained a passive, dependent role, taking care of the household while Bill aggressively confronted and exchanged experiences with the larger world outside.

It is my opinion, however, that Pat Loud's feelings of dependency on Bill and his strength was also an illusion. There is an important difference between actual dependency and helplessness due to paucity of inner resources and the illusion of dependency. Pat is not a helpless woman. She assumed the dependent role (like her mother) to comply with a cherished dream, and with what she perceived to be the requirements of the culture in which she lived. She sustained a façade of that role (like her mother) so as to nurture a family of five children and, I suspect, to bide her time—her children-growing-up time.

I say a façade because even in that pseudodependent role I suspect that Pat, like her mother, also provided the strength and fabric necessary to nurture her family.

Most men retain much of the small boy; I suspect Bill was no exception. Despite business competence, and a show of benevolent family despotism and paternalism, many men remain very immature emotionally. Like small boys, they feel it's safe to experiment outside, provided their wives (as surrogate mothers) are minding the store, keeping a home going—a safe refuge to run back to if the playing outside gets too rough.

Some time prior to the television experience, Pat became aware of Bill's involvement with other women. With anger and regret, she then realized that her illusions could no longer be sustained. Only then did she begin to listen to some of the yearnings that had been within her since college. She even tried dating other men. She realized that her children were growing up and would leave for lives of their own in the not-so-distant future. She knew that the evolution of her family was taking a revolutionary turn; she needed no television experience to bring home this growing insight.

With all these factors clearly in mind, Pat says, "I began to think about how I had always loved books and about an old dream I had about settling in a big city and becoming a research historian."

In April, 1972—after the television project was finished (but before it appeared on TV), Pat made the big step to the outside, and I'm sure it was a gigantic step for any woman who has had the responsibility of raising five children. Pat took a job as an associate editor of a newsletter containing correspondence from people eluci- dating events of current social interest, people who may not other- wise have the opportunity to be heard. These include views on Indian affairs, ecological problems, new social forces, and other wide-ranging important areas.

Today, Pat is thoroughly involved, fascinated, and open to her own growth and development. She is particularly keen on the job because it operates democratically. There is no "chief"—not even a symbol of one. Pat and her co-workers work and make decisions equally, an extremely important consideration to her at this time.

Pat Loud in no way degrades or minimizes her marriage to Bill Loud. She still cares very much for him and wants the best for him. She feels that her ex-husband has many fine assets, as well as limitations. She says that he is inconsistent, but she agreed with me that being inconsistent is human. She knows that vast changes have taken place in her and in her family, and that there is no turning back. While she continues to care about Bill, she demon- strates her good health by now caring more about herself. This is how it should be.

She has no illusions about her current and instant fame. She is well aware of its dangers and pitfalls, but realizes that it's too late for regrets. She enjoys her instant celebrity status to some extent— and the recognition and interesting contacts it brings—but she will try to take a firm stand against becoming chronically addicted to it.

She says quite openly, "I was naive to become involved in the project to start with." She seems well aware that withdrawal symp- toms, including depression and self-hate, can be devastating. She hopes the TV program helps other people to realize that their prob- lems are not unusual, and that this realization will make them more self-accepting. This may be because she has already received many warm and grateful letters.

Pat Loud is deeply concerned for her children. She hopes that the TV experience doesn't hurt them. Her oldest son Lance, now twenty- one, suffered from suspected polio when he was five. To Pat's great relief, this problem was overcome. She has always felt especially protective of him and is aware that, despite surface bravado, he is particularly sensitive and vulnerable. She has heard him announce to the TV world that he is a homosexual, that he has moved to New York, and that he is happy in his life. Despite her son's pronouncements, she worries about him.

Pat Loud is a very involved, concerned, and loving mother, but she is making every effort *not* to hold on to her children. She hopes to help them to realize themselves and to cut umbilical ties. Her middle two sons, Kevin, twenty, and Grant, eighteen, have their own rock band. While she wishes them every success, she is grateful that they have not become part of any kind of rock drug scene. Her oldest daughter, Delilah, likes dancing, but, like her mother, Delilah, now seventeen, is most interested in graduate work in history and hopes to study abroad. Pat totally approves. Michele, now fifteen, starts senior high this fall and is still interested in dancing and poetry. "I will miss the kids terribly when they have all left," Pat says. "Five children and their many friends have filled my life and house for years."

Their leaving will be particularly painful because Bill is gone, too.

At the moment, however, the children—except Lance—are still there and Pat has much in common with them. They are all growing, groping, struggling, and seeking to give birth to themselves. So is Pat Loud. She is eager and hungry to learn, to grow, to communicate.

After meeting Pat Loud, I am particularly suspicious of the effects of TV editing. I also suspect that the presence of the TV camera and crew in the privacy of one's home makes for disturbing and unnatural influences. (Pat admits to being less than free in their presence, and also to some "playing to the camera" in the last days of filming.) Considering this, perhaps it is not possible to produce a television documentary of an American family. Television may be just too distorting.

In any case, Pat Loud is not a typical American woman, wife, or mother; but then neither is anyone else. We share feelings, moods, yearnings, frustrations, problems, sorrows, and joys. Learning about each other we learn about ourselves, and learning about ourselves we learn about each other. But we still remain individual and different. Individuality is one of the great human privileges. Pat Loud is an individual and a very interesting person. She was interesting before she became famous. Nearly all people are interesting without becoming well known, but trying to know them is necessary to learn how interesting they really are.

Index